THE CANDIDATE'S DILEMMA

THE CANDIDATE'S DILEMMA

Anticorruptionism and Money Politics
in Indonesian Election Campaigns

Elisabeth Kramer

SOUTHEAST ASIA PROGRAM PUBLICATIONS

AN IMPRINT OF CORNELL UNIVERSITY PRESS   ITHACA AND LONDON

Southeast Asia Program Publications Editorial Board
Mahinder Kingra (ex officio)
Thak Chaloemtiarana
Chiara Formichi
Tamara Loos
Andrew Willford

Copyright © 2022 by Cornell University

All rights reserved. Except for brief quotations in a review, this book, or parts thereof, must not be reproduced in any form without permission in writing from the publisher. For information, address Cornell University Press, Sage House, 512 East State Street, Ithaca, New York 14850. Visit our website at cornellpress.cornell.edu.

First published 2022 by Cornell University Press

Library of Congress Cataloging-in-Publication Data

Names: Kramer, Elisabeth, 1981– author.
Title: The candidate's dilemma : anticorruptionism and money politics in Indonesian election campaigns / Elisabeth Kramer.
Description: Ithaca [New York] : Southeast Asia Program Publications, an imprint of Cornell University Press, 2022. | Includes bibliographical references and index.
Identifiers: LCCN 2021043570 (print) | LCCN 2021043571 (ebook) | ISBN 9781501764028 (hardcover) | ISBN 9781501764059 (paperback) | ISBN 9781501764042 (pdf) | ISBN 9781501764035 (epub)
Subjects: LCSH: Elections—Corrupt practices—Indonesia. | Political campaigns—Corrupt practices—Indonesia. | Political corruption—Indonesia. | Indonesia—Politics and government—1998–
Classification: LCC JQ779.A4 K73 2022 (print) | LCC JQ779.A4 (ebook) | DDC 364.1/32409598—dc23/eng/20211128
LC record available at https://lccn.loc.gov/2021043570
LC ebook record available at https://lccn.loc.gov/2021043571

Contents

Acknowledgments	vii
List of Abbreviations	ix
Notes on Currency and Indonesian Terms	xi
Introduction	1
1. Competitive Elections and Campaign Behavior	25
2. Corruption and Leveraging Anticorruptionism	47
3. Standing His Ground	68
4. Bowing to Pressure	91
5. Experienced and Pragmatic	114
6. Campaigns, Context, and Consequences	135
Conclusion	157
Notes	171
References	181
Index	199

Acknowledgments

I am grateful to the many people who have played a part in writing this book, both in facilitating its creation and enriching my own journey. After four years of research, two and a half of them spent doing intense fieldwork, and several more spent writing and rewriting, the list of those to whom I owe a debt of gratitude is very long indeed.

I am forever indebted to a number of contacts and informants in Indonesia, who will remain anonymous. I am especially thankful to my "case study candidates," who let me follow them for over a year as they campaigned. Through this I had so many unique experiences, from catching a ride in a private jet, eating BPK at a roadside diner with local "gangsters," to being looked after tenderly by a candidate's sister as I shivered from fever during a horrendous bout of food poisoning. I admit here that objectivity could never be the aim of this book, as I sought to see the campaign through their eyes. Their successes and failures played out before me—real people living the real consequences of political campaigns in real time, and I thank them for opening their world to me.

I also thank Michele Ford, who encouraged me to finish this manuscript. Michele was a constant reminder that this book is important and went out of her way to give me the professional support I needed to finish it. I also wish to thank Simon Butt and Vivian Honan for feedback on drafts, input, and proofreading. I am grateful to Edward Aspinall, Allen Hicken, and William Liddle for their early comments on this research, which were instrumental in the creation of this book. I deeply appreciate the anonymous reviewers whose extensive comments immensely improved this monograph. Many thanks also to Sarah Grossman from Cornell University Press for bearing with me through revisions and shifting time frames.

I wish to thank the team at the Sydney Southeast Asia Centre (SSEAC) at the University of Sydney for being wonderfully supportive colleagues and friends. Thanks to Thushara Dibley for being a great fellow deputy, Natali Pearson and Kristy Ward for being my book club buddies, and the rest of the SSEAC team (past and present): Sam Bashfield, Imogen Champagne, Ariane Defreine, Merryn Lagaida, Minh Le, and all the postdoctoral fellows, visiting scholars, and research assistants who have come through the center. I also wish to acknowledge the support of colleagues in the Department of Indonesian Studies at the University of Sydney (past and present): Novi Djenar, Vannessa Hearman, Dyah

Pitaloka, and Adrian Vickers. Also, thanks to Susan Park for her ongoing academic mentorship. I acknowledge that this book was largely written on the lands of the Gadigal people of the Eora Nation, where the University of Sydney currently stands. This always was, and always will be, their land. Sovereignty was never ceded. I must also acknowledge that several chapters of this book were first drafted while I was a visiting fellow at Chiang Mai University in Thailand, and so I thank Phil Hirsch and the team at the Regional Center for Social Science and Sustainable Development (RCSD) for their hospitality.

My extended stays in Indonesia were a necessary pleasure, made even more delightful by a cast of excellent friends, some visitors, and others based in Indonesia long term. In particular, I want to thank Dylan Alban, Fatima Astuti, Ben Elberger, Brooke Nolan, Alfira O'Sullivan, Ank Palmer, and Josh Stenberg, who were sometime travel companions in Jakarta and beyond. I would also like to thank the immigration official who refused to issue my exit permit in 2013, forcing me to collect five letters from different offices across Jakarta. The fact that I was able to do this in three days (without providing any inducements to officials) in the week before *Idul Fitri* is a memory I draw on often to remind me of my resourcefulness.

Also special thanks to Keith Foulcher for being a most wonderful teacher and to Wayne Palmer, Charlotte Setijadi, Claudia Stoicescu, and Tiffany Tsao for being much-needed pillars of strength over the years. Thanks to my parents, Tini and Michael, with an extra special thanks to Michael (aka "Dad") for coming to the field with me in 2014. To John Fenech, my favorite person—writing this book would have been so much harder without you and there are no words for how much I appreciate you in my life.

Finally, I would like to dedicate this book to my dear grandmother, Sheila Howard Kramer, who passed away in 2017. Her strength and resilience were, and remain, great sources of inspiration.

Abbreviations

5D	*Datang, duduk, diam, dengar, duit* (term used to describe corruption among New Order parliamentarians, literally meaning "come, sit, be quiet, listen, money")
Bawaslu	Badan Pengawas Pemilihan Umum (Electoral Supervisory Board)
BPK	Badan Pemeriksa Keuangan (National Audit Agency)
Bulog	Badan Urusan Logistik (State Logistics Agency)
CSIS	Centre for Strategic and International Studies, Indonesia
dapil	daerah pemilihan (electoral district)
DPD	Dewan Perwakilan Daerah (Regional Representative Council)
DPR	Dewan Perwakilan Rakyat (National People's Representative Council)
DPRD I	Dewan Perwakilan Rakyat Daerah tingkat propinsi (Regional People's Representative Council, provincial level)
DPRD II	Dewan Perwakilan Rakyat Daerah tingkat kapubaten/kota (Regional People's Representative Council, regency or city level)
Gerindra	Partai Gerakan Indonesia Raya (Great Indonesia Movement Party)
Golkar	Golongan Karya (Party of Functional Groups)
Golput	*golongan putih* ("white group" or people who choose not to vote in elections)
Hanura	Partai Hati Nurani Rakyat (People's Conscience Party)
INES	Indonesian Network Election Survey
KKN	korupsi, kolusi dan nepotisme (corruption, collusion and nepotism)
KPK	Komisi Pemberantasan Korupsi (Corruption Eradication Commission)
KPKPN	Komisi Pemeriksa Kekayaan Penyelenggara Negara (Commission to Examine the Wealth of State Officials)
KPU	Komisi Pemilihan Umum (General Election Commission)
LSI	Lembaga Survei Indonesia (Indonesian Survey Institute)
LSN	Lembaga Survei Nasional (National Survey Institute)

MPR	Majelis Permusyawaratan Rakyat (People's Consultative Assembly)
Nasdem	Partai Nasdem (National Democratic Party)
NGO	non-governmental organization
PAN	Partai Amanat Nasional (National Mandate Party)
PDI	Partai Demokrasi Indonesia (Indonesian Democratic Party)
PDIP	Partai Demokrasi Indonesia Perjuangan (Indonesian Democratic Party of Struggle)
PEKUNEG	Tim Penerbitan Keuangan Negara (Team to Regularize State Finances)
Pemilu	pemilihan umum (general election)
PKB	Partai Kebangkitan Bangsa (National Awakening Party)
PKI	Partai Komunis Indonesia (Indonesian Communist Party)
PKK	Pembinaan Kesejahteraan Keluarga (Family Welfare Development)
PKS	Partai Keadilan Sejahtera (Prosperous Justice Party)
PNI	Partai Nasionalis Indonesia (Indonesian Nationalist Party)
PPATK	Pusat Pelaporan dan Analisis Transaksi Keuangan (Center for Financial Transaction Reports and Analysis)
PPP	Partai Persatuan Pembangunan (United Development Party)
PRD	Partai Rakyat Demokratis (People's Democratic Party)
PSI	Partai Sosialis Indonesia (Indonesian Socialist Party)
Rp	rupiah (Indonesian currency)
SMRC	Saiful Mujani Research and Consulting
TGPTPK	Tim Gabungan Pemberantasan Tindak Pidana Korupsi (Joint Team to Eradicate the Crime of Corruption)
TII	Transparency International Indonesia
Tim Tastipikor	Tim Koordinasi Pemberantasan Tindak Pidana Korupsi (Coordination Team for the Eradication of Corruption)
Tipikor	Pengadilan Tindak Pidana Korupsi (Anticorruption Courts)
TPK	Tim Pemberantasan Korupsi (Anticorruption Team)
UGM PUKAT	Universitas Gadjah Mada Pusat Kajian Anti-Korupsi (University of Gadjah Mada Center for Anti-Corruption Studies)
USD	United States dollar

Notes on Currency and Indonesian Terms

Rupiah (Rp.) is Indonesia's national currency. Monetary amounts throughout this book have been given in US dollars wherever possible. Conversions are estimates due to currency fluctuations occurring between 2012 and 2014, when the bulk of this research was undertaken. Where US dollar amounts have been given, these are approximates based on the historical conversion rate found at OANDA (www.oanda.com). Where amounts have been rounded to avoid cumbersomely large numbers, this is indicated in the text.

Where appropriate, key Indonesian terms for specific phenomena discussed in this book are given both in English and Indonesian language.

Any study of Indonesia politics or history is sure to be full of acronyms and portmanteau, which are commonly used in Indonesia, especially in spoken language. This book has given the full name of any organization or term followed by any common acronym or portmanteau in parentheses upon first appearance in the text. A list of relevant Indonesian abbreviations used can be found at the beginning of the book.

THE CANDIDATE'S DILEMMA

INTRODUCTION

I saw the poster on the road outside the town of Malang, East Java. A candidate from the National Awakening Party, running for a seat in the Batu Regency legislature had superimposed his head on the body of a knight in shining armor. Below his gleaming metal sword read, in bold, "100% Anti Money Politic [*sic*]." The poster, with its over-the-top imagery and videogame aesthetic, made me chuckle. But it also echoed the campaign rhetoric I had been observing over the months leading up to the April 2014 legislative elections. The symbolism on the poster combined religion, morality, and nationalism in an exaggerated but familiar way. This heroic figure in his Islamic *peci* (a hat often worn by Muslim men in Indonesia) and gleaming armor, with an Indonesian flag attached to his sword, was ready to vanquish the enemy of the people that is money politics.

This crusader against money politics ultimately failed in his bid for public office. But his campaign slogan resonated with me, though perhaps not for the reason he would have hoped. The imagery on his poster may have been something of a parody, but its sentiment was recognizable not only in local electoral campaigns but also at the national level. The underlying message that candidates wanted to convey to voters through their rejection of money politics was that they were "clean" (*bersih*) and had integrity—characteristics that distinguished them from the archetypal candidates, who either visited the village simply to give voters money or goods, or sent emissaries with envelopes of cash, only to vanish once elected. The anticorruption candidates claimed to be different: they were committed to making things better for ordinary people, and they hoped that this stated commitment would attract voter support.

This book tells the story of national legislative candidates who, like our knight in shining armor, wanted to present themselves as challengers to the status quo. It is not uncommon for political hopefuls to proclaim their rejection of money politics, playing on Indonesians' widespread dissatisfaction with corruption, which is evident in all crevices of government. Using money to influence voters is explicitly outlawed. In practice, however, Indonesia's democratic system is characterized by an array of economic incentives given to voters during election campaigns and corrupt behavior among those elected. The shift to democratization following the end of the Suharto regime (post-1998), while offering many benefits to Indonesian citizens, also intensified political competition in elections—and, subsequently, the ubiquity of money politics.

Individual campaigns cannot be divorced from the political environment in which they occur, and attention to the dilemmas that candidates face allows us to assess the real impacts of both formal and informal institutions and systems on democratic elections. By integrating an investigation of individual campaigns with a theoretical consideration of the role of context within campaign decision making, this book generates new ideas about the nature of election campaigns from both a systemic and a personal (candidate) perspective.

The Electoral Campaign Dilemma

Electoral campaigns, when political parties and candidates battle each other for votes and power, represent an integral feature of contemporary democracies. In theory, democratic elections offer an opportunity to hold legislators to account and to punish those who have not acted in the best interests of those they represent (Warren 2004). They are subject to myriad interests, ranging from national and international concerns, elites, political parties, and civil society down to the everyday concerns of ordinary citizens. However, at their heart are the individual candidates who vie for selection. Election campaigns are hard-fought, expensive, and time-consuming. So that these efforts do not go to waste, candidates must campaign effectively. But what an effective campaign looks like varies depending on the political landscape—and the way candidates interpret that landscape as they campaign to win voter support. The lives of those who genuinely want to win become consumed by the question, what am I willing to do to ensure that voters choose *me*? The answers to this question are what ultimately guides their campaign decisions, set against the backdrop of their individual circumstances.

Elections have enormous influence over access to power in leadership, policy priorities, and the overall welfare of states and citizens. How candidates act before, during, and after elections underscores their own attitudes toward democracy and commitment to the rule of law. Elections are, ideally, "free and fair." But how do democratic ideals play out in a reality where money politics, and more specifically vote buying, is endemic? In the case of Indonesia, what does this mean for candidates who themselves believe, and want voters to believe, that they can challenge the status quo? In this book, I take as a starting point the puzzle of how those vying for a seat in Indonesia's national legislature make decisions about their campaigns, telling this story through the eyes of three self-identified anticorruption candidates. The core dilemma is how these candidates navigate the pressure to engage in money politics. To explore this dilemma, I address a series of interrelated questions that interrogate the context behind the decisions they must make as they navigate the electoral terrain: How have post-1998 democratic changes affected individual engagement in legislative politics and the way that candidates campaign? What is the appeal, at least for some, in engaging with anticorruptionism or running as an anticorruption candidate? And finally, how do self-identified anticorruption candidates negotiate the pressure to engage in money politics and the ethical dilemmas that this might generate?

Two key elements contribute to the complexity of this puzzle. First, Indonesian elections offer a paradox: the coexistence of a high prevalence of strategies that can be broadly defined as "corrupt," along with a plethora of anticorruption rhetoric. The country's political history of corruption and the nature and norms of contemporary electoral politics foster this paradox. The mobilization of anticorruption rhetoric, which positions candidates within a moral framework which they should be adhering to the law, is at odds with what most voters understand to be the inherent nature of Indonesian elections: that those competing for votes are more interested in serving themselves than their constituents, and that bribing voters is simply part and parcel of electoral campaigning. The juxtaposition of anticorruption rhetoric against observable behavior during electoral campaigns amplifies the visibility of the paradox. At the same time, the paradox, as it exists within individual campaigns, reflects the disconnect between seemingly universal ideas that money-driven strategies undermine democratic ideals and localized campaign norms that position the exchange of money, goods, or other promises as a crucial element in a candidate's prospects of success.

A simple answer to this paradox could be that voters simply do not see the cash payments or bribes that they accept during a campaign as corruption and therefore do not see their actions as being comparable to those of candidates, politicians, and bureaucrats who engage in corrupt activity while holding official positions. But even if the paradox itself can be explained in such simplistic terms, this does not prevent it from having a profound effect on how candidates campaign. The disjuncture remains a challenge for anticorruption candidates to navigate. Even if voters do not condemn candidates for engaging in money politics per se, such activity still puts the candidates in a difficult position. Candidates who give gifts or make patronage promises feel the lingering consequences of their decisions long after election day, with money to recoup, debts to pay, and promises to keep.

The resulting tension guides the second element of the puzzle—how candidates make decisions about their own campaigns and what influences those decisions. Not all candidates will choose to position themselves as being against money politics, or indeed against corruption more broadly. But those who do must establish the parameters of what is moral and acceptable in their campaign. This determination can shift as candidates move from planning to electioneering, where they may face increasing pressure to choose between their ideals and what they perceive to be a political reality. Yet, while candidates may encounter similar pressures arising from electoral institutions, their parties, and voters, each necessarily responds in a unique way. The process of negotiation is personal, shaped by candidates' operating context and their process of reconciling pragmatism with idealism. For self-identified anticorruption candidates, who must negotiate complex social relationships and demands in order to remain competitive, it can result in a spectrum of compromises. Voters may not have much sympathy for those facing these dilemmas—after all, no one is forcing these candidates to run for office. But the dilemma itself exposes an even more fundamental issue in Indonesian politics: if candidates feel compelled to make such compromises before they even enter government, how might they behave once in public office?

Corruption and Money Politics

Throughout this book, I explore particular candidates' attitudes and responses to the phenomenon of *money politics*, a term commonly used in Indonesia. The phenomenon is positioned within broader discourses about corruption—an issue that has frustrated Indonesians since independence and fostered the rise of an anticorruption movement following the resignation of President Suharto in 1998 (Aspinall 2019; Kramer 2019). Although there are ongoing debates about how best to define corruption (Heywood 2017; Rose 2018; Rose-Ackerman 2008), the term is generally a catch-all for a range of distinct social pathologies that includes mismanagement of public resources, weak government institutions, and complex relationships between political actors and public economic assets (Cheng and Zaum 2008). One widely used definition of corruption describes it as the abuse of public roles for private gain (Johnston 2005). Another identifies it as behavior that deviates from the formal practice of a public role for personal gain or that violates the rules of exercising influence (Nye 1990). These definitions are criticized for overgeneralizing the problem, failing to adequately define what exactly constitutes "abuse" or "personal gain" (Philp 2008, 311–312).

Processes of defining corruption also involve determining who has the authority to decide what corruption is and what acts are corrupt. These endeavors are complicated by the fact that conceptualizations of corruption based on the law, morality, and social norms are not necessarily congruent. Legal definitions of corruption are found in the statute books, whereas moral definitions are often (but not exclusively) drawn from religion and culture to categorize "evil" actions (Marquette 2012, 14). In Indonesia, these ideas fuse in legislation that tacitly recognizes the immorality of money politics, specifically banning the use of financial incentives or other types of rewards in return for votes. Meanwhile, sociological definitions of corruption are derived from norms that define acceptable and unacceptable behavior within society, a determination that ebbs and flows as norms shift with time (Leys 1990).[1] Because legal and sociological ideas of what is corrupt do not always align, we sometimes see situations where behavior is illegal but licit (Abraham and van Schendel 2005). Regardless of how corruption is defined, however, there is normative agreement that it has negative political and economic effects on ordinary citizens (Johnston 1996).

Abundant academic studies address the different functions of money in politics (Stratmann 2005).[2] Indeed, one would be hard-pressed to find examples where money *does not* play a role in determining who gets elected to public office. Money politics is not necessarily illegal, as there are plenty of legal ways for money to influence electoral outcomes. For example, in the United States, super political action committees (super PACs), although legal, have come under scrutiny for their role in facilitating unlimited spending on political campaigns with contributions from corporations, wealthy individuals, labor unions, and other interest groups (Shattuck and Risse 2020). Although this form of campaign financing is deemed legal, it invites criticisms about how access to donors and unchecked donations can privilege candidates who are well connected or bolster the interests of certain groups over the broader interests of the electoral district. Where corruption fits in this discussion is a pertinent question, especially when a lack of transparency surrounds where money has come from or what it is used for. Furthermore, even if money is used legally in election campaigns, there may still be debate about whether it has been used in moral or socially acceptable ways.

Looking at the topic of money politics, which influences elections all over the world, begs the question of why study this issue in Indonesia? Studies identify comparable challenges in neighboring countries, including Malaysia (M. Weiss 2016), the Philippines (Canare, Mendoza, and Lopez 2018; Colmenares 2017;

Hicken et al. 2019), and Thailand (Phongpaichit and Baker 2004). Farther afield, studies from other countries confirm that the Indonesian experience has parallels in other parts of the world.[3] It is impossible to conclude whether the situation in Indonesia is better or worse than of other countries, but it is undeniably a pressing concern—at least for those who would like to see freer and fairer elections. It is not surprising, then, that the role of money in elections has attracted attention among scholars of Indonesian politics.

While Indonesia is far from alone in its experiences with money politics in elections, it offers a particularly rich case. Indonesia is a large country, with over 193 million voters going to the polls in 2019.[4] It is also a relatively new democracy, transitioning in 1998 from authoritarianism. In addition, it stages some of the world's most complex single-day legislative elections, in which voters select representatives for local, provincial, and national legislatures, as well as the national Regional Representative Council. This book takes advantage of these circumstances to investigate issues that have bearing on Indonesia's democracy today. At the same time, it offers lessons for other countries that experience similar concerns—emphasizing that untangling the influence of context, and how individual decisions interact with that context, can help in understanding how things have come to be the way they are.

Definitionally, money politics and corruption are, of course, not synonymous. But the concepts are interrelated and are often conflated in Indonesian electoral campaigns. Money politics generally describes the array of activities—including vast spending on election campaigns, such as distribution of cash payments, goods, or services to voters, and promises of future benefit to voters or electoral officials—used to gain competitive advantage in an electoral race (Norris and Van Es 2016). The main subset of money politics that this book engages with is vote buying, though it will touch on other activities as well. Early definitions of vote buying conceptualized it as simply an exchange of money for votes (J. Weiss 1988). However, definitions now incorporate transaction-based strategies in which a candidate offers an economic incentive, such as a direct transfer of cash, goods, or services, in return for the promise of votes. These transactions often occur before the election, which also makes candidates vulnerable to betrayal, especially in the context of a secret ballot.

Vote buying, like the term corruption, is a catch-all term, with academic observers such as Aspinall and Sukmajati (2016) preferring the more nuanced terminology of patronage and clientelism in their analysis of money politics in the Indonesian case. Although clientelism and patronage are sometimes used interchangeably, there is a definitional distinction between the two. Patronage refers to the distribution or promise of public benefits (Hutchcroft 2014), whereas clientelism describes personal power relationships through which material benefit—

including both state resources and those provided through personal funds—is used to secure political backing. Thus, patronage relationships can be viewed as a specific type of clientelism (Berenschot and Aspinall 2020). However, despite this lack of precision, money politics and vote buying are common parlance in discussions about Indonesia. Reflecting this reality, I use these terms throughout this book to describe the exchange-based campaign activities that I observed.

There are specific laws that prohibit vote buying during election campaigns in Indonesia. Law No. 10/2008 on the General Election of Members for the People's Representative Council (DPR), Regional Representative Council (DPD), and the Regional People's Representative Councils (DPRD I and II) identifies a host of activities that could be dubbed money politics.[5] In no uncertain terms, it forbids the use of financial inducements as tools of persuasion during an election campaign. It also requires candidates to conduct themselves in accordance with the law, and, at least in theory, it may impose sanctions on those deemed to have breached legal standards. But beyond legal definitions, engaging in money politics implies that a person has used the resources at the person's disposal—position and/or access to funds—to manipulate democratic processes and circumvent a "fair election" in which candidates are judged on their capacity to best represent the interests of their electoral district. Moreover, if elections occur within a system where the exchange of cash, goods, or promises for votes is a precondition for support at the ballot box, those who are unable to offer such inducements are necessarily disadvantaged, regardless of their capacity and commitment to genuinely represent the concerns of their constituents.

Much of the groundwork on the issue of vote buying in Indonesia and the mechanics behind it has been covered by Aspinall and Berenschot (2019) and Muhtadi (2019) in their investigations of Indonesia's 2014 general election. Aspinall and Berenschot's work (2019, 3) offers a case for the role of informal politics—the use of personal networks to amass votes—in Indonesia's elections. They observe conduct of candidates through this clientelist lens, with a focus on how the relationships that candidates build and the money they distribute sit within a context where politics, personal relationships, and self-enrichment are intertwined. Using qualitative interviews and a national survey, their book ultimately seeks to make more definitive assessments of the prevalence of clientelism and the reasons it occurs. Aspinall and co-authors Rohman, Hamdi, and Triantini (2017) also offer a rationale for why a political candidate may decide to adopt a money politics strategy. They argue that "market logic" guides decisions in which candidates will target their vote-buying efforts toward "loyalists" to ensure that they at least turn up to vote. In contrast, the core focus of Muhtadi's (2019) work is on determining the prevalence of vote buying and motivations to "sell" votes. He concludes that vote buying is both "imprecise" and subject to "leakage," since candidates distribute money to voters who may ultimately select someone else. Nevertheless, he argues, the number of voters who respond favorably to vote buying may still be enough to secure victory in a tight competition, therefore providing candidates with an incentive to engage in money politics.[6]

My analysis draws on these studies. However, it departs from their approach to focus in more depth on the decision-making process for candidates. Whereas other works on this topic often start with the aim of explaining what money politics looks like, its prevalence, or why it happens, I begin with candidates who *want* to present themselves as anticorruption candidates and seem to be against money politics, tracing how their campaigns proceed from this starting point. This study also differs from, but complements, others on this subject in its approach and methodology—and particularly in its extended case studies of individual candidates. With a finer focus on the struggles of individuals, it becomes possible to see the tension between performance, practice, and principles against a backdrop where money politics is so common. A close charting of individuals' election journeys highlights different aspects of the campaign, including the role of identity and values, changes in behavior, the emotion behind decisions, and the personal toll of competing for public office. In analyzing the case studies, I draw on a shared literature with the aforementioned works but also on theories of agency and deriving advantage in decision making as outlined in works by C. Campbell (2009), Cook and Emerson (1978), and Swartz (1997).

Even though this book focuses on a single campaign perspective—that of candidates—it is important to acknowledge the ongoing debate surrounding where the impetus for vote-buying behavior comes from and to look for ways that this study may contribute to that debate. This question has caught the attention of scholars hoping to move beyond the chicken-and-egg conundrum of money politics: is it *vote buying* or *vote selling*? Vote buying implies that the ultimate responsibility for transactions intended to secure votes in elections lies with candidates. However, an alternative possibility is that the primary driver of this behavior is the willingness, indeed the *desire*, of voters to derive material benefit from the election process itself. Vote selling, sometimes described as "demand-driven vote buying," is the act whereby a voter promises to vote in a certain way, causing a candidate to agree to pay them (Rieber 2001). Interestingly, while Indonesian law expressly criminalizes candidates for vote buying, the legislation on elections overlooks the culpability of voters in this transaction and there are no explicit sanctions against individual citizens who sell their vote. The outcome of both vote buying and vote selling is exclusionary in that it favors candidates who have higher social standing, better financial resources, and more political influence, with implications for the quality and competence of lawmakers (Keefer and Vlaicu 2017; Shattuck and Risse 2020). Thus, research on the motivations and experiences of candidates in electoral campaigns feeds into wider discussions about the nature and quality of democracy in a given place. In the concluding chapter, I return to this discussion and outline what this study has shown vis-à-vis debates about vote buying and vote selling in Indonesia.

Anticorruptionism

In developing this book, I expanded upon the term *anticorruptionism* to describe the campaign strategy adopted by several political parties and some individual candidates in Indonesia. I drew from Sampson (2010), who originally coined the term to describe the resources, including people, knowledge, and symbols, that are mobilized to agitate for corruption eradication. While my usage differs slightly from Sampson's, it captures a similar intent—the framing of debates about corruption within discourses of morality. There is a further distinction to be made between anticorruption efforts and anticorruptionism, in the sense that *efforts* are actual attempts to hold institutions and their representatives accountable, whereas anticorruptionism exists primarily as a rhetorical tool.[7] Clearly, there is some intersection between what influences anticorruption efforts and anticorruptionism. But in this book, I focus more on what drives image creation and the use of rhetoric, rather than analyzing candidates as stakeholders in the broader project of combating corruption.

When anticorruption rhetoric and discourse are used in politics, they play into a whole range of "public-service related" values such as trust, honesty, humanity, equity, and responsibility, which Collins (2012, 6) describes as moral "non-negotiables." These exist within an ethical discourse that is, as Kleinman (1999, 363) contends, "an abstract articulation and debate over codified values . . . [usually] conducted by elites, both global and local." Mobilizing anticorruptionism not only speaks to a (declared) commitment toward fighting corruption but is also intended to present the candidate as having "good" values. This seemingly principled opposition toward evils such as bribery, vote buying, graft, siphoning government funds, and nepotism goes some way to explaining why anticorruption symbols are so prevalent in elections around the world, including in Indonesia. Whether this ethical discourse is accepted or prioritized by the communities that candidates are trying to win over, and what it looks like once it has been adjusted to accommodate local understandings of value, fairness, and the political system, is a different matter altogether. Some voters may buy in to the anticorruption ideal wholeheartedly, but, more likely, many will not.

Harnessing anticorruptionism in a campaign is not necessarily an ideological pursuit. When referring to "anticorruption candidates," I am talking about the strategic image individuals wish to present at a specific time, which may or may not reflect a firm ideological commitment to opposing corruption. For some candidates, appeals to anticorruptionism may be purely instrumental. As Aspinall (2005a, 118) observed of the 2004 national legislative and presidential elections, the "dominant discourse of the elections was democratic, against corruption and even pro-change . . . [but it] was merely an empty rhetorical device intended to mask continued elite dominance." Candidates like this are likely to respond quite differently to pressure to buy votes than candidates who hold a deep commitment to corruption eradication. This distinction also explains, in broad terms at least, why a candidate might begin their campaign with an anticorruptionism platform, then switch tactics as soon as cracks begin to appear. There will always be politicians who are willing to pay lip service to hot-button issues but abandon this rhetoric when it stops serving their interests (Edelman 1988; Petrocik, Benoit, and Hansen 2003). Indeed, this use of corruption as an election issue seems to be common in Indonesia, particularly in the centralized political party campaigns that are created and directed from Jakarta (Kramer 2015), but it is rarely supported by any concerted commitment to policing candidate behavior throughout campaigns.

In chapter 2, I explore more closely why anticorruptionism has become so popular among some parties and candidates and the challenges that it has presented, given Indonesia's unique political history. The theoretical literature on campaign strategies helps, to some extent, to explain the appeal of anticorruptionism as an electioneering strategy. Election campaigns provide an opportunity for politicians to chase votes by advancing ideas that they believe will resonate with voters—the hot-button topics that people are angry about and want to see addressed (Rohrschneider 2002). While professing a moral motivation to fight corruption may create a good sound bite, there are also more practical reasons why candidates might choose to focus on corruption in their electoral campaign. First, it is useful when attacking opponents, especially incumbents, to be able to lay charges of impropriety or corruption against them, promoting campaigns focused on moral character, personal finances, family life, and daily habits (Welch and Hibbing 1997). It is perhaps not surprising, then, that members of smaller, less dominant parties often appeal to voters in this way, claiming they are best placed to banish electoral fraud and corruption in situations where the large political parties who have held power are perceived to have failed (McCann and Domínguez 1998). Second, drawing attention to corruption issues during the early stages of campaigning, especially in relation to electoral fraud, provides a basis to later question unfavorable results (McCann and Domínguez 1998), much like was seen in Donald Trump's 2016 and 2020 presidential campaigns in the United States (Cottrell, Herron, and Westwood 2018). But even if instrumentalism influences the perceived utility of anticorruptionism, this does not mean that candidates are necessarily disingenuous in their use of the strategy. For some, the seeming utility of anticorruptionism may in fact align with personal values, and these personal values remain a driver for adopting this specific strategy.

Campaigns and Context

A working democracy requires an informed citizenry, and campaigns play an essential democratic function in *informing* voters about the competing political parties, their candidates, and their stance on key issues (Banducci, Giebler, and Kritzinger 2017; Lau and Redlawsk 2001; Nadeau et al. 2008). But for political parties and candidates, election campaigns are also about *persuading*. Achieving one's political interests is accomplished "by getting others to accept your view and perspective" (Hall 1972, 51), and political parties and candidates that are serious about winning strive to maximize the persuasiveness of their campaigns.

To achieve this goal, campaigns require the investment of time, money, and human resources in their construction and execution. Election campaigns are not created out of thin air—in fact, in today's age of professionalized elections, they are likely to be strategically imagined, carefully constructed, and purposefully delivered. The persuasiveness of campaigns lies in tapping into what will appeal to voters in an environment where many voters have neither the time, nor the enduring interest, to sift through vast swaths of information about political parties, candidates, and pressing issues (Downs 1957; Schmitt-Beck and Farrell 2002). Even though campaign communication and marketing can play an integral role in the mechanics of a campaign, what candidates *do* is equally important in determining voter attitudes and responses. Within these parameters, vote buying is also a campaign strategy, relying on voters' openness to illegal behavior and the attraction of cash, goods, or promises in return for political support.

Election campaigns are generally seen as comprising four basic elements (Norris 2002, 128): the messages the campaign wishes to communicate, the channel(s) of communication employed to relay these messages, the impact of these messages on target audiences, and the feedback loop from the audience to the campaigning organization. I extend on these elements—and particularly on the notion of the feedback loop—to consider campaigns as exercises that reflect ongoing, subjective assessments of how candidates decide what is persuasive, what is useful, and what actions are acceptable or unacceptable. Thus, campaigns can be understood and interpreted as ongoing responses to the sociopolitical environment in which they are constructed and individuals' interpretations of this environment.

Beyond information and persuasion, campaigns also have another, more personal function. They are in essence performative attempts by individual candidates to establish a specific image and a reputation. As such, campaigns become an *embodiment* of the appearance, personal values, and ethics of those who create them. As Mahler (2006) contends, entering the political world is a choice. Many candidates view it as a personal "vocation," a calling that requires them to present an image of themselves to the world. While the decision to run for office may stem from a variety of reasons, an individual's perception of what is moral and what is right will guide what strategies the candidate chooses, while also influencing the emotional toll the candidate undergoes, in the quest to win. Most politicians will publicly claim that they are driven by a desire to fix certain problems. Regardless of whether this is a sincere motivation, their conduct in the public eye invites scrutiny and will lead to suppositions about who they are as a person. How candidates respond when their campaign strategy—indeed, their self-image—is challenged, says much about who they are and the tenacity required to go against the electoral grain. A considered focus on individual contexts provides a meaningful lens for understanding how candidates make strategic decisions at various stages of their campaign. In the cases of the candidates profiled in this book, the dilemma of how to negotiate their campaigns in the face of money politics opens up discussions about how context drives decision making in elections. At the same time, it encourages a closer look at the role of individuals within the electoral environment and what underpins responses to this dilemma.

Every electoral campaign offers a unique context, and each campaign is imagined and produced accordingly. Borrowing from Van Dijk (2008, 4), I use the term context to describe the agglomeration of different factors that bear influence during an electoral campaign. Several facets of this understanding of context are especially pertinent for the analysis to come. First, contexts are always subjective (Edelman 1988; Van Dijk 2008). When attempting to make meaning out of the processes that shape the construction and execution of electoral campaigns, one must remember that strategies are based on interpretations of the world as held by candidates, campaign advisers, and other agents involved. A second important element is differentiating between macro and micro contexts, which I offer as a practical means for classifying the influences that exist during campaigns. At the macro level, context is driven by historical situations or sociopolitical structures, while at the micro level, influences may be specific to a party or individual. In terms of context, the root causes of vote buying, patronage, and clientelism are also complicated. Institutions have a large part to play in encouraging such behavior. Different aspects of the electoral system, including candidate-centered electoral rules, party organization, and access to government resources, all play a role in normalizing vote buying (Hicken 2007). The macro context, fueled by Indonesia's recent political history and the nature of its democratic transition, certainly creates a fertile environment for vote buying. However, these factors alone cannot explain exactly why candidates take the paths that they do, nor the nuances and differences in each individual campaign.

A third factor is that context is highly dynamic and develops "in parallel with interaction and (other) thoughts" (Van Dijk 2008, 18). The relevance of certain influences to the electioneering process may wax and wane, transforming the electoral campaign context as they do. These processes are not lineal but rather shaped by different factors interacting at different points in time. Taking this into account invites us to ask what contextual factors might lead a candidate to pivot strategies and what role temporality plays in campaigns. The dynamism of electoral contexts also offers hope: what we see today is not a measure of how things will always be. Pinpointing the circumstances under which a candidate makes a particular decision can provide a starting point for disentangling the contexts that might lead to a similar, undesirable decision for candidates in elections to come.

Positioning Candidates in Campaigns

Within the campaign sphere there are three key groups of actors: (1) the candidates themselves and their campaign team, (2) the voters, and (3) the political parties that candidates represent. While the first two spheres are central to campaign development, the influence of political parties can vary significantly. For some candidates, upholding party standards and channeling existing party rhetoric may be very important, while others may view the party as merely a vehicle for entry into the electoral race. There are arguments that other groups could also be included as campaign actors—for example, electoral bureaucrats, members of the media, and those representing corporate interests—but I very much focus on the experiences of candidates in this book. From this perspective, I discuss how the candidates I followed initially conceived their campaigns, encountered and interpreted voters' desires, and the extent to which their party shaped their campaign. Although I offer some reflections on candidates' opinions with regard to voters' motives, I do not make claims about why voters make the decisions that they make.

The behavior of candidates is not an automatic response to the political landscape in which they find themselves. While establishing the systemic factors that influence candidate behavior is important, there is some danger in generalizing candidate behavior. There is a need to move beyond assumptions that political identity is somehow fixed, to ask more meaningful questions: "On what basis, at different times and in different places, does the nonfixity become temporarily fixed in such a way that individuals and groups can behave as a particular kind of agency, political or otherwise? How do people become shaped into acting subjects, understanding themselves in particular ways?" (Dirks, Eley, and Ortner 1994, 32). I must acknowledge here that it may seem that I also risk falling into this trap of generalizing and essentializing identity by referring to and writing about "anticorruption candidates." However, readers will later see this label questioned—especially in the case study chapters. Also, in campaigns, just as in everyday life, different spaces and occasions demand different behavior (Hetherington 1998). Therefore, to gain a deeper knowledge of candidates and what fuels their decisions, we must look at their behavior over time and across different circumstances; otherwise, we risk developing a static image of political behavior.

The dynamism of an electoral campaign is in part the product of private negotiations through which candidates reconcile their values and expectations with the influences around them. While party platforms may offer some guidance, in Indonesia, candidates' own values and interests largely determine the identity and discourse that they adopt in their campaigns. A study of individual campaigns provides insight into both how local understanding of politics and elections influences the actions of candidates and the discordance between the ethical ideal (against money politics) and local morality (permissive of money politics), as well as the impact of this disjuncture in a specific campaign. It also reflects the role that values play in elections and the psychological work involved in reconciling ideals and reality. Values determine what a candidate wants (and is willing) to say and do during a campaign. These stances are then interwoven with other identity markers such as religion, ethnicity, and gender to create a narrative about the candidate and what the candidate wishes to represent to voters.

Decision making can be viewed through the prism of agency, since a candidate has the ability to make decisions that promote their interests and the capacity to maintain a program of action that serves these interests (C. Campbell 2009). The fact that "anticorruption" candidates consider—and sometimes end up—engaging in vote-buying behavior in some form or another reflects the realities of Indonesia's democracy. But anticorruption candidates have more at stake than rivals who have not expressed any moral sentiment about vote buying, or corruption more generally. Many candidates may have no qualms about engaging in vote buying as a campaign tactic and therefore their decision-making process about whether to engage in the practice will likely be driven by means rather than morals. For anticorruption candidates, however, the decisions they make about whether to engage in money politics are additionally complex precisely because they want to portray an image of being more moral than their rivals. Indeed, they often hold the belief that they *are* more ethical candidates.

The terms under which candidates will create strategies, or shift existing strategies, vary significantly from person to person, depending on their resources, personal circumstances, self-identity, and sense of morality. For candidates who wish to market themselves as "clean," the dilemmas are jarring—giving money to voters in return for votes is not just illegal or wrong but also expensive, and the returns are uncertain. But if their rivals are doing it and the strategy appears to offer a competitive edge, then where does that leave them? Do the ends justify the means? How can they reconcile the meeting with a village head where they lamented together how terrible those other, corrupt, politicians are, only to agree soon after to fund a new irrigation system? For candidates who are more utilitarian in their approach to anticorruptionism, seeing it as a means for gaining competitive advantage rather than a reflection of their core beliefs, the decision to shift strategies is much easier.

We can broadly categorize their potential responses to pressures to engage in money politics by looking at two core factors: the candidates' personal commitment to rejecting money politics and the perceived utility of an anticorruption identity. A host of considerations influence these factors. Assuming that candidates feel external pressure from voters (and perhaps also from their campaign team or political party) to use money to gain support, decision making outcomes can be categorized in four general domains (see figure 1).

This typology categorizes candidates seeking to campaign on an anticorruption identity in terms of the decisions they make throughout their campaigns in relation to money politics. Some candidates will begin and end their campaigns in the *acceptance* quadrant, setting out on their campaign without an

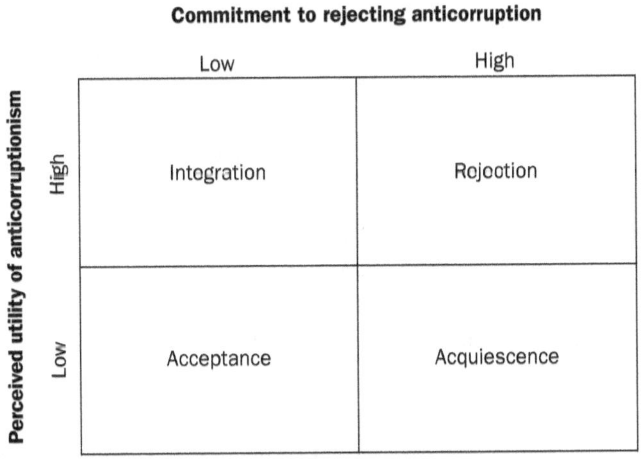

	Commitment to rejecting anticorruption	
	Low	High
Perceived utility of anticorruptionism — High	Integration	Rejection
Perceived utility of anticorruptionism — Low	Acceptance	Acquiescence

FIGURE 1. Outcomes of decision-making in candidate responses to money politics.

interest in using anticorruptionism as a campaign tactic. Acceptance of vote buying is where a candidate simply understands this to be normal, has no ethical objection to it, and has no desire to engage with anticorruptionism. Acceptance also denotes that the candidate has the resources to meaningfully participate in vote buying, which will not be the case for all candidates. The candidates who fall into this sector would likely believe that vote buying is expected by voters and attempting to campaign on anticorruptionism is not a viable, winning alternative to this strategy. In addition, candidates who are using anticorruptionism in their campaigns for utilitarian reasons—and initially perceive its utility as high—may easily shift to an acceptance of vote buying when they no longer feel they can derive advantage from mobilizing an anticorruption stance.

Depending on context, some candidates may be able to *integrate* vote buying into their campaigns alongside anticorruption discourse, leading to a simultaneous use of anticorruptionism and vote-buying strategies. In looking at cases of integration, we can study more closely what circumstances allow a candidate to continue to use anticorruption rhetoric while also engaging in money politics. Candidates who have a deep commitment to anticorruption values are likely to continue to *reject* vote buying because their personal commitment to the ideal makes the other options highly undesirable. Rejection can also stem from a lack of resources, where a candidate simply does not have the option of using this strategy. But if a candidate has the means and feels subjected to sufficient external pressure—for example, the absence of other advantages such as deep ties to the voter base—the candidate may ultimately *acquiesce*, even if they originally intended to reject vote buying. Acquiescence describes a situation where a candidate has a stated, perhaps even genuine, moral commitment to rejecting vote buying and presenting themselves as an anticorruption candidate but changes tack at some point in the campaign. Of the four quadrants, acquiescence is one that candidates can move into during the course of a campaign, but it is not a starting position.

Using this typology to classify candidates can help clarify the nexus between anticorruptionism and money politics. However, such categorizations are at best a rudimentary form of labeling. More interesting questions include what might compel a candidate to move from one quadrant to another? Conversely, we can consider what allows some candidates to not deviate from their initial strategies and remain in one quadrant throughout their campaign. Particularly in the case of a "rejection" of vote buying, what are the circumstances under which a candidate develops this response and stays the course? This approach to understanding and analyzing candidates and their decision making during campaigns can be used to interrogate case studies in places beyond Indonesia where vote buying is also endemic. Through this lens we can consider how context and personal values influence campaign decision making over the course of an election and refine our understanding of how candidates respond to external pressure in their campaigns by interrogating campaign decision making over an extended period of time.

Approach and Methods

In many ways, electoral campaigns hold a mirror up to the societies in which they take place. They reflect the prevailing political sentiments of the moment, capturing a snapshot of what seems to matter and to whom. An in-depth study of campaigns—those who manufacture them and the spaces in which they occur—can tell us a great deal about the conceptualization, mobilization, and infusion of values within them. It also offers insight into how "macro contexts" intersect with the politics of the personal, shaping the production of campaigns. Exploring electoral campaigns as they unfold provides an opportunity to observe just how complex campaign development can be in establishing a distinct and marketable political identity and communicating it to voters in a persuasive manner.

I adopt an extended case study approach that draws heavily on political ethnography, a method based on closely observing actors in real time (Baiocchi and Connor 2008; Mitchell 1983, 194). Ethnographic approaches have long been embraced by political scientists, albeit increasingly from the margins as a consequence of a narrowing understanding of "what constitutes legitimate research" in political science (Schatz 2013, 1). In pushing back against quantitative gatekeeping, I contend that political ethnography has much to offer in studying politics, power relations, and decision making and can meaningfully contribute to attempts to understand the political world. Concurring with Dirks, Eley, and Ortner (1994, 32) and Kubik (2013), I believe that studying the politics of specific issues and environments requires us to acknowledge that identities are not fixed, that agency and motivations ebb and flow over time. This understanding is at the heart of the extended case study, which integrates long-term engagement in fieldwork to "invite the researcher to 'see' differently," allowing "heterogeneity, causal complexity, dynamism, contingency, and informality to come to the fore" (Schatz 2013, 11).

In terms of methodology, my project was guided by the work of Burawoy (1998, 5), who suggests we extend a "reflexive" approach to case studies and embrace engagement as a means for gaining knowledge rather than attempting to remove the researcher from the equation, as is common in the positivist tradition. Burawoy's conceptualization of case study methodology argues that the researcher must enter into "dialogue" with participants, with local processes and extralocal forces, and with theory, using these three mechanisms to build a more complete picture of what is happening and why. The researcher is present and conscious that their presence has consequences. This awareness requires the researcher to build a narrative based not solely on what the researcher sees and hears but also on what the researcher understands about the context and the theoretical frameworks that might explain it. After my observations were completed and all were noted in the many fieldwork journals I accumulated during my time in Indonesia came the task of "extending out from process to force" (Burawoy 1998, 19) to trace the source of differences between the case studies and allowing the opportunity for theoretical expansion.

The core narrative of this book is based on the physical presence I established at my sites, designed to help me understand the "around chains, paths, threads, conjunctions, or juxtapositions of locations" (Marcus 1995, 105). Combined with extensive reading on available literature about Indonesian politics, corruption, and theories of campaigns and candidate behavior, my strategy was to immerse myself in Indonesian politics in the lead-up to the 2014 elections. Beginning in 2011, I began to compile data on political parties' references to corruption in the media. Then, from December 2011 to March 2012, I spent three months in Jakarta conducting interviews with members and employees of political parties. At the same time, I began preliminary interviews with candidates from several political parties. All this preliminary groundwork provided a footing in the contemporary context of elections and the influence of anticorruptionism and money politics in the way decisions are made. After familiarizing myself with the "bigger picture," I decided on my case studies, which set the scene for the rest of the project fieldwork.

I based myself in Indonesia from June 2012 to August 2013 and February to May 2014 to undertake multisited observation for my extended case studies. This involved shadowing the main actors over time to observe the processual aspects of their campaigns. In determining my time frame, I drew from Bowler and Farrell (1992, 11), who argue that an "electoral campaign" incorporates the periods of preparation and planning, along with execution, leading up to the vote. While the official campaign period for general elections in Indonesia is short (in 2014 from March 16 to April 5), candidates spend a much longer period strategizing and organizing their campaigns. This approach contributed to a reflexive process of intersubjective interrogation between the participants and observers (Burawoy 1998). Being the explorer myself, I was able to catalogue actions and emotions in real time and locate them within the campaign landscape.

This aspect of the research focused on individuals and their actions while simultaneously positioning them within the vast networks of formal and informal organizations that both inform and result from political interactions—an approach sometimes referred to as "action theory" (Vincent 1978). To better understand the challenges faced by candidates and their engagement with vote buying, I conducted a minimum of six formal interviews with each of them over the course of campaign planning and execution. I also shadowed these candidates over several one- to two-week periods in the twelve months leading up to voting day, in all spending between one and two months with each candidate in their electoral districts. During my time on the campaign trail, I attended strategy meetings with campaign staff, meetings with polling consultants and brokers, logistical planning and procurement discussions, and community meetings and rallies, as well as being present during the "off" outside of campaign activities. The latter provided an opportunity to ask questions and reflect on the day's events. Being in the field with candidates also made it possible to observe their networks and ties to other candidates competing across the different levels of government, with local party branch offices, and with other political actors such as governors, regencies, and the police. This allowed me to build a picture of the embeddedness of candidates in intricate and complex webs of relationships, including with voters, their parties, and broader institutions, and how these relationships influenced their campaign decisions in relation to money politics.

Existing research of elections and money politics shaped much of the study, with many excellent works cited throughout the chapters of this book. This body of research had an early influence in drawing my attention to the paradox of corruption in Indonesian elections and the ongoing pervasiveness of vote buying, patronage, and clientelism. However, my "dialogue" with theory was ongoing throughout the research, reflected in the many ideas I toyed with in choosing how to approach the topic and the data collected. In early iterations of this project, I focused on the symbolic aspects of campaigning and anticorruptionism as a campaign tool. But as the study progressed, I found myself wanting to understand why particular circumstances generate certain campaign decisions for individuals. The field research made it clear to me that these decisions were not simply a response to external structures but instead were a much deeper reflection of who these candidates are as people. The project developed further in response to this insight.

As already discussed, much of the prevailing theoretical literature that underpins research on electoral campaigns takes, as its starting point, the premise that campaigns are primarily exercises in informing and persuading the public about candidates, political parties, and their platforms. This body of literature—in the realm of electoral studies—emanates primarily from Global North liberal democracies such as the United States, the United Kingdom, and western Europe. While aspects of it are relevant in the Indonesia context, it is also apparent that platform and policy discussions are often divorced from the day-to-day realities of individual campaigns, where positionality and personality play a much more prominent role. Moreover, the current academic trends toward study of media in campaigns, including television, print, and social media, felt less relevant as candidates prioritized individual meetings and establishment of broker networks over strong media engagement. But what I felt was most acutely missing from the literature was a means for explaining why some campaigns I observed changed over time. Building on this lacuna in the literature, I articulated a third "function" of campaigns, relating much more to the individual lens and world view, that is, campaigns also reflect an embodiment of individual candidates: their networks, wealth, charisma, gender, and their moral nonnegotiables. Candidate decisions about the use of anticorruptionism and vote buying are not simply a function of what a candidate thinks will be informative or persuasive to voters but also what is *possible*—practically and psychologically—for them.

The Case Studies

There was much speculation in the lead-up to the 2014 election that money politics would play a decisive role in the voting results (Reuter 2015). There was also a juxtaposition between the prevalence of illegal campaign practices and intense use of anticorruptionism by several political parties. My initial efforts focused on understanding how rhetoric about corruption became a strategy for some political parties and candidates in their electioneering. To do so, I centered my analysis on the use of anticorruptionism as an electoral strategy among candidates from emerging political parties that were competing in the general elections either for the first or second time. These newer parties promoted themselves as being committed to corruption eradication, while accusing more established parties as either unable or unwilling to take the steps necessary to decrease levels of corruption across political and bureaucratic spheres.

As the project progressed, I became increasingly interested in how the context of electoral campaigns could explain the paradox of corruption in election campaigns and how this paradox affected individual political candidates' day-to-day decisions as they planned their campaigns and, subsequently, their approach to and engagement with local voters. To this end, I selected three candidates—running in the provinces of East Java, North Sumatra, and South Sulawesi—who permitted me to observe their campaigns closely in the period leading up to the election (see figure 2).[8] At one level, the selection of these candidates represents a confluence of timing, good luck, and their openness to observation. More important, however, they were selected because when I first met them, they expressly stated that they planned to present themselves as staunch anticorruption figures. Two of the candidates vehemently rejected vote buying

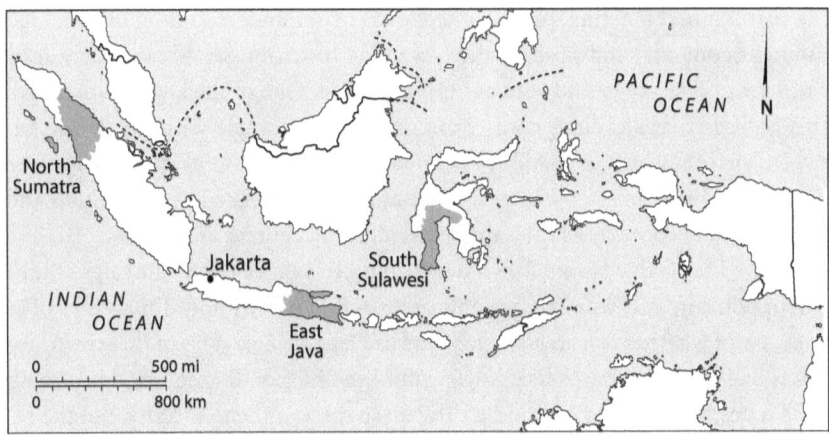

FIGURE 2. Locations of study field areas. Map by Bill Nelson.

and money politics. The third presented himself as a corruption fighter, though his attitude toward money politics was less clear when we first met. All of the candidates had a strong bond to their political party, something that is, by all accounts, uncommon among the majority of Indonesian candidates. As such, they were not chosen to be representative of a "typical candidate"—if there even is such a thing. Rather, they were selected precisely because of their commitment to anticorruptionism as a campaign tactic.

While the case studies tell us much about the nature of campaigns and the dilemmas that candidates face, they also allowed me to engage and extend theoretical discussions of political behavior. At first, I was hoping to collect a body of data on "atypical" candidates to allow an exploration of contradictions against a backdrop of what is normal or expected of subjects in a particular situation (Mitchell 1983). However, although I initially posited that anticorruption candidates would represent behavioral anomalies, I cannot say that they in fact were. I witnessed several of the expected activities and behaviors I had already heard about—the exchange of money, promising of club goods, and the like—which fit neatly with examples of vote buying offered by other researchers. It was my anxiety over whether this long-trodden path would simply lead me down the exact same roads as others before me that I turned my attention to Burawoy's (1998, 19) comparative strategy, using my case studies to trace the source of difference, making sense of each case in its connection to other cases rather than attempting to reduce cases to instances of "general laws." With this focus, my case studies could bring something new to the table. My decision to follow candidates who all stated at the outset that they intended to present themselves as anticorruption candidates, and with a seemingly genuine commitment to the issue on first meeting, provided scope for better understanding the role that different contexts, and positionality, can play in shaping how campaign decisions around strategy and vote buying are made. One of the key arguments of this book is that although many candidates must grapple with the divide between what they hope is possible and what campaign realities show them to be possible, the outcomes of this tension are as much influenced by individuals and their personal contexts as they are by overarching context above them.

While I hope this book offers a new perspective on election campaigns, anti-corruptionism, and vote buying, this approach is not without limitations. The question of whether research participants are reliable narrators of their own stories is one that all researchers grapple with. Even in spending so much time with candidates, a researcher can find it difficult to discern their sincerity. But the research approach of this project does a lot to counter this concern by situating personal interactions within broader interactions, in talking to people around the candidate, and in observing "official" campaign behavior and comparing this to what is happening behind the scenes. A second caveat is about generalizability. While the candidate experiences at the center of this book tell us much about the nature of campaigns and the dilemmas that candidates face, they are also unique and not intended to be representative of all candidates' experiences. Indeed, one of the key arguments of this book is that although candidates may face common challenges, their responses are shaped by unique, individual circumstances.

A third caveat is that this book does not set out to attribute responsibility for the prevalence of vote buying in Indonesia. From the candidates' viewpoint, the attitudes of voters and the perceived inconsistencies between ethical ideals, local moralities, and campaign norms can be confusing and frustrating. The candidates often *described* vote buying as a voter-driven phenomenon, but that is not to say that it *was* a voter-driven phenomenon. If anything, the case studies reflect the complexity of expectations and assumptions on both sides and discourage a simplistic attribution of blame. The case studies show both offers and requests for money, goods, and promises. Telling the story from a candidate perspective allows the reader to better understand the candidates' assessment of the situation and how they respond, but it offers only conjecture, based on other texts and personal observations, to explain the rationalization processes used by voters when they decide to demand goods or money. There are some excellent works that do tackle this subject, including Muhtadi's research on the 2014 elections (2019). Finally, in my discussion of candidates' personal struggles, I do not intend to portray them as heroic protagonists battling unreasonable demands. While candidates might claim that vote buying is demand driven and they are vexed by the phenomenon, they remain implicated by their decision to participate in it.

Outline of Book

At the heart of this book are personal stories that tell us not only how three individual candidates navigated the challenges of running in an election but also about the way that political systems, both formal and informal, shape electoral campaigns. Before turning to these personal stories, however, it is helpful to first explore how democratization has shaped Indonesia's political history and institutions in recent times and what implications this has had on elections. Chapter 1 begins this task by situating electoral campaigns against the backdrop of Indonesia's transition to competitive elections since 1998, tracing the evolution of the electoral system and proposing a model of how it—and other factors such as campaign norms, resources, and values—shape the decisions that candidates make. Chapter 2 then turns to a history of corruption issues in Indonesia and the politics that has made it both an enduring concern and an electoral issue. In doing so, it underscores why developing an anticorruption persona may have become a priority for some candidates in the lead-up to the 2014 elections.

The three chapters that follow offer extended narratives of individual campaigns undertaken in South Sulawesi, North Sumatra, and East Java. Even though faced with similar (though not identical) pressures to engage in money politics, each of these self-identified anticorruption candidates took very different paths over the course of their campaigns. Beginning with Ambo in South Sulawesi, we find a candidate who maintained a firm anticorruption stance throughout the campaign. We then explore the story of Ayu, who—having initially held quite an idealistic view on the fight against corruption—eventually succumbed to pressure from voters and adopted vote-buying strategies. As Ayu did not win a seat, her case also sheds light on the risks of money politics and the personal costs of bowing to pressure, both financially and emotionally. The final case is that of Bontor, an incumbent in North Sumatra. Bontor presented himself as a staunch anticorruption campaigner, even calling for the death penalty for corruption. Yet, at the same time, he leveraged his ethnic networks, channeled funding from local programs to his supporters, and distributed small payments to voters. His ability to comfortably rationalize the integration of these strategies stands in stark contrast to the other candidates. The fact that he easily retained his seat attests to the anticorruption paradox, whereby a candidate can frequently and openly criticize corruption while also buying votes and developing clientelistic networks, without any consequences at the polls.

The final chapter assesses the challenges that these candidates faced, situating them within an analytical framework of campaign decision making that highlights the competing objectives of election campaigns, which simultaneously aim to inform, persuade, and embody the candidate. It expands on the typology presented in this introduction, focusing on the circumstances that may lead an anticorruption candidate to reject, integrate, or acquiesce to money politics strategies, in the process laying bare the broader challenges posed during a campaign. In the book's conclusion, I reflect on what the cases tell us about the candidate's dilemma and how we can better understand candidates' decisions about vote buying through a multifaceted context lens. I also offer some ideas about the implications of this research beyond the case studies and the scope for replication in studying other election campaigns, both in Indonesia and elsewhere. Finally, I end with some thoughts on what this study tells us about the prospects for elections and democracy. In this last section, I discuss what this research can tell us about demand-driven vote buying, an ongoing question among academics studying Indonesian elections. Using the insights from this study, I identify ways to better understand the actions of those running for office and what these actions can tell us about democratization in Indonesia.

1
COMPETITIVE ELECTIONS AND CAMPAIGN BEHAVIOR

Electoral campaigns are imagined and created against a vast backdrop of institutions and norms that shape how candidates access the electoral system, gain nomination, and interact with the system during their campaign. To analyze the individual experiences of electoral candidates, it is important to first understand the broader context in which they are operating and the myriad influences that guide their thinking as they move through their campaigns. By tracing the recent history of electoral campaigns, we can gain a better understanding of how political contexts have changed and what this has meant for candidates competing for seats in the national legislature. In this chapter, I provide an overview of the changing electoral context in light of Indonesia's democratic transition since 1998. By locating the experiences of candidates within this dynamic political environment, I bring into focus existing electoral institutions and the effect they have on candidates competing for public office at the national level. In the second part of the chapter, I expand this discussion of context to identify key factors that shape an individual candidate's political campaign, laying the foundation for my analysis of individual accounts of campaign creation and decision making in the context of the 2014 election.

The political transition that began following the resignation of President Suharto, the authoritarian leader who ruled Indonesia from 1966 to 1998, prompted a shift in how elections and political campaigns were conceived and conducted. The post-1998 period of political reform, commonly referred to as Reformasi, saw sweeping changes to Indonesia's political institutions, including a move toward more competitive elections. At the same time, the lingering influence of over thirty years of autocratic rule has been difficult to escape, and Suharto's New Order continues to cast a long shadow over the democratization process. More than three decades of authoritarian rule has left its mark. The dominance of wealthy elites and the existence of local systems of patronage and clientelism that took hold well before Reformasi have been difficult to overcome (Blunt, Turner, and Lindroth 2012; Hadiz and Robison 2013). The effect of this dominance is evident in the ongoing power of elites and patronage systems, in the registration processes and structures of political parties, and in patterns of political participation among voters. As actors caught between the New Order legacy and the more contemporary shift toward democratization, candidates must deftly negotiate this context if they have any hope of winning office.

Although the democratization process has had varying impacts on the overall quality of democracy, it has undoubtedly generated increased space for broader engagement in electoral politics.[1] Moving beyond the three-party system of Suharto's regime, elections now incorporate multiple parties, which compete in elections at the national, provincial, and district levels. There are many more seats available, and consequently many more legislative candidates participate in general elections. The scope for inclusion in elections is larger than it has ever been. For example, quotas have now been implemented that ensure that at least 30 percent of each party's candidates in any electoral district are women (Shair-Rosenfield 2012).[2] This new diversity of candidates operates in an environment where personal identity and social networks play a vital role in how campaigns evolve. Furthermore, with an open-party system in place since 2009, most candidates have even less reason to rely on their political parties to channel votes to them. Never has the individual campaign been more important.

Elections in Indonesia

Indonesia has a long history of "depoliticization" of the masses, which has undermined citizen engagement in politics and fostered the norm of voting networks based on patronage, personal relationships, and vote buying that we see today. Moreover, the political party system, which has its roots in the New Order, places controls on eligibility while also barring individuals from competing as independent candidates in legislative elections. This means that political parties continue to act as gatekeepers, determining who can gain access to political office. Individual candidates now compete under electoral rules introduced for the 2009 elections that see them competing against candidates from both their own party and those from rival parties. These key features, as well as other elements of the electoral system, created a unique political landscape for candidates to navigate as they planned and conducted their campaigns in 2014.

New Order Legacies

We can trace many problematic aspects of Indonesia's electoral system to institutions and practices that developed under President Suharto's decades-long rule. Suharto rose to power after Cold War tensions between the Communists and the military boiled over into an attempted coup and subsequent counter-coup in 1965.[3] He solidified that power through a range of means, including both strong-arm tactics and the use of symbolic, but democratically inconsequential, elections. Suharto ruled Indonesia until 1998, when he resigned amid economic and social turmoil. There was evidence of growing concern over the government's brutality toward its own citizens, including repressing calls for democracy in Aceh and East Timor, as well as violence against labor and other human rights activists (Dibley and Ford 2019). Government corruption also fueled public discontent (Liddle 1996; Schütte 2009), as the blatant wealth of Suharto's family and cronies grew increasingly obvious. This discontent was intensified by the Asian Financial Crisis of 1997–1998 (Hill and Shiraishi 2007; Wie 2003). Indonesia's economy had experienced highs and lows during the 1990s but nothing of the scale triggered by the monetary crisis.

Drastic price increases of key basics, such as fuel and household goods, led to mass civilian protests across the country, especially in the capital, Jakarta. On May 12, 1998, soldiers opened fire on protesters, killing four students from Trisakti University and injuring several others (Bird 1999). Public outrage at the deaths sparked further riots in Jakarta and several major cities. Suharto family enterprises and those of Chinese Indonesians became targets for arson and looting, with hundreds perishing in shopping mall fires (Siegel 1998). Suharto lost the support of not only ordinary citizens but also the business elite, many of whom fled the country. Political allies also rebelled, with fourteen cabinet members refusing to continue serving under Suharto. Finally, the military, under Commander in Chief Wiranto, withdrew its support for the president, while Islamic leaders also advised him to resign (Aspinall 2005b; Ricklefs 2001). Suharto stepped down on May 21, 1998, and was replaced by his protégé, Vice President B. J. Habibie, until new elections could be conducted.

The experience of 1998 notwithstanding, elections played an important role in symbolically legitimizing Suharto's presidency. The institutionalization of the electoral system, and the role that candidates played within that system, reflected Suharto's motivation to stack the legislature heavily in his favor. The primary function of the People's Consultative Assembly (Majelis Permusyawaratan Rakyat, MPR), the overarching government body, was to elect the president and vice-president. It consisted of one thousand members including the four hundred elected representatives and one hundred military appointees who made up the National People's Representative Council (Dewan Perwakilan Rakyat, DPR). The other five hundred delegates, including representatives from each of Indonesia's provinces in the Regional Representative Council (Dewan Perwakilan Daearah, DPD) and other appointees from functional groups, were appointed by Suharto.[4] Dubbed "Pancasila Democracy,"[5] after the state ideology adopted when Indonesia achieved independence from the Dutch, the system promoted consensus-based decision making over a more adversarial strain of democracy and did not foster a strong oppositional voice.[6]

The New Order regime also took steps to distance organized politics from the everyday lives of Indonesian citizens, discouraging political party allegiances beyond the broad "streams" (*aliran*) that they represented.[7] All civil servants and their families were required to vote for the regime's political vehicle, Golkar (from Golongan Karya, Party of Functional Groups), which Suharto promoted as a movement to represent the political interests of a broad range of social groups, rather than a political party per se. Other citizens could also support Golkar or choose to cast their vote for one of two other alternatives—an Islamist party, the United Development Party (Partai Persatuan Pembangunan, PPP), or the secular-nationalist Indonesian Democratic Party (Partai Demokrasi Indonesia, PDI).[8] Beyond this, successive elections fostered the government's ideal of citizen participation—a "floating mass" of voters who were "allowed to vote every five years but would otherwise refrain from political activity" (Schwarz 2004, 33). This was underpinned by attitudes of New Order elites who felt that, owing to the political upheaval before 1965, Indonesian citizens were "not ready" for modern democracy (Haris 2004, 20). Ali Moertopo, Suharto's head of Special Operations in the 1970s, even coined the term *deparpolisasi*, meaning "the freeing of people from political party allegiances," to describe the intended outcome of the process (Bourchier and Hadiz 2003, 48). This semiofficial doctrine was particularly evident in rural areas, with political parties banned from establishing branches below the regency level. Thus, Indonesia's rural masses were almost entirely divorced from politics between 1973 and 1998, except for the brief campaign period before elections (Anderson 1990, 115), concentrating political activity in cities and fostering an urban–rural rift in political engagement that remained in place well after the end of the New Order.

Elections—or *pesta demokrasi* (festivals of democracy)—were little more than a symbolic inclusion of citizens in the political process. Between 1973 and 1998, they were "heavily rigged affairs" (Eklöf 1999, 6) designed to validate Suharto's ongoing presidency. Golkar won at least 60 percent of the votes in each of these elections. Suharto's position was bolstered by military appointments to the legislature, making it inconceivable that he could lose power as a consequence of an election result (Crouch 2010, 44). These elections were closely surveilled with "harsh methods" employed to ensure Golkar's victory, including "threats, coercion, unlawful detention, destruction of property, and outright physical abuse" affecting candidates, election scrutineers, and voters (Eklöf 1999, 91). So, if the primary purpose of elections during this time was to lend legitimacy to Suharto's regime, what did it mean to be a legislative candidate in the New Order?

Suharto's need to control electoral outcomes had a direct impact on who could run for office. All candidates were screened by the military and national intelligence agency to assess, as Moertopo euphemistically claimed before the 1972 elections, that they had the right "attitudes and . . . capabilities to fulfil their political tasks" (Bourchier 2014, 164). Candidates were expected to toe the government line at all times (Crouch 2010, 44). At the same time, because political engagement was so far removed from day-to-day life, only individuals who were tenacious and calculated in advancing their party status ended up running for office (Fionna 2014, 114). For the privileged few who were able to secure nomination, legislative seats also became a marker of esteem, offering access to patronage networks and opportunities for embezzlement, bribes, and kickbacks (Robison 1981). People asserted that parliamentarians primarily followed the "5Ds," an abbreviation for "*datang, duduk, diam, dengar, duit,*" which translates as "come, sit, be quiet, listen, money" (Sebastian 2012, 470).

Holding a prestigious parliamentary seat may have offered status and opportunities for personal enrichment, but the seats themselves held little real democratic function. As such, candidates were rarely ideologically motivated. Those competing were certainly not compelled to present any real platform to mobilize voters. Campaigns and elections were merely a hurdle to accessing the perks of public office. By the same token, voters had no real impetus to choose one candidate over another (Robison 1981), given that the composition of legislature made no real difference to the state of Indonesian politics or to government policies. Candidates in some areas may have benefited from *aliran* preferences, where the population would traditionally vote for the PPP or the PDI. Others may have chosen Golkar as an expression of gratitude for the benefits they had received as a result of Suharto's development agenda.[9] However, the "floating mass" represented a largely politically unengaged populace. Without any real policies to offer voters, and a general understanding that politicians were simply in office to rubber-stamp government decisions, campaign tactics were about leveraging relationships or offering better incentives than other candidates—a theme that has endured well after the fall of the New Order.

Changing the System

The immediate post-Suharto period saw a dramatic political shift that brought with it high public expectations for change and an opportunity to enact sweeping democratic reforms. The transitional government was determined to prove its democratic credentials. It made several far-reaching policy amendments, lifting restrictions on civil society and the media, implementing political decentralization, and initiating electoral reforms. Decentralization measures devolved power from Jakarta back to the regions, giving cities and districts more control over their budgets and resources, while also dampening the threats of separatism posed by anti-Jakarta backlash in outer islands (Nordholt 2004, 564). This decentralization agenda had immense consequences for local politics, as competition for power at the local level took on a new significance (Hadiz 2003). Included in the measures was the establishment of provincial and local legislatures, which served as new sites of political and electoral competition, while also greatly expanding the number of legislative positions available to be contested.[10]

In terms of electoral reform at the national level, new laws enacted in 1998 reduced the concentration of power, placed a two-term limit on the presidency, expanded the power of the legislature, and diminished the military presence within it (Bird 1999).[11] Although the new laws did not change the basic structure of representation established under the New Order—maintaining the existence of the MPR—they opened elections for the DPR to multiple parties and for the DPD to individual candidates.[12] There were still some restrictions on party eligibility, but these reforms drove the final nail in the coffin of Suharto's three-party system, with forty-eight parties qualifying to field candidates in June 1999. These new parties had only a narrow window to recruit candidates and organize their campaigns, and the election results were dominated by the established parties, with the PDI offshoot, the Indonesian Democratic Party of Struggle (Partai Demokrasi Indonesia Perjuangan, PDIP) and Golkar securing the most votes by a healthy margin. Despite this, the elections were heralded as "democracy restored," with twenty-one parties securing seats in the national legislature in a relatively peaceful and open competition (Liddle 2000). The process also benefited from relaxed media controls, allowing for openly publicized debate in which candidates could level all manner of criticisms at the government (Hara 2001).

Elections for members of the national legislature are significant for two main reasons. First, the elections dictate the lawmaking power and influence that parties have. The more seats a political party wins, the greater the party's ability to create or amend national legislation. Second, the number of seats won by a political party in the national legislature influences their ability to nominate a presidential candidate. With these motivations in mind, the Indonesian government has continued to "tinker" with the parameters of electoral contests since 1998 (Morgenbesser and Pepinsky 2019, 16), making changes to party eligibility, presidential nomination, and electing candidates. Party eligibility in elections has become a battleground for existing political parties keen to maintain systems that work in their favor. The laws guiding party eligibility to both compete and to take their place in the national legislature have been amended several times (Shair-Rosenfield 2019).[13] After the 1999 election, new, stricter eligibility criteria were introduced, ostensibly making elections more manageable by deterring "hopeless parties" but also favoring the three New Order parties (Crouch 2010, 78). Regulations for eligibility required parties to have at least one thousand registered members, a permanent regional office in each province and in 75 percent of districts or municipalities, and a chapter in at least half of each of the sub-districts, answering to the permanent office (although these chapters did not need to be permanent). Forming a new party that met all of these requirements took time, money, and resources, not to mention the ongoing costs once the party had been validated. Establishing a viable, competitive political party was very expensive and burdensome, with substantial costs in establishing and maintaining the expected number of branches across the archipelago. In short, even with a more open government, it remained hard for new parties to get a foothold in this system.

Regulations passed in 2003 allowed only parties that had won either a total of 2 percent of seats in the DPR or 3 percent of seats in at least half of the provincial and local legislatures to contest a subsequent election. This excluded all but six of the parties that had competed in 1999 from competing in the 2004 general election. For the 2014 election, parties had to clear a minimum threshold of 3.5 percent of the total national vote to assume any seats in the legislature, even if party candidates had obtained enough votes to win an individual seat.[14] The eligibility threshold was also narrowed in 2014, requiring incumbent parties to have secured at least 3 percent of the total number of seats in the DPR in order to contest the subsequent election. The Electoral Supervisory Board (Badan Pengawas Pemilihan Umum, Bawaslu) was empowered to make a final determination as to whether parties met these requirements.

In 2014, the parties that qualified based on these threshold requirements included the New Order–related parties the PDIP, the Golkar, and the PPP, as well as the newer Islamic parties the National Mandate Party (Partai Amanat Nasional, PAN), the National Awakening Party (Partai Kebangkitan Bangsa, PKB), and the Prosperous Justice Party (Partai Keadilan Sejahtera, PKS). A number of successful new parties were created primarily to serve as vehicles for the leadership ambitions of their founders, such as the Democratic Party (Partai Demokrat), Gerindra (Partai Gerakan Indonesia Raya, Great Indonesia Movement

Party), Nasdem (Partai Nasem, National Democratic Party), and Hanura (Partai Hati Nurani Rakyat, People's Conscience Party).[15] The latter three were established by political elites who had been unable to achieve their aspirations for power within Golkar, driving them to create their own political parties (Sherlock 2013; Tomsa 2009).

Another key change in the political system related to the nomination and election of the president, which also had implications for the relationship between national legislative elections, political parties, and presidential candidates. In 1999, the president was elected by the People's Consultative Assembly, meaning that political parties had direct influence in determining the presidency. Although the PDIP won the most seats in the DPR, its presidential nominee, Megawati Sukarnoputri, was bested by a coalition of opposing parties and representatives from the DPD, which chose Abdurrahman Wahid to be Indonesia's first elected president of the post-Suharto era.[16] Megawati did become president following Wahid's impeachment in 2001, but the dissatisfaction sparked by this process eventually led to a constitutional amendment that introduced a direct plebiscite to select the president. Parties still had the right to nominate presidential candidates, but those candidates then had to win at least 50 percent of the popular vote across Indonesia and a minimum of 2 percent in every province. If no candidate won a 50 percent majority, there was to be a second runoff election between the two leading candidates to determine the presidency.

Eligibility criteria to nominate a presidential candidate became hotly contested, and more-established parties sought to secure a competitive advantage by advocating for high nomination thresholds that would disadvantage parties with a smaller presence in the national legislature. For the 2004 presidential elections, political parties had to garner at least 5 percent of the popular vote or 3 percent of seats in the legislative elections of April 2004 to nominate a presidential candidate. With this new rule, the legislative elections took on a renewed significance, as the more seats won, the more opportunity a party would have to put forward a presidential candidate without having to form a coalition. At the same time, the direct presidential elections introduced in 2004 paved the way for a shift that put presidential candidates at the forefront of legislative campaigns, particularly at the national level (Gunn 2019). Political parties and candidates could promote themselves by referencing their presidential nominees, urging voters to support their preferred presidential candidate by choosing their party. The role of established parties was entrenched even further in 2008 when the eligibility to nominate was again amended, with political parties now needing at least 25 percent of the popular vote or 20 percent of seats in the DPR to put forward a presidential candidate. Not all political parties, particularly those with a smaller presence in the national legislature, were happy with the nomination threshold, but it has persisted. An updated 2017 law on elections (Law No. 7/2017) maintained this threshold despite heated debate in the legislature. In more recent times, before the 2019 elections, the Constitutional Court decreed that the legislative and presidential elections must occur simultaneously. Thus, legislative elections were held separately from the presidential contest for the last time in 2014.[17]

A third major change in the electoral system was the introduction of the open-party list in 2009. Under this arrangement, citizens could vote directly for individual candidates instead of having to vote for a political party, as had been the case since 1972. This regulation has arguably had the most significant impact on how individual elections campaigns are run.[18] Before its introduction, parties would rank each candidate to determine their position on the ballot, and the first-ranked candidate would receive a seat if the party won the requisite number of votes. If the party garnered sufficient votes to be allocated multiple seats, then these seats would be awarded to candidates based on their position on the party list (Johnson Tan 2012). This closed-party list system meant that candidates had to ingratiate themselves with decision makers in their political party to be allocated a winnable position on the ballot. But while political jockeying took place to secure a plum spot on the list, candidates from the same party were not in direct competition once campaigning began. The fact that every candidate on the list had an interest in soliciting as many votes as possible for the party provided an incentive to work collectively, fostering greater cohesion among a party's candidates during the campaign (Muhtadi 2019).

Up to the 2004 elections, party list ranking had been crucial to a candidate's political prospects. However, this all changed in December 2008 when the Constitutional Court ruled that voters had the right to direct their vote to an individual candidate (Aspinall 2010, 108). This decision had ramifications for both party and individual campaigns. Under the previous system, political parties had total control over how votes were apportioned—to the extent that candidates with low levels of local support could obtain a seat if they had party backing (Crouch 2010, 63). With the new system, political maneuvering to obtain official party positions became less crucial (Johnson Tan 2012, 171). As a result, the power of local branch leaders, who played a pivotal role in both recruiting candidates and determining the order of the party list, diminished. While a high ranking remained desirable, a candidate's position on the party list became primarily a status symbol—reflecting the candidate's standing in the party and, in some cases, the level of party support the contender could expect to receive—with little practical significance if the candidate could not attract enough personal votes.

Individual Candidates in Elections

The post-1998 democratization process changed the engagement of candidates in elections in several ways. Despite some restrictions that continued the New Order tradition of excluding some groups—for example, the Electoral Commission requirements on physical fitness introduced in 2004, which may disadvantage potential candidates with a disability (Dibley and Tsaputra 2019)—post–New Order elections have included a more diverse range of actors.[19] The new system allowed for candidates who would have faced great difficulty in participating during Suharto's regime, if not being outright barred, such as labor unionists (Caraway and Ford 2020) and other civil society activists (Tomsa and Setijadi 2018). In addition to facilitating more competitors running for office, post–New Order electoral reforms drastically changed the nature of engagement for legislative candidates in national elections. Whereas under Suharto candidates were generally party cadres, representing their party's interests and vetted to ensure allegiance to the existing system, the new electoral system, and particularly the introduction of the open-party list, placed an emphasis on candidates as individuals, rather than simply representatives of a larger party machine.

This focus on individual candidates has contributed to an increase in celebrity candidates, with television, film, and music stars, as well as business and civil society leaders, turning their hand to politics. Hoping to capitalize on their preexisting reputation, political parties actively recruit celebrities and use them as "commodities" to draw voters who are already familiar with these people (Ahmad 2020). The attraction of having a candidate with a base of supporters who may be inclined to choose them regardless of how much effort they put into their campaign is clear. And even though the success of such candidates has been mixed (Firmansyah 2017), the trend has continued. This speaks to parties' desires for "instant" candidates, rather than nurturing candidates internally through ongoing recruitment and cadre training (Fionna 2014, 204). In short, candidate selection may sometimes be motivated by the *massa* (mass of dedicated voters) that a candidate could offer a political party, rather than an alignment of values or ideology.

While it is in parties' interests to give their candidates for the national legislature the best possible chance of success—both in terms of power over lawmaking and ability to put forward a presidential nominee—candidates are, for the most part, left to fend for themselves. In the absence of robust party platforms, most candidates go in search of the party that will offer them the most advantage (Aspinall 2013, 40). Political parties, in many cases, are simply the vehicle that allows candidates to pursue electoral success. They may also offer some advantage in terms of party identification—particularly in terms of the Islamist-pluralist ideological divide that characterizes Indonesian political parties (Fossati et al. 2020). Although Islamic parties have not been able to outperform their secular-nationalist rivals in elections (Nastiti and Ratri 2018), they stand as identity markers for voters who wish to see a religious influence in national politics (Tanuwidjaja 2010). Parties that have their roots in the New Order—the PDIP, the PPP, and Golkar—also continue to benefit from old *aliran* concepts, though there are continuing debates of how much this advantage has declined in the post-Suharto era (Ufen 2008; Fossati et al. 2020). Furthermore, because the number of party members wanting to run is often less than the number of seats available in any given electoral district, parties often approve outsider candidates, who also represent a revenue-raising opportunity since many parties charge a fee in return for their backing (Mietzner 2013, 85). In any case, any advantage offered by alignment with a particular party is hardly sufficient to base an entire individual campaign on, given the backdrop of the open-party list system.

The introduction of the open-party list is often held responsible for the significant increase in money politics in Indonesian elections, as it fostered "vigorous" intraparty competition among candidates (Aspinall 2014a) and an increase in campaign costs (Mietzner 2015, 588; Indrayana 2017). Candidates nominated by each party stand for election in a specific electoral district, known in Indonesia as a *daerah pemilihan* (dapil). As each national electoral district is allocated between three and ten seats, parties commonly field multiple candidates in the same race. Without the mediating influence of parties to determine how votes are channeled, individual candidates must fight harder to stand out from rivals, especially those from their own party. With voters able to direct their support toward an individual, there is more incentive to focus on self-promotion, rather than party promotion, and to explore ways to boost support in ways that set a candidate apart from others. As Muhtadi (2018a, 2019) has shown, while vote buying is an uncertain strategy, it can also yield enough support to obtain a victory, especially in competitions where the winning margins are narrow. In this political landscape, the individual campaign, and the strategic decisions taken, are imbued with increased significance as candidates vie for voter attention. The strategies they develop to capture citizens' interest depend heavily on their operating context, which, in turn, can determine the extent to which they engage in money politics. Beyond the election itself, the nature of the open-party list also provides additional incentives to engage in corruption once in office as the costs of intraparty competition trigger the need for more financial resources in a campaign (Chang 2005, 716; Hicken 2007).

Context and Candidate Campaigns

Electoral campaigns are guided by three underlying aims—to inform, to persuade, and to offer a personal and negotiated embodiment of the candidates themselves. It helps in understanding how individual candidates construct their campaigns to first map the influences that shape the context of a particular election bearing these factors in mind. Integrating insights from a broad range of election campaign literature, I take a holistic approach to what influences electoral campaign context, considering it as an outcome of both an overarching, systemic environment to which all candidates are subject within a particular geographical location and the particularities of an individual candidate's circumstances. A helpful way to approach mapping the existing context for any political party or candidate is to first consider the various factors that influence campaigns across all candidates and then examine the ways in which they relate to each individual candidate—thus establishing the context for the election. These factors guide what is possible, what is acceptable, and what is desirable during a campaign.

Several key factors shape the way a campaign is imagined and produced. Most prominent among them are the macro factors of the overarching political institutions in place at the time of the election, campaign norms, and the salience of political issues. Micro factors, which are specific to individual candidates, include the resources available, personal values, and identity (see figure 3).

Every electoral campaign offers a unique context, and an individual campaign strategy is imagined and produced in response to this context. The relevance of particular factors to the electioneering process may wax and wane, transforming the electoral campaign context as they do, and context should therefore be understood as a dynamic space unique to each campaign. How these factors manifest and play out in a specific election race underpin crucial decisions made throughout the campaign process. At the same time, vigilant candidates who are engaging closely with voters quickly and repeatedly respond to citizen input. As such, their campaign strategies may change over the course of a campaign.

Institutions

Institutions represent the overarching structural influences on an election. In articulating the campaign "environment," Bowler and Farrell (1992, 8–9) point to the type of political system in place, the existing electoral laws, the number of parties involved in the election, and the independence of the media. These institutions set the scene for what is possible during an electoral campaign by determining the rules of engagement in terms of what is legal, what is acceptable, and what candidates can get away with. At the same time, they may be far

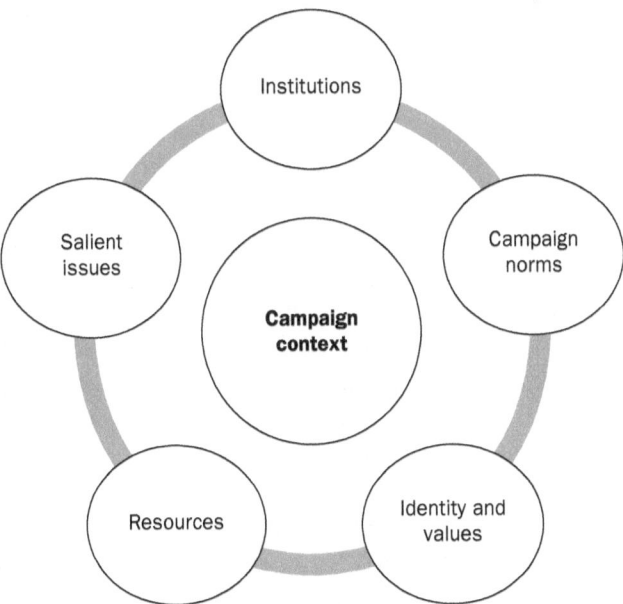

FIGURE 3. Factors that influence candidate campaign context.

from impartial, even in long-established democracies. Institutions are controlled by people who may use their power to shape them in various ways, for example, by passing rules that limit participation, gerrymandering, enacting discriminatory regulations on campaign funding, and using incumbency to pander to voters (Ely 1998). In Indonesia, the barriers to political party eligibility in elections are a clear example of this, offering political advantage to incumbent parties while making it extremely difficult for new parties to enter elections and be competitive in them. At the same time, while these influences are overarching in nature, their impacts can also be uneven. For example, electoral laws may be strictly applied in one area but lax in another, depending on the various attitudes among election oversight agencies between districts.

As "inherited structures" (MacKinnon 2011, 31) that apply to all candidates in one form or another, the prevailing political system and the nature of political parties set the parameters of what is possible when choosing a campaign strategy. It is these institutions that determine which political parties are eligible to compete and that dictate the rules to which the parties and candidates are beholden as they make practical decisions about how their campaign will run. These inherited arrangements determine whether elections are even possible and, if they are, the extent to which they can be free and fair. They also determine the breadth and depth of electoral competition. For example, states dominated by a single party may still hold elections with some limited participation from opposition parties, but the system is designed to ensure that the ruling party remains in power. In multiparty states, the depth of competition varies according to the openness of each country's political system. In Indonesia, elections are "free and fair," according to Freedom House, though they are undeniably affected by money and elite influence.[20]

The nature of parties themselves also contributes to the institutional context of a particular campaign. Political parties, in theory, set expectations of how their candidates should behave during a campaign, the standards to which they must adhere, and the rhetoric they are required to espouse. The more institutionalized a party is, the more likely it is that it will have mechanisms for punishing those who breach these rules (Panebianco 1988). Depending on how coordinated a party is and the control that party leadership is able to exert, candidates may be required to align with certain policies to project party unity and ensure uniformity across different candidate campaigns. However, this is not always the case. In Indonesia, the official party offices are relatively disengaged from local campaigns and there is little attempt to ensure that campaign codes of conduct and ethics are followed. As a consequence, candidates have relatively free rein over their actions, and the influence of a political party on a candidate's campaign will vary significantly depending on their ties to the party and their commitment to party ideals.

The nature of the relationship between parties and candidates in Indonesia is symbiotic, but not without problems. On the one hand, individual candidates cannot run as independents and require party endorsement to compete in elections. On the other hand, political parties cement their power by having the highest number of individual candidates elected to the legislature. Political parties have been accused of exploiting candidates, requiring payments in return for nomination and a proportion of their salary if they are successful in gaining a seat (Simandjuntak 2012, 105; Fionna 2014, 93). Conversely, Indonesian candidates often see a political party as simply a vehicle for nomination, rather than as an organization that they believe in and want to represent. Moreover, representing a political party can involve simultaneously dealing with complex intraparty power relationships, such as infighting among party members at the branch or head level, as they campaign. With no option to compete independent of party nomination, candidates must navigate the power struggles that political party structures foster.

While not a formal institution in the same sense, the media is also relevant (Chiang and Knight 2011; Farrell and Schmitt-Beck 2003). Although candidate engagement with the media can vary significantly, there are many electoral contexts where the media plays a crucial role in facilitating communication with voters, as well as in shaping public discourse. Media outlets collate and disseminate information about political parties and candidates, which voters then use to decide whom they will support (Farrell and Webb 2000). The forms of media coverage that candidates can access may also be restricted either through official or unofficial censorship or, in some cases, self-censorship by reporters (Schedler 2002). Even where the media is relatively free, it can also be partisan and offer biased coverage of candidates or their parties. The way that media outlets describe elections—whether it tends toward covering campaign policy or process (such as campaign rallies, visits, and whistle-stop tours)—has the potential to privilege some candidates over others (Cushion and Thomas 2018). The presence of media barons in the senior membership ranks of some Indonesian parties has ensured privileged access and reportage in television and print media for those parties and, possibly, some of their candidates.

Print, radio, and television are no longer the only kinds of media that must be considered in assessments of electoral campaigns. There has been a proliferation of academic studies that address the role of social media in elections, especially since Donald Trump (the "Twitter President") won the 2016 US presidency (Ott and Dickinson 2019). With voters liking (or disliking) and sharing campaign content online, and with the traditional media paying more and more attention to what is "trending" on sites such as Twitter, there is now more space for citizens to determine the direction of campaigns (Jungherr 2016). Globally, Indonesia has the fourth-largest number of Facebook users, with around 60.5 million registered accounts (Ross 2014). It also had approximately 20 million active Twitter users, according to figures released by Twitter in June 2014 (Lukman 2014). Social media has the potential to continually change the game, offering instant and unfettered access to official party statements as well as those made by individual party representatives. These platforms provided a means of direct communication with voters in the lead-up to the 2014 elections, without needing to go through journalists, editors, and media outlets more generally. It is, of course, up to individual candidates how much they wish to engage with social media (or other types of media) during their campaign.

Campaign Norms

Campaign norms are influenced by what behavior has occurred, and been accepted, in the past and how this feeds the expectations of voters in the present. This baseline understanding may include a whole range of norms, for example, how campaigns teams are set up, how candidates engage with media, what campaign paraphernalia is produced (such as banners, flags, t-shirts, calendars, or other such objects), how candidates engage with each other, how candidates interact with voters, and a whole host of other expected activities that are part of a campaign. These unofficial processes can shape a campaign in one of two ways: candidates can choose either to conform to them or to challenge them. The relative appeal of candidates to voters depends very much on how they execute their campaign. In this context, candidates must weigh the pros and cons of using particular strategies. Established patterns of normal and expected campaign behavior are sure to factor in to candidate decisions.

Candidates approach campaigns with a tacit understanding of what a campaign should look like, perhaps related to their own previous experience as a candidate (or that of their campaign advisers) or based on their past experience as a voter. In contexts like Indonesia's, it has become normal for campaigns to draw on preexisting patterns of candidate–voter relationships characterized by patronage. Clientelistic practices were common throughout the New Order and have continued through the democratization period. As Hicken (2011, 290) contends, clientelism is "highly adaptable to different political, economic, and cultural environments." However, it is stronger in contexts where patronage networks have been normalized. There are many states in which exchanges of goods or services are an integral part of the electionscape, so much so that those candidates not participating in these rituals are automatically excluded from contention by voters (Callahan 2005; Vicente and Wantchekon 2009; Vaishnav 2017).

The prevalence of these informal, but normalized, arrangements may mean one of three things for candidates. If they are established politicians, they must ensure they deliver on their promises to brokers and clients in order to guarantee they get support at the ballot box in the next electoral cycle. They must consider how best to reinforce or renew these ties to ensure that loyalties are preserved. If they are newcomers, they may see the development of a patronage/broker network as a priority for their campaign, in which case they may need to focus on establishing the kinds of connections that could grow into a reliable support network in the lead-up to the election. Conversely, if candidates do not have an established patronage/broker network and do not wish to entangle themselves in such a system, they must seek out campaign strategies that will allow them to circumvent this and other campaign practices associated with patronage. In the Indonesian case, they will likely still use influencers during their campaign—family, friends, or other professional/social contacts—but avoid relationships where campaign support is necessarily predicated on payment or is clientelistic in nature. Candidates who wish to break from established campaign norms may seek to turn their nonconformity to their advantage, presenting their refusal to comply as part of their appeal. Whether this strategy wins over voters, however, is a separate issue.

In the case of money politics in Indonesia, Aspinall, Mietzner, and Tomsa (2015) argue that although vote buying itself may not guarantee success, its absence may guarantee failure. Thus, although challenging campaign norms may become a centerpiece of a candidate's campaign, it is not without risks. In Indonesia, eschewing campaign norms is risky because the expectations of voters may be tightly bound to their experiences of candidate behavior in previous elections. Norms are established through ongoing patterns of campaign behavior and their acceptance (albeit sometimes tacit) by voters. Putnam (1966) contends that accepting the community's "political standards" and reflecting these in a campaign affects how citizens respond to politicians. In other words, deciding how to tailor a campaign to the expectations of local voters can form an important part of campaign strategy and presenting oneself as someone who does not conform may alienate the people to whom a candidate is trying to appeal. By the same token, if a candidate rejects local norms, the candidate must think deeply about how to counter the backlash this might invoke.

Salient Issues

Voters make sense of the campaign messaging created for them during elections by contextualizing and understand campaign issues in terms of relevance to their own lives and the world around them. If candidates want to build an issues-based campaign, they may choose to play upon "salient issues," namely things that voters care about with the potential to influence their voting choice (Bélanger and Meguid 2008; Wlezien 2005). Promoting certain issues within a campaign can act as an "information shortcut" for voters, who can use a candidate's campaign platform as quick way to determine if they are worth supporting (Downs 1957). Campaigns can avoid the hard work of convincing voters that their platform is significant by selecting an issue that is already meaningful to them, in other words "salient" (Bélanger and Meguid 2008; Druckman, Jacobs, and Ostermeier 2004). In Indonesia, the way that salient issues emerge through campaigns varies tremendously. Some candidates do not bother with issues-based campaigns at all, directing all their energy toward establishing the relational networks and finding ways to distribute funds to help them to win. However, others see leveraging issues as a potential means for establishing a comparative advantage over rivals, sometimes even in conjunction with forms of money politics.

Candidates who want to incorporate issues into their campaigns may focus on contemporary "trending" issues or on issues with a long political history. Long-established issues tend to resonate with the populace because they have been problems for a long time and the importance of addressing them is clear.

By contrast, trending issues—which may be social, political, economic, or something else entirely—capture the imagination of large groups of people at a specific point in time. During some elections, trending and long-established issues may coincide, as was the case in the 2014 elections with the issue of corruption. Corruption has a long history of salience in Indonesia, stretching back to the colonial period.[21] However, it was also a trending issue in 2014, courtesy of numerous corruption scandals throughout the Yudhoyono presidency, which contributed to a rise in public skepticism toward politicians and distrust of the judiciary, legislature, and the police. These scandals played into broader discourses of institutionalized wrongdoing and undemocratic behavior, thus creating what some candidates saw as a highly desirable issue to integrate into their own campaign rhetoric.

Salient issues also exist at various scales. For example, the state of global markets can have a real impact on national and local politics in one election, especially if they have led to high inflation rates, job insecurity, or other issues that are influencing the day-to-day lives of voters, but be of little concern in another election (Garrett 1998). There may be recent national scandals that capture the public's imagination and prompt campaigners to integrate a discussion of the case, and their response to it, in their electioneering. At the same time, there will be issues that resonate primarily in a local area—such as environmental degradation or protection issues in a specific place. The fact that such issues are geographically contained means they are unlikely to get much airplay in national campaigns, but local candidates may seize upon them to boost their credentials within their electoral district. Regardless of scale, the point is that these issues become key talking points for a period; campaign discussions of the issue and the responses to it are like time stamps, representing a particular moment.

Candidates must also consider how their campaign messaging to voters and self-promotion intersects with the salient issues of the day. What issues can they credibly purport to represent? This will depend on their track record and public persona. The term "track record" (*rekam jejak*) is often used by candidates in Indonesia when discussing how they can legitimately present themselves to voters.[22] Another reason to position oneself as an anticorruption candidate, apart from its salience in the Indonesian context, stems from practicality. While some legislative candidates are wealthy or able to access funding and support through networks, there are many candidates who do not have such resources. For these candidates, salient issues take on an additional importance because their ability to win office relates to their ability to persuade voters using limited monetary incentives. Without the financial resources to buy eye-catching advertising, fund expensive rallies with entertainment, or distribute gifts to voters, a candidate needs to determine what rhetorical tools will work best. Anticorruptionism is an opportunity for the resource-poor candidate, allowing them to present themselves as humble and virtuous because they are *not* throwing money at voters and instead presenting themselves as someone who will not be influenced by money should they be elected, something that they hope voters would appreciate.

Resources

Having made the decision to compete in an election, a candidate's available resources have a profound impact on how electoral campaigns are constructed. Individuals with money, time, and political experience are significantly more likely to run for office, motivated by a range of incentives (Fox and Lawless 2005). In much of the existing literature, campaign resources are defined in terms of campaign financing (Moon 2004; Snyder 1989). However, here I extend the definition to include capital (personal, party funds, donations, and credit), physical resources (such as offices and transportation), and human resources (such as campaign paid staff and volunteers). Social capital also constitutes a type of resource—for example, close links to media outlets that can prioritize coverage, celebrities willing to provide an endorsement, or extended business or social networks that can be harnessed for electoral support. While most candidates are likely to have access to resources from several of these categories, there is often great disparity between what candidates have available to them.

Political parties are permitted to solicit donations and receive state subsidies (Mietzner 2015). But, in general, the party funds available to individual candidates for campaign purposes are limited, if they even exist at all. The relationship between candidates and their political party may, to some extent, dictate their access to such financial resources. Candidates who hold official positions within a party might have access to some internal funding and use of the party machine for campaign organization (Aspinall and Berenschot 2019, 87). However, the vast majority of candidates are left to fund and coordinate their own campaigns, with very little oversight from the political party that they purport to represent. A candidate's ability to access funds—whether they have money of their own or must seek out donations or loans—influences what options are available to them in promoting their candidacy to voters. It can also determine whether vote buying is a viable campaign strategy. Candidates who have access to substantial amounts of capital but do not have strong personal ties to the community may be inclined to bribe voters. Candidates with fewer financial resources who cannot envisage winning simply through buying votes rely heavily on volunteered services from friends, family, work colleagues, or the local community rather than paid staff. For example, a candidate who has been active in a particular social movement may be able to harness civil society and other social networks in their campaign, using their credibility in the field to garner support and votes (Dibley and Ford 2019).

Resources can also include relationships and networks within a candidate's own electoral district. Local candidates often leverage existing personal connections to generate a support base. To borrow a term from Bourdieu (1996), the "capital" that candidates possess due to their personal and professional networks guide the options that are available to them. For instance, a candidate who is also a wealthy businessperson with numerous employees can leverage these employment ties for votes or turn to business partners for additional support. Through such webs of influence, candidates can source votes, funding, and campaign staff or volunteers. In some situations, these personal networks may be developed in brokerage systems, in which candidates use networks of "champions" to advocate for them, hinged on the establishment of trustworthy relationships with the broker (Stokes et al. 2013, 75). Alongside paid and volunteer staff, brokers are often part of a candidate's campaign team (Aspinall and Sukmajati 2016).[23] The use of brokers is sensible, as a national electoral district is large and a candidate's energy is finite. Finding brokers who will advocate on behalf of a candidate can greatly extend that reach. Hence, the establishment of a robust network of brokers can be a significant resource for candidates. However, there are dangers associated with the use of brokers, many of whom are more interested in exploiting the campaigns for their own benefit rather genuinely supporting a candidate in whom they believe, which is common in Indonesia (Aspinall 2014b).

Identity and Values

Candidates must decide what aspects of their own identity they will infuse into the campaign—what will set them apart from others and give them a competitive advantage? They must decide not only who they are as people but also what they stand for as politicians. The reality, at least in Indonesia, is that political parties do little to foster a set of values that candidates can use to guide their campaigns. And even if Indonesian political parties did have robust policy platforms, candidates cannot rely solely on the appeal of their party in an open-list system where voters chose candidates directly. This leaves candidates to be guided by their own core values—to choose what virtues, or "family of virtues," they wish to project, especially in response to the general skepticism that many citizens have toward politicians (Clarke et al. 2018, 193). They must craft an identity that draws upon facets of their individual identity, experience, and values, using these to develop and project an image that they believe will win them support.

In their effort to win, candidates must reconcile their values and expectations with the influences around them. These beliefs and values are interwoven with identity markers such as religion, ethnicity, and gender, which candidates can use to create a narrative about themselves. For example, a candidate may choose to highlight his or her religion to appeal to those with a similar faith or emphasize their commitment to gender equality in order to attract women voters who feel they are inadequately represented in current political debates. It may be that they build their reputation as a "family person," appearing at rallies accompanied by an overtly supportive spouse and/or children to hammer home that they embody wholesome family values. Moreover, expressions of identity may vary depending on who the candidate is speaking to. For a religious crowd, the candidate may play the pious believer, while for a military crowd they may highlight their support for increased military spending. The identities are not necessarily contradictory; they are simply part of the ever-changing campaign spaces created throughout the electoral competition.

If the portrayal of candidates' values does not align with their broader campaign strategies, they risk presenting an incohesive image and undermining their "authenticity" (Stiers et al. 2019). Credibility can be determined by the reputation of the party the candidate represents, or by their personal history and values, and how these characteristics mesh with their stance on particular issues. For example, it could be jarring to voters to find that a candidate running on an antiestablishment platform had received substantial campaign donations from large corporations, or for an anticorruption candidate to engage in overt vote buying. While it may not necessarily scuttle their chance of winning, it could lead voters to think twice about their trustworthiness as candidates.

Conversely, a candidate's willingness to break the law is also tied to their values. It is worth noting here that illegal activities do not have to be extreme. In Indonesia, candidates regularly give out t-shirts, food, and donations (among other things) to curry favor with voters. Though technically illegal, in practice these activities are so widely accepted that even a highly moralistic candidate would most probably engage in them. Thus, a candidate's willingness to "bend" the rules during their campaign does not *necessarily* reflect a complete disregard for the rule of law. It is, rather, the result of a negotiation between the electoral context, the desire to win, and a candidate's own moral compass.

With the background context to Indonesian elections set out in this chapter, we can better understand the landscape of the 2014 campaign. So far, we have explored Indonesia's political history as it pertains to elections—how they were organized, who was permitted to run for office, and the involvement of citizens—from the Suharto regime, through Reformasi, up to the 2014 elections. Having examined the democratization process, we can see that post-1998 political reforms significantly changed the way that elections are conducted. But at the same time, these new processes did not sufficiently address preexisting campaign norms and expectations. The increasing emphasis on personalized campaigns has strengthened the hold that money has over electoral outcomes. Personality and candidate networks have become more prevalent as a key campaign strategy for those who cannot afford to buy votes, or as a means for supplementing vote-buying strategies. Outlining the various influences on campaigns and how they are constructed provides an important understanding of the broader realm in which legislative candidates operate and the many challenges they face. We can imagine many dilemmas regarding how to engage with their political party, how they present themselves, what rhetoric they use, and how best to capitalize on their individual identity. Campaign behavior, and the electioneering it engenders, reflects a host of dynamics that converge over time in the lead-up to election day.

In the next chapter, we will explore a key influence on Indonesia's campaign context—political corruption and its relationship to political parties and elections. Corruption and efforts to combat it have played out on the public stage for many decades, affecting political institutions and solidifying its place as a salient issue. Offering a brief political history of corruption in modern Indonesia, the chapter helps us to better appreciate why some candidates might reject or be drawn to anticorruptionism as a strategy. Underscoring the value of anticorruptionism as part of an electoral campaign strategy, and its pitfalls, we gain further insight into some of the motivations for, and challenges surrounding, anticorruptionism in the context of electoral campaigns.

2
CORRUPTION AND LEVERAGING ANTICORRUPTIONISM

Every regime change since the founding of the modern Indonesian nation-state has had some link to Indonesians' dissatisfaction with corruption. Entrenched in the state's systems of government since Dutch colonial times, each new administration has been presented with the challenge, and opportunity, of combating existing networks of corruption, collusion, and nepotism (*korupsi, kolusi, nepotism*, KKN), for which Indonesia has become renowned. Corruption has shaped not only the business of politics but also how Indonesian citizens view their government. This historical backdrop of corruption and counter-corruption efforts colored and constrained the nature of democratic change throughout Reformasi. It also shaped the development of norms and practices in electoral politics, as well as the behavior of politicians once they enter government.

Corruption influences electoral politics in Indonesia in two distinct ways. First, the ongoing pervasiveness of corruption has shaped how election campaigns run. Vote buying in its many permutations—as discussed in the introduction to this book—has become an electoral norm. Reformasi saw a rise in the number of political parties and candidates vying for office. Elections became more hotly contested than ever following the introduction of the open list system, further heightening the importance of cash handouts, as well as the distribution of goods, favors, and donations during electoral campaigns, and developing systems of patronage that could help to generate support at the ballot box. The need for money in elections, and how it is later recouped, has led to a complex web of political behaviors. Money politics has turned electoral contests into sites of illegal, though rarely prosecuted, practices and provided an impetus for further corrupt behavior among politicians who are elected. It is hard to ignore accusations that ongoing corruption in government is fueled, in part, by the costs of elections and political parties' need for financial resources (Dick and Mulholland 2016; Lewis and Hendrawan 2019; Reuter 2015). In a world where it costs so much to enter public office, there will invariably be some who seek a healthy return on their investment, with far-reaching consequences for the way corruption influences democratic practice.

The second way that corruption influences elections is that it offers an opportunity to leverage the ongoing discontent created by abuses of political power. Opposition parties can appeal to voters for support, claiming they are best placed to banish corruption in situations where the incumbent government is perceived to have failed (McCann and Domínguez 1998). Meanwhile, candidates new to electoral politics, those outside of elite circles of power and those without the financial resources to effectively engage in money politics, can capitalize on anticorruption rhetoric to condemn rivals while presenting themselves as challengers to the status quo. It is useful when attacking opponents, especially incumbents, to lay charges of impropriety or corruption against competitors and promote campaigns focused on moral character, personal finances, family life, and daily habits (Welch and Hibbing 1997). Being able to market oneself as a candidate who represents citizens' interests through an explicit anticorruption agenda can be a powerful tool for gaining popular support.

Looming in the background here are political parties. Elections are but one segment of a bigger picture, in which jostling to cement power, and derive advantage from that power, drive much of what happens once politicians take their seats in the legislature. How elections are won—if there are outstanding promises to be fulfilled or personal funds to be recouped—no doubt colors the way that legislators behave. Beyond this, the behavior of individual legislators, most visibly in terms of corruption allegations, also influence public perceptions of political parties and elections. Political parties may attempt to disassociate themselves from criminal allegations, but whether voters are persuaded by "lone wolf" explanations for individual politicians giving or accepting bribes, colluding with contractors, or embezzling cash, is another question. Political parties may also claim throughout an election, as we have seen among several parties in the Reformasi era, that they reject all forms of corruption and antidemocratic behavior, promoting themselves as true representatives of citizens' interests. To understand why individual candidates adopt anticorruptionism in their campaigns, it is helpful to take a broader view of the role that political parties play in shaping anticorruptionism as a strategy.

In this chapter, I focus on the political history of corruption and anticorruptionism leading up to the 2014 election, explaining how it came to be a salient issue and how it has influenced national politics in the post–New Order period, both in terms of the behavior of elected officials and voter responses to this behavior. With the resignation of Suharto in 1998, it seemed that Indonesia might finally be able to make some headway in eradicating corruption. But hopes for better government transparency and accountability mechanisms to undo the influence of corruption during the New Order dissipated over the ensuing years. Corruption continued to permeate government activity, attracting media attention and giving rise to public frustration in spite of more democratic electoral systems and the establishment of a much-lauded Corruption Eradication Commission (Komisi Pemberantasan Korupsi, KPK) in 2003. While the chapter highlights a number of corruption scandals that are illustrative of a range of different types of corruption beyond money politics in elections, it also establishes corruption as a salient electoral issue and provides context for the motivations in highlighting corruption during a campaign. Since corruption remains embedded in systems of government, and with citizen dissatisfaction continuing to affect trust in political parties and their representatives, the potential benefits of anticorruptionism for electoral candidates becomes clear. But it also underscores how failure to live up to this rhetoric has come to undermine public confidence in politicians and foster apprehension about their motives for entering public office. Furthermore, this chapter brings into focus that corruption was a *live* issue in 2014, and one that influenced campaign decisions for political parties and their candidates alike.

An Historical Perspective

Corruption and anticorruption efforts have a long history in Indonesia, with the first government-led corruption investigation taking place in the 1920s when colonial leadership investigated officials who had accepted kickbacks and embezzled from the treasury (Wertheim 1963). The rise of Indonesian nationalism and the desire for independence among advocates for an Indonesian republic were linked to, among other things, ongoing frustration with corruption within the Dutch administration (Smith 1971). The uneven access to prosperity engendered by corruption became yet another source of grievance against the Dutch, as ideologies of equality and social justice came to the fore within the nationalist movement (Kahin 2003). But while nationalists identified corruption as a colonial problem, there was more to come.

Following independence, Indonesia, like many fledgling post-colonial states, continued to grapple with problems of entrenched corruption within government (Cribb and Brown 1995; Khan 1998; Smith 1971). As political parties competed for power, their members often seemed more interested in self-promotion and preservation than in stamping out corruption. Parties began to play an important patronage function, and several ministers used their position to help family members, repay personal debts, and create lucrative business opportunities (Feith 1962). Recognizing potential career benefits, many bureaucrats also joined political parties. In fact, by the end of 1950, most civil servants were also party members (Feith 1962). Party leaders were obliged to distribute favors and material rewards to their loyal supporters through cabinet posts, business opportunities, overseas junkets, houses, and cars, which led to factionalism and the rise of intraparty competition. Politicians who refused to distribute patronage risked facing opposition in the legislature and a limited career. At the same time, army leaders rationalized military involvement in commercial activities as subsidizing the inadequate budget received from the state while collecting profits for both the military and themselves (Cribb and Brown 1995; Penders 1974). With so many government officials deriving personal and institutional wealth from practices that seemingly went against democratic ideals, corruption became even more embedded in the Indonesian government.

As the parliamentary system began to disintegrate, some political actors began capitalizing on cases of corruption to discredit their rivals.[1] Among the chaos of parliamentary politics, anticorruptionism emerged as a means for self-promotion and attacking opponents. The media, with its lower threshold for evidence and propensity for sensationalizing charges, proved to be a ready vehicle for airing accusation of corruption (Feith 1962).[2] Complaints of corruption became a mainstay of Indonesian politics in the transition from parliamentary to Sukarno's "guided" democracy (1957–1966). Eager to justify his new regime, Sukarno blamed greedy and immoral individuals for the failure of parliamentary democracy. In his 1959 Independence Day address, he admonished those who had used their positions in state enterprises for personal gain:

> those bodies [have become] the nest of people who filled their own pockets till they bulged, people who became wealthy, people who became millionaires. There must be an end to this! Such a situation must be changed! . . . It may not be allowed to happen again that . . . a few speculators or a few profiteers can shake our whole national economy. (Sukarno 1964, 52)

In the same speech, Sukarno asserted that "Whoever scoops up wealth at the expense of the public, whoever disrupts the public economy, will be arrested, will be sentenced to death!" (Sukarno 1964, 55). In his 1961 Independence Day Address, he referred to the prominence of corruption within the government, classifying it as one of the "three si's—**tjari promosi, birokrasi, korupsi** [emphasis in original]"—seeking promotion, bureaucracy, and corruption. He went on to proclaim it would be better if "such people were pushed aside!" (Sukarno 1964, 153).

Having established a new political regime of "Guided Democracy" in 1957, Sukarno also boosted his own claims as an anticorruption crusader by achieving what none of the previous cabinets had been able to do: establish an anticorruption law.[3] In 1960, an official government definition of corruption was codified, alongside defined punishments for related crimes, through Law No. 24/1960 on the Determination, Prosecution and Inspection of the Criminal Act of Corruption. In the first paragraph of the act, corruption was broadly defined as having two facets. First, it involved a violation of the law causing an economic loss for the state, a region, or any other legal body that uses state funding and concessions. Second, corruption involved the abuse of position or authority for self-enrichment, or that of another person or body. The passing of this legislation was hardly a feat given that Sukarno held close to dictatorial power over the government. It proved difficult, however, to focus public attention on Sukarno's anticorruption efforts as the country plunged into economic and social chaos.[4]

Calls for change mounted as the Indonesian Communist Party (Partai Komunis Indonesia, PKI) and the military both competed for power in a heightened Cold War landscape. In the end, the military triumphed, after the events of September 30, 1965—in which PKI supporters attempted a coup and assassinated six army generals—brought this rivalry to a head (Anderson and McVey 1971). While the coup failed, it unleashed a chain of events culminating in the rise of Suharto, an army general and Indonesia's second president (Crouch 1980).[5] On March 11, 1966, Sukarno signed an order granting Suharto full authority to "restore the peace." Between June and July 1966, the national parliament ratified Suharto's position and called for elections to be held in 1968 (Ricklefs 2001, 349–351). Now at the helm of a newly ratified government, Suharto began the process of consolidating his support. This included an early anticorruption drive aimed at winning over the Indonesian people.

The Suharto Era

In the early days of the New Order, Suharto was eager to build an image that would set him apart from previous politicians (Elson 2001, 140; Juwono 2016). Along with promises of development and prosperity, anticorruptionism was an important part of this effort. Suharto promised that he would support "not only good government but also clean government" (Robertson-Snape 1999, 589). Responding to popular sentiment, establishing an anticorruption reputation became a core aim for the new regime as it worked to validate its claims to power and distance itself from the previous government (Feith 1994; Ricklefs 2001). Between 1965 and

1970, "there [were] few burning issues of comparable horsepower [as corruption] for opponents or critics of the regime" (Mackie 1970, 88). Student groups rallied around the issue and threatened vigilante action against "corruptors." A number of newspapers fueled public concern, including Mochtar Lubis' *Indonesia Raya* and *Nusantara*, as well as other student publications such as *Harian Kami* and *Mahasiswa Indonesia* (Crouch 1980, 294–295).

Concerned about public order, the government banned all non-approved demonstrations in January 1970. Subsequent meetings between student leaders and cabinet ministers led to promises that anticorruption measures would be a government priority (Dahm 1971; van der Kroef 1971). Acting on this promise, Suharto established a corruption investigation taskforce, called the Commission of Four, led by former Prime Minister Wilopo, and involving former Vice President Hatta. The commission was charged with investigating the extent of the corruption in the government and providing recommendations for its eradication (Elson 2001; Mackie 1970). Further emphasizing his commitment, on February 2, Suharto released a public statement in the newspaper *Kompas*, decrying the effects of corruption:

> Corruption and deviant actions in the economic field in general not only conflict with the law and with security, but are clearly incompatible with morals, and puncture the feeling of justice [sic]. Corruption blocks the implementation of the state's programs, damages the principles and reduces the authority of the government apparatus, if it is not curbed, lessened and suppressed as much as possible. (cited in Elson 2001, 195)[6]

Despite Suharto's public anticorruption rhetoric, progress was slow. He was in a difficult position, as he required the support of military and business leaders who had benefited from the existing status quo (Mackie 1970). Having come to power under such tumultuous circumstances, Suharto needed to assert the legitimacy of his regime but, although an anticorruption agenda appealed to Indonesian citizens, he still had to shore up support from elites in order to consolidate his authority.

This prompted a shift in strategy in the mid-1970s, characterized by an increasingly authoritarian government that abandoned corruption eradication and performative forms of persuasion—turning, instead, to intimidation, repression and, at times, violence. Vocal anticorruption protests were quashed in the public sphere, while corruption in government remained an "open secret" (*rahasia umum*). From the 1980s, Suharto's family and his cronies engaged in increasingly brazen business dealings, with privileged access to loans from state banks, government funding, and concessions (Elson 2001, 279). The Suharto family established a complex network of foundations (known as *yayasan*) to mask corruption and launder money (Setiyono and McLeod 2010). Bribes could be paid into a foundation owned by a member of the family to escape detection (Vatikiotis 1993). "Donations" by state-owned enterprises were also channeled into foundations to siphon funds from the government (Aspinall 2005b, 93). By the early 1990s, Suharto had created a network of supporters who were not only extremely wealthy but also heavily dependent on him for business favors (Liddle 1996). His own family's assets were worth an estimated USD 2–3 billion (Vatikiotis 1993, 50).[7]

While Suharto's patronage networks were strong, his support from other interest groups was never guaranteed. At various times, there were criticisms of the regime from military leaders and political opposition (Aspinall 1995).[8] Pressure mounted as international support for the regime weakened with the end of the Cold War. Students' insistence that the government address inequality, human rights, and corruption mounted, as did condemnation from Islamic leaders. In the late 1980s and early 1990s, Suharto attempted to appease dissenters through a policy of "openness" (*keterbukaan*), which saw press censorship relaxed, the establishment of a commission for human rights, and some tolerance of political protests, demonstrations, and government critiques (Bertrand 1996). Some opposition politicians took the opportunity to draw attention to corruption within Suharto's circle of elites.[9] But while some felt emboldened to speak out about the government's failings, the regime maintained that it was steadfastly addressing the issues of corruption.[10]

By 1994, the openness experiment was over, heralded by the sudden closure of three major media publications, *Tempo*, *Detik*, and *Editor*, which had published a series of negative reports about a decision by B. J. Habibie, then-Minister for Research and Technology, to purchase East German warships (Mallarangeng and Liddle 1996). The press had also begun to investigate a number of potentially embarrassing corruption scandals linked to Suharto's inner circle, providing additional impetus for the media closures (Bertrand 1996). Opposition parties continued to condemn the government's failure to address corruption, but this criticism was not without consequences.[11] However, the government's efforts at repression could not contain mounting criticism of the regime, which erupted in 1998, after the Asian financial crisis forced Indonesia into an economic crisis (Bird 1998; Hill and Shiraishi 2007). By the time Suharto resigned on May 21, 1998, the extent of corruption among his family and cronies was abundantly clear, and citizens were hopeful that a new, democratically elected government could implement new transparency and accountability measures to better hold politicians and business elites to account.

Early Reformasi

As the regime change unfolded, it was clear that something had to be done to address public frustration with the corrupt practices that had become the norm during the Suharto years. Now interim president, Habibie quickly approved two bills that sought to curb the public's frustration with corruption. He signed Law No. 28/1999 on the Establishment of a Commission to Examine the Wealth of State Officials (Komisi Pemeriksa Kekayaan Penyelenggara Negara, KPKPN) in May 1998, and Law No. 31/1999 on the Eradication of the Crime of Corruption three months later (Butt 2011b; King 2000). These laws authorized investigations into the dealings of politicians and bureaucrats who could be reasonably suspected of corruption, and the establishment of an anticorruption commission within two years (Butt 2011b). The laws were well-received, but the upheaval of the early Reformasi period and upcoming elections soon overshadowed these anticorruption efforts. As a result, the KPKPN was not set up until January 2001.

In the meantime, the MPR passed a resolution committing to investigate corruption during the New Order, including that of Suharto and his family (Bird 1999). Although Suharto claimed to have few savings and denied owning offshore bank accounts, four of the foundations he controlled had been valued at over USD 310 million in 1995. In December 1998, seven more foundations were found to be worth "quintillions of rupiah" (Ricklefs 2001, 409). Subsequent investigations conducted during Habibie's term as president found no evidence to suggest that Suharto's wealth had been gained through inappropriate means (Elson 2001). Perhaps it was too much to expect the former Suharto protégé to demand an open and frank assessment of Suharto's wealth. In any case, the "show" of the investigation was unconvincing, leading to public demand for a more thorough inquiry (Hadiz 2000, 27).

Habibie opted not to run as a presidential candidate in the 1999 general elections, which were the first elections since 1955 in which party representation was not restricted. Several parties participated, the major ones being (in order of votes garnered) PDIP, PKB, PPP, and PAN. After a protracted debate, the MPR chose Abdurrahman Wahid as president (Liddle 2000). Wahid was a well-respected religious figure associated with Indonesia's largest Islamic organization, Nadhlatul Ulama and a human rights crusader, who had previously stated that combating corruption should be a government priority (King 2000). Acknowledging the public pressure to institute reforms across the police force, judiciary, and the public prosecutor's office, Wahid identified corruption eradication as a core goal of his administration (Hadiz and Robison 2013). The Wahid government established the Joint Team to Eradicate the Crime of Corruption (Tim Gabungan Pemberantasan Tindak Pidana Korupsi, TGPTPK) as a stop-gap measure while provisions could be made for the establishment of the KPK. Wahid also passed a Presidential Decree in 2000 that established the National Ombudsman's Commission, which was tasked with receiving complaints from the public regarding the conduct and decisions of public officials (Sherlock 2002). In addition, efforts were made to reinvigorate the state audit institutions and improve oversight of government spending (Hamilton-Hart 2001).[12]

Wahid's anticorruption rhetoric jarred with his ongoing leniency toward New Order elites (Barton 2006). With a new leadership installed, citizens expected punishments for Suharto and his associates. Public perception was that the financial crisis had been intensified by government corruption under Suharto and he needed to be held accountable (Hamilton-Hart 2001). Pressure mounted to reopen the investigation into his behavior during Wahid's presidency. In August 2000, Suharto finally faced corruption charges. But they were dropped in February 2001, when defense lawyers and the presiding judges agreed he was too ill to face trial. It was widely understood that, regardless of the outcome, Wahid intended to pardon Suharto if he was found guilty, which further undermined his anticorruption credentials (Brown 2003; King 2000). Suharto's immediate family also escaped largely unscathed, with the only family member tried being Tommy Suharto. Indeed, the only other member of the Suharto clan charged and jailed for corruption was Suharto's half-brother, Probosutedjo, who was convicted in 2003 for misappropriating approximately USD 4.3 million from a government reforestation project (*Kompas*, February 19, 2001).

Tommy—who had come to represent the excesses of the New Order, with his "playboy lifestyle" and penchant for luxury vehicles (Tupai 2005)—was sentenced in late 2000 to eighteen months imprisonment for swindling the State Logistics Agency out of approximately USD 8.3 million. There was a public outcry against the leniency of the sentence. Tommy went into hiding after his appeal was rejected (Brown 2003; Crouch 2010, 202) and was eventually found in a residence on the outskirts of Jakarta, almost a year after his sentencing. Once imprisoned, reports of special treatment and outings to nightclubs fed popular suspicions that the rich remained "above the law" (Hainsworth 2007). Tommy was later convicted to a further fifteen years in prison for hiring hit men to murder the chief judge involved in his conviction, Syafiuddin Kartasasmita, which they succeeded in doing (Brown 2003, 243). He was released in 2006, having served just four years of his fifteen-year prison term. Meanwhile, the two men found guilty of the actual shooting were sentenced to life in prison, further solidifying perceptions that the Suharto family were not being held accountable for their crimes (Crouch 2010).

Wahid's reluctance to condemn Suharto and his family disappointed those who believed that bringing New Order corruptors to justice was an important step in moving toward a new democratic era. This reluctance also undermined his reputation as a democratic leader intent on redressing past corruption crimes (Liddle 2000). Then, in 2000, allegations of corruption were leveled at Wahid himself when it appeared that funds given to the National Bureau of Logistics by the Sultan of Brunei as humanitarian aid to support those affected by conflict in the province of Aceh, was allegedly loaned to associates of Wahid (Barton 2006; Liddle 2001).[13] The incident left Wahid vulnerable to attacks from a national legislature that could no longer support his rule and an impeachment process began in February 2001. Five months later, he was dismissed from the presidency and replaced by Megawati.

When Megawati became president, she too spoke about the importance of eradicating corruption. During Megawati's presidency, the law on the Corruption Eradication Commission (Law No. 30/2002) was passed by the national legislature, which also approved the establishment of a specialized Anticorruption Court (Pengadilan Tindak Pidana Korupsi, Tipikor) (Schütte 2012). Originally a chamber of the Jakarta District Court, Tipikor was designed exclusively to hear corruption cases. However, progress in establishing these new institutions was slow and they were not in full force until 2004. Megawati herself did not appear to view corruption as an institutional issue, instead blaming individuals, whom she claimed needed to exercise better moral judgment (Sherlock 2002). Megawati's support for other anticorruption initiatives, like TGPTPK investigations, was hesitant, presenting a roadblock to investigators who needed presidential approval before they could question senior government officials. In March 2001, a team of three Supreme Court judges annulled the law allowing for the TGPTPK altogether. What remained of the institution was subsumed into the KPK in 2003.

The stalled progress on corruption issues across all levels of government was symptomatic of Megawati's performance as president and the need to balance forces of power within the government (Crouch 2010). Like Wahid, Megawati needed to appease Golkar and the military in order to sustain support for her leadership. Unlike Wahid, she chose to pacify her reluctant supporters rather than confronting them and her ambivalence toward fighting corruption became increasingly evident as her term progressed (Brown 2003; Sherlock 2002). In addition, the PDIP itself gained a reputation for corruption during Megawati's time in office, with members using their new-found authority for their own benefit (na Thalang 2005). According to Wanandi (2004, 124), members of Megawati's own family were also possibly involved in corruption, though none were arrested on corruption charges in the two decades that followed. Even with her political pedigree and her reputation as a critic of the New Order, Megawati was unable to convince the Indonesian people that she was the leader they needed to see Indonesia through the challenges posed by the country's democratic transition, and she was defeated by Susilo Bambang Yudhoyono—a former general and minster in Megawati's own cabinet—in the 2004 presidential elections.

First Yudhoyono Term

In 2004, both Yudhoyono and Megawati pledged that they would combat corruption (Ananta, Arifin, and Suryadinata 2005), however, with a poor track record, Megawati had little credibility on the issue. By contrast, Yudhoyono was able to paint himself as being committed to combating corruption in the lead-up to the election. Surveys taken at the time suggested that corruption eradication, along with the economy and social welfare, were the highest priorities for Indonesian citizens (Aspinall 2005a) and support emerged for new leadership. Reflecting this sentiment, Yudhoyono's Democratic Party gained 7.5 percent of votes in the legislative elections, while PDIP's vote declined from 39 percent in 1999 to 19 percent in 2004. Yudhoyono went on to secure a decisive victory in the second round of the presidential election, attracting 60.6 percent of the popular vote in a run-off against Megawati (Liddle and Mujani 2005).

Newly installed as president, Yudhoyono embarked on a much-lauded anticorruption drive. He authorized the KPK to investigate senior officials and parliamentarians and in 2004 announced new measures to "accelerate" the eradication of corruption. During his first year as president, Yudhoyono signed off on investigations into fifty-seven officials (Crouch 2010). The first Tipikor trial—which involved former Acehnese governor Abdul Saleh, who was sentenced to ten years imprisonment in April 2005—was seen as a landmark trial (Crouch 2010). A slew of high-profile corruption cases were subsequently mounted, including some that Megawati had previously refused to approve. By 2006, seven governors, sixty-three district heads and thirteen national parliamentarians had been investigated and/or arrested (McGibbon 2006).

Yudhoyono steadfastly supported the KPK and the anticorruption courts throughout his first term in office (2004–2009). Acknowledging its limited resources, Yudhoyono approved the formation of an additional body called the Coordination Team for the Eradication of Corruption (Tim Koordinasi Pemberantasan Tindak Pidana Korupsi, Tim Tastipikor) in 2005. Drawn from the attorney-general's office, the police, and the Finance and Development Board, the team brought cases to the ordinary courts instead of the anticorruption courts and answered directly to the president. It also led to some high-profile prosecutions including that of Megawati's Minister of Religion, Said Agil Husin Al Munawar, who was charged and convicted of embezzling funds designated to help Indonesian citizens undertake the *Hajj* pilgrimage to Mecca.

As convictions began to mount, critics accused Yudhoyono of focusing his anticorruption crusade on rival parties. Nor did the investigations reach the highest echelons of power in the government and business (Crouch 2010). Nevertheless, with his relatively clean background and less overt involvement in patronage politics, Yudhoyono was able to use these convictions to boost his already-high popularity.[14] Mobilizing his clean image and commitment to fighting corruption, Yudhoyono and the Democratic Party repeatedly used anticorruption rhetoric in campaign advertisements leading up to the 2009 legislative elections, where the Democratic Party increased its number of seats. Recontesting the presidency for a second term, Yudhoyono spoke of his ongoing commitment to eradicating corruption, while members of his party appeared in a (later infamous, due to allegations of hypocrisy) national television campaign featuring the tagline "say no to corruption!" (*katakan tidak pada korupsi!*). On the back of this campaign, Yudhoyono secured a resounding victory in the first round of the presidential election and was sworn in for a second term in October 2009.

Political Parties and the Facade of Anticorruptionism

The Democratic Party was not the only party to mobilize anticorruptionism in the lead-up to the 2009 election, as the issue continued to garner media and public attention. Indeed, several parties stressed their commitment to combating corruption to establish their legitimacy in that electoral race. These commitments became a millstone when members of several parties became ensnared in very public corruption scandals. The scandals that struck these parties had an especially severe impact on already negative perceptions of the trustworthiness of politicians. The veil also began to lift on the shady dealings of government officials. Corruption investigations began to ramp up, with a number of officials investigated and officially identified as "suspects" (*tersangka*) by the KPK. The most damaging corruption scandals for political parties were those involving legislators or members of their leadership teams. As elected representatives, members of the legislature are entrusted with pursuing the public interests and protecting citizens, which they were clearly not doing if they were taking bribes or embezzling state funds. Some party leaders who were not members of the legislature also faced corruption claims, adding to the overwhelming sense that political parties were not acting in the best interests of the citizens they purported to represent. Among the parties hit hardest were the Democratic Party, PKS, and Golkar.

The Democratic Party

The Democratic Party suffered a decline in popularity in the 2009–2014 term, in part because of multiple corruption scandals involving its members (Honna 2012). In one case, Muhammad Nazaruddin, a thirty-three-year-old national legislator representing East Java and national treasurer for the Democratic Party, was accused of accepting bribes in relation to the construction of an athletes' village in South Sumatra, as part of the 2011 Southeast Asian Games (SEA Games). The case came to be known as the Wisma Atlet (Athletes' guesthouse) scandal and was one of the most-reported corruption scandals of that year. It was particularly salacious because Nazaruddin fled the country, only to be pursued in an international manhunt by the KPK and arrested in Colombia in August 2011 (Mahi and Nazara 2012). He was sentenced to four years and ten months imprisonment for accepting approximately USD 365,200 in return for rigging construction tenders for the athletes' village. The ruling prompted outrage among anticorruption campaigners for its leniency, given that the prosecution had recommended a seven-year sentence (Rolisman 2012). Though the verdict did not link the bribe to the party more broadly, Nazaruddin implicated several colleagues during his trial, implying that other legislative representatives from the Democratic Party were involved in systemic corruption.

Nazaruddin's accusations were damaging because he and many other corruption suspects from the Democratic Party were young recruits who had been heralded as a new generation of politicians. His allegations had serious repercussions for certain colleagues, including Angelina Sondakh, a former beauty queen and a star party recruit in 2009. She was found guilty of accepting around USD 217,400 in bribes in return for awarding construction contracts to specific bidders. In January 2013 she was sentenced to 4.5 years imprisonment and fined USD 43,500. Her case was closely followed by the media, with some coverage resembling that given to celebrities by the paparazzi (Kramer 2013).[15] Also indicted, though in a separate sports-related case, was Democratic Party politician Andi Mallarangeng, then Minister for Sports, who resigned from his position in December 2012 following accusations that he had abused his ministerial power in the tendering of construction works for the Hambalang sporting complex, a facility for elite athletes on the outskirts of Bogor, resulting in state losses of USD 40,300 (approximately). Mallarangeng was accused of accepting close to USD 850,000 in bribes in exchange for awarding tenders to specific construction companies, and he was eventually arrested by the KPK in October 2013. He was convicted of abuse of authority in July 2014 and sentenced to four years in prison and fined USD 17,400 (*Jakarta Post*, July 18, 2014).

Even more damaging for the Democratic Party was the indictment of its chairperson, Anas Urbaningrum, for using money obtained through the Hambalang project and other government projects to fund his 2010 campaign to become party leader (Mahi and Nazara 2012). Although Anas was not an elected official, the scandal inferred that corruption had pervaded the upper echelons of the party and cast further doubt over its carefully curated anticorruption image. Yudhoyono rejected this suggestion, proclaiming corruption to be the exception rather than the rule. Anas was eventually convicted for his role in the Hambalang scandal and for money laundering, in September 2014. He was sentenced to prison for eight years and fined over USD 26,000. In their verdict, the Tipikor judges appeared to reflect popular sentiment, stating that Anas had "failed to support the spirit of society in fighting graft" (*Jakarta Post*, September 24, 2014).

Having once claimed to be a bastion in the fight against corruption, the Democratic Party was particularly susceptible to criticism when corruption among its own members was exposed. These scandals contributed to the party's declining popularity (Fealy 2013; Masduki 2018). Public concern about the party's integrity grew when WikiLeaks cables published in 2012 suggested that Yudhoyono had personally intervened to influence judges and prosecutors to protect officials close to him. Despite this, Yudhoyono was elected to the chairmanship of the Democratic Party in 2013 in an attempt to restore confidence in the party's leadership following Anas's downfall (Nehru 2013). Not surprisingly, the party shied away from anticorruptionism in its campaign for the 2014 elections, choosing instead to focus on Yudhoyono's track record as leader (Akuntono 2013). But the damage, it seems, was done. The Democratic Party had won 20.9 percent of votes in the 2009 election, but this fell to 10.19 percent in 2014.

The Prosperous Justice Party

The Democratic Party it was not the only political party to fall victim to corruption scandals and find itself facing allegations of hypocrisy in the 2009–2014 term. Similar charges were leveled at other political parties, including PKS. As a self-proclaimed Islamist party of reform, PKS had spent years fostering a clean image and cultivating an anticorruption reputation. The party campaigned heavily on a platform of moral transformation in the lead-up to the 2004 and 2009 elections. Following the 2009 elections, it joined Yudhoyono's ruling coalition in the national legislature, gaining a few ministerial positions, including leadership of the Ministry of Agriculture. It was this position that ultimately undermined the party's anticorruption image prior to the 2014 election, through the so-called *Beefgate* scandal.

In January 2013, PKS chairperson Luthfi Hasan Ishaaq and legislator Ahmad Fathanah were accused of accepting bribes from a beef import company, PT Indonguna, in return for increasing their beef import quota. Ahmad was arrested by KPK representatives in a five-star hotel room in Jakarta on January 29, 2013. He was in possession of a suitcase containing close to the equivalent of USD 87,000 (Cochrane 2013), allegedly a payment for Luthfi from PT Indoguna executives. Luthfi and Ahmad were charged with accepting bribes and money laundering in March 2013. The case became a full-blown sensation when it was revealed that Ahmad had been caught with a naked college student (Subkhan 2013). Both men strenuously asserted their innocence, though no plausible alternative explanation for the suitcase of cash was ever offered.

Media scrutiny intensified as more details of the case became public, painting an increasingly negative picture of individual party members and the party as a whole. PKS rallied support from its cadres, contending that hostile political interests seeking to damage the reputation of PKS were at play. The party launched a counterattack upon the KPK, claiming that the anticorruption agency had lost its independence and become a puppet of PKS's political rivals (Kramer 2014). The KPK attempted to seize five party vehicles belonging to Luthfi in May 2013, claiming that they may have been purchased with proceeds from corruption. Party officials refused to hand over the vehicles, instead lodging a police complaint claiming that KPK officials had abused their power, entered PKS's premises by force, and failed to produce a warrant for the seizure of the cars.

The illegal import quota deal, and the party's subsequent attacks on the well-respected KPK, took a toll on the party's image. However, the scandal was overshadowed by an increased focus upon the private lives of the PKS figures involved. Ahmad was eventually linked to over forty-five women, despite having two wives. It was alleged that he had given these women expensive gifts, possibly in exchange for intimate relations. There was also speculation that the women could themselves be tried for money laundering, though this did not eventuate. During the course of the investigation, it was also revealed that Luthfi had married for a third time, this time to a high school student. Many Indonesians were critical of the relationship between the fifty-two-year-old and the teenager, further damaging Luthfi's public reputation (Ucu 2013). The incorporation of such personal details in the case also cast doubt on the morality of these PKS members who, in addition to facing legal charges of corruption, were tainted in the court of public opinion (Kramer 2014).

After a highly publicized trial, Ahmad was found guilty of corruption on November 4, 2013, for receiving grants and incentives on behalf of Luthfi. The Tipikor sentenced him to fourteen years in prison and fined him the rupiah equivalent of almost USD 87,000 or an additional six months in prison. Once this verdict was passed, Luthfi attempted to shift the blame to Ahmad. Luthfi's own trial began later, and during questioning he claimed that Ahmad—his friend since the 1980s, when they had studied together in Saudi Arabia—had deceived him and used his name to make unsavory deals without his consent. Luthfi claimed that he had, as Ahmad's friend, attempted to protect him by denying that either of them had been complicit in illegal activity. The defense plea fell on deaf ears, and Luthfi was sentenced to sixteen years' imprisonment in December 2013, and a choice between paying a fine or spending an additional year in prison. Luthfi immediately announced that he would appeal the sentence, but his 2014 appeal saw him receive an even harsher sentence of eighteen years imprisonment. Hoping to restore its reputation before national polling in April 2014, PKS distanced itself from Luthfi, stating that it planned to focus on the upcoming elections and would not seek to intervene or influence the case in any way. But while the strategy may have mitigated complete electoral disaster for the party, PKS's share of the national vote still dropped (to just 6.79 percent) and it lost seventeen seats in the national legislature.

Golkar

The third party to be severely hit by scandal during Yudhoyono's second term as president was Golkar, the former ruling party of the Suharto era and consistently one of the best-represented parties in the legislature since Reformasi.[16] Golkar was implicated in a sensational scandal involving the arrest and conviction of Akil Mochtar, the chief justice of Indonesia's Constitutional Court and former national legislator for Golkar, for accepting bribes.[17] The Mochtar scandal dominated the national headlines from early October 2013, when rumors began circulating that the KPK had been investigating him. He was soon charged with receiving almost USD 350,000 for favorable rulings in disputes over the outcomes of district elections in Gunung Mas, in Central Kalimantan, and Lebak in the province of Banten. Later, he was tried for accepting bribes to fix eleven electoral rulings (Setuningsih and Cahyadi 2014). He was also charged with money laundering via his wife's company (Amelia 2013). Mochtar was sentenced to life imprisonment for receiving over USD 5 million in bribes and laundering almost USD 14 million during his tenure as a Constitutional Court judge.

The case provoked a particularly visceral outcry because the Constitutional Court, unlike other judicial institutions, was widely respected by the Indonesian public. The court's previous chief judge, Mahfud MD, was renowned for his hardline stance against corruption. The scandal was also unexpected because Mochtar had promoted himself as an anticorruption crusader, at one point stating that those guilty of corruption should have a finger cut off (MacLaren 2013).

The surprise his arrest generated echoed through international media reporting. For example, *The Australian* reported that "Akil Mochtar's arrest has raised anger about high-level corruption to a new pitch and the court's founding chief justice has called for the death sentence" (Alford 2013).

The case was also damaging for Golkar.[18] Not only had Mochtar previously represented the party in the national legislature, but several Golkar officials were implicated in the case against him. In March 2014, Chairun Nisa, a Golkar legislator from Central Kalimantan, received a four-year prison sentence and a fine of almost USD 8,700 for brokering a deal between Golkar members and Mochtar. As the investigations continued, Banten's governor, Ratu Atut Chosiyah, also made headlines when her younger brother was linked to the case. Atut herself was tried in August 2014 for allegedly paying Mochtar approximately USD 87,000 to secure a Golkar victory in the regency of Lebak when the party appealed the local electoral results in the Constitutional Court. Although prosecutors sought a ten-year prison sentence for Atut, she was only sentenced to four years' imprisonment and a fine of USD 17,400. There was widespread public outrage at the light sentence, especially on social media, where netizens complained that it undermined the deterrent effect that a harsher punishment would have otherwise achieved (Soares 2014). Mochtar's arrest and conviction were portrayed as a gross betrayal of trust, while Atut's conviction confirmed the ongoing use of bribery to fix political outcomes, demonstrating that corruption still reached the highest echelons and continued to undermine democratic processes.

As a party, Golkar had never openly described itself as being anticorruption, not least because its ties to Suharto and the New Order meant that such a claim would ring false. But Mochtar's case had much broader implications for perceptions of corruption in Indonesia. The case demonstrated that party politics and corruption reached far beyond the legislature and ministries to include the courts. While the judicial system was already perceived as being rife with corruption, being run by a "judicial mafia" (Butt and Lindsay 2011), the Constitutional Court had stood apart as one of the country's more trusted government institutions (Butt 2015b). With this image shattered, all parties, not just Golkar, would find it difficult to establish that they were genuinely interested in fighting corruption and were not simply part of a self-serving political machine.

Voter Perceptions

By 2014, the high expectations that accompanied the end of the New Order had largely dissipated. Corruption continued to permeate Indonesia's government, and many of those who appeared to champion corruption eradication had themselves been found to be corrupt. Frustration mounted as economic and political elites continued to benefit from poor accountability mechanisms, easily bribed officials, and the use of patronage. The maintenance of exclusive systems of personal enrichment not available to ordinary people created a sense of distrust toward those in public office, and suspicion at their motivations. A rash of corruption cases within the bureaucracy confirmed that corruption was not only a legislative issue but also commonplace among civil servants, police officers, and judges. Being linked to corruption scandals was also a contributing factor in the decline of Yudhoyono's popularity (Aspinall 2015; Sulaiman 2014), as well as several other political parties, and fostered a general distrust of key institutions including the legislature.

Not unexpectedly, these revelations provoked widespread public dissatisfaction not just with the legislature but with the government overall. Surveys conducted during this period indicate that citizens were displeased with the government's performance on corruption despite growing numbers of convictions, from twenty-seven in 2007 to fifty-nine in 2013.[19] A number of surveys undertaken in 2012 and 2013, leading up to the 2014 election, reflected the depth of public discontent with progress on the government's anticorruption agenda, highlighting disappointment with Yudhoyono and parliament (table 1).[20] Regular surveys conducted by the Indonesian Survey Group (*Lembaga Survei Indonesia*, LSI) over a longer period confirm that public satisfaction with the government's anticorruption endeavors had declined. In 2008, a survey revealed a 77 percent approval rate for the government's work on combating corruption. By 2011, this number had fallen to 44 percent (*Lembaga Survei Indonesia* 2012). At the same time, a LSI study in the 2014 election found that the qualities of "honest" (*jujur*) and/or "corruption-free" (*bebas korupsi*) were the most desirable qualities in a legislative candidate.[21,22]

Dissatisfaction with the government's performance on corruption did not necessarily mean, however, that voters saw elections as the means for resolving the problem. Voters' trust in political parties had also declined. This growing discontent was illustrated by the public's increasing reluctance to align themselves with a party (Fealy 2011).[23] Surveys conducted in 2011 by LSI found that only 20 percent of respondents considered themselves to "belong" to a party, compared to 86 percent in 1999 (*Lembaga Survei Indonesia* 2011). The SPACE survey conducted in July 2013 suggested that, nine months out from the election, a large proportion of citizens felt no party loyalty and were open to voting differently in 2014 than they had in 2009. Another 43 percent of those surveyed were not planning to vote at all. As many as 47.7 percent of respondents in a Saiful Mujani Research Center poll in March 2014 chose not to nominate a preferred party. While it is impossible to identify a single reason for this lack of party loy-

TABLE 1. Surveys addressing corruption issues in Indonesia (July 2012–December 2013)

RELEASED	INSTITUTION	FINDINGS
July 2012	CSIS	77% of respondents believe the majority of government officials are corrupt.
Jan. 2013	Biro Pusat Statistik	On average, respondents rate corruption in the Indonesian government as 3.5 out of 5 (with 5 being very corrupt, 0 meaning no corruption).
July 2013	Lingkaran Survei Indonesia	52% of those surveyed say they do not trust politicians.
Sept. 2013	Indonesian Network Election Survey	86% of respondents believe that all political parties are corrupt.
Oct. 2013	Lembaga Survei Nasional	55.9% of respondents believe corruption eradication is the most important issue facing the government (the highest-ranking issue in the survey). 55.4% of respondents believed that the state of the nation had not improved during Yudhoyono's second term and 25.9% believed it had gotten worse.
Dec. 2013	Indikator	41.5% of respondents believe that political parties are the primary group responsible for preventing money politics.
Dec. 2013	Transparency International	Corruption Perceptions Index finds that national parliamentarians are perceived as the most corrupt figures in Indonesia.

alty, or indeed political engagement more broadly, the apparent prevalence of corruption across all parts of government certainly contributed to cynicism among voters.

A sense of disappointment with parties' failure to effectively address corruption and improve transparency, even within their own ranks, was also evident in public discourse. According to Tama S. Langkun, a researcher at Indonesian Corruption Watch, "the public is waiting for the government and House to show their good intentions," but were continually disappointed by the decisions being made by their political representatives (quoted in *The Diplomat*, March 20, 2014). Moreover, media attention on the many corruption cases involving political parties during the 2009–2014 period illustrated that it was not only widespread but involved all arms of government. These cases reflected both continuing problems with governance and the rule of law, and the absence of generational change that had been anticipated with the new wave of post-Reformasi recruits. Political commentators and anticorruption activists alike had hoped that post-Reformasi youth taking over from old guard civil servants would bring with them new ideals that would discourage involvement in corruption. However, these hopes faded when young politicians indicted for corruption were joined by young public servants also charged with graft-related crimes (Yogi Prabowo 2014).[24]

This disappointment was reflected in the results of the 2014 legislative elections, which heralded a change in fortune for a number of Indonesia's national political parties. PDIP, which had previously been in opposition, was the favorite to win a majority. Even though it fell short of expectations, it still won more national legislative seats than any other party (Hamid 2014).[25] The main casualty was the Democratic Party, which lost eighty-seven seats and its dominance in parliament. PKS, which had gained a significant number of votes in 2009, became the only Islamic party to lose seats. The decline in popularity for both the Democratic Party and PKS appeared to be closely tied to numerous corruption scandals—though also questions about the morality of individuals members in the case of PKS—which tainted the parties' anticorruption credentials in the lead-up to the election.[26] This decrease in votes may potentially reflect the electoral consequences for politicians and their parties of making anticorruption claims but failing to live up to them. But, perhaps more likely, it simply reinforced that political promises had little weight and voters were right to be suspicious of them.

Corruption and the need to fight it have been persistent themes in Indonesia's political history, from colonial times to the present day. Alongside an increase in political corruption scandals was a rise in money politics during Indonesian elections. Although these scandals served to foster an increasing skepticism among Indonesian citizens toward the activities and motives of the politicians that were entrusted to represent their interests, the ongoing use of money as a tool of persuasion during voting was, perhaps, a more visible indicator of the state of democracy in Reformasi Indonesia. It was a particularly hot topic in the lead-up to the 2014 elections, with many surveys conducted before the elections revealing that voters were disillusioned by, and suspicious of, political parties and their candidates.

This chapter has offered a general overview of some key corruption issues in Indonesia and illustrated how these issues have been co-opted by different actors and heighted some of the inherent dangers of invoking rhetoric that does not live up to expectations. While the chapter discusses several forms of corruption, well beyond the vote-buying focus of the chapters to follow, it provides some background for understanding why corruption was a salient electoral issue and the potential benefits and pitfalls of anticorruptionism as a campaign strategy. A closer look at the historical context of corruption and anticorruptionism goes some way to explaining why an anticorruption identity would be so appealing for political hopefuls, potentially generating support from voters exasperated by the extent of government corruption scandals. For political parties and their candidates, constructing an anticorruption identity would be challenging given the negative press received over the preceding years and voters' skepticism about the motivations of political parties. At the same time, being seen to represent a break from tradition was a useful rhetorical tool for those competing in the 2014 elections, especially new parties who could, essentially, enter the electoral campaign with a clean slate.

Understanding the opportunities and challenges presented by anticorruptionism allows us to put the decisions and dilemmas faced by candidates during the campaign development in perspective. The salience of corruption as a political issue—built on its long political history and impact on politics in Indonesia, but also the specific context of the 2014 election—certainly influenced the decision of some candidates to make anticorruptionism a campaign focus. Presenting oneself as being staunchly committed to fighting corruption and staying "clean" became a catch-cry for many political parties, especially newer ones. Concentrating public attention on corruption to fuel disdain for those in power seemed beneficial for new parties, allowing their candidates to position themselves within dominant discourses explaining why corruption was so prevalent. They seized upon narratives holding that corruption impeded national and social development and was driven by selfish materialism, drawing a black-and-white comparison with existing parties. Claims that Indonesia needed new and tough leadership, fronted by committed and trustworthy individuals (such as themselves), were the crux of this messaging.

This chapter also introduces new questions about how voter behavior and candidate experiences during elections intersect with a broader dissatisfaction with the behavior of political parties and elected representatives. With corruption established as a prominent issue, and citizens seemingly unhappy with the status quo, one could assume that anticorruption candidates who are persuasive in their campaigns would reap some benefit from these attitudes. But while the shadow of political corruption and party reputation loom large, candidates ultimately decide how much of a role these discourses will play in their campaigns. There were individual candidates who attempted to position themselves in contrast to *other* politicians who had been unable to resist the temptation of using their authority for their own gain. In some cases, this led to an integration of anticorruptionism—a broad rejection of corruption and a promise that they would be different. Others extended this strategy to establish themselves as clean campaigners who would not countenance illegal behavior that would tarnish their identities before they even made it to public office. These candidates had to negotiate their own use of anticorruption rhetoric and the establishment of their candidate image within a context where money politics was illegal but common during elections. As we will see in the following chapters, the end result of this negotiation varied significantly, depending on the individual circumstances of each candidate.

3

STANDING HIS GROUND

A candidate's decision to run on an anticorruption platform—to present themselves as clean (*bersih*)—could reflect deeply held personal values or constitute a cynical grab for the moral high ground. In either case, it is accompanied by a host of assumptions about how voters will respond to anticorruptionism as a campaign message. In 2014, candidates understood, based on public surveys and media portrayals, that the public were tired of corrupt politicians taking advantage of their public position to take kickbacks, rig tenders, embezzle funds, and provide favors to their associates. Some candidates imagined that they could leverage this dissatisfaction, at least amongst a subset of voters, by demonstrating that they themselves were honest, clean, and ready to do a better job than their rivals. In reality, however, while the use of anticorruption rhetoric could form a basis for strategy, campaigns required candidates to strategize beyond simply telling voters they opposed corruption.

This chapter follows the campaign of Ambo,[1] a candidate running in 2014 for the national legislature, who was determined to win without resorting to payments (in cash, club goods, or local projects) to voters or establishing patronage relationships based on promises of kickbacks once in office. In following Ambo's campaign journey—the development of his strategy, the challenges he encountered, and his responses—we come to better understand how an election campaign played out for one self-described "anticorruption candidate" (*caleg antikorupsi*). We learn what factors guided him as he resisted turning to money politics in order to win in a context where the practice is not only normalized but seemingly demanded by voters. We also come to appreciate how his relationship to his party, his own values, and his ties within his electoral district shaped his response to these pressures. Ultimately, we witness the victory of this candidate, who did his utmost to maintain his commitment to anticorruptionism until election day. This does not mean that he made no compromises, but—in staying true to the parameters of his campaign—he rejected vote buying as a strategy to the very end.

The Candidate

I first met Ambo in Jakarta in early May 2013. I had been put in contact with him by another member of his party who, after hearing about my interest in anticorruption candidates, told me that Ambo was *the* person to talk to. Ambo was an up-and-coming leader within the party. He had previously won a seat in the national legislature representing a different party. Soon after resigning from the legislature, he took on a leadership role in his new party.[2] Although he had been based in Jakarta for almost two decades, he was planning to run for a seat in his home district, a traditional Golkar stronghold. The party had high hopes that he would be elected and was planning not only to give him the use of local party offices and allocate party cadres to his campaign team (commonly referred to as *tim sukses* in Indonesia) but also to provide him with funds to run his campaign.[3]

Having set up a meeting via text message, we met at the party headquarters in Central Jakarta, where the candidate had his own office by virtue of his standing as a senior party leader. After navigating the office security process and handing my identification over at the front desk, I met a secretary who escorted me to Ambo's office. Greeting me with a serious but amicable demeanor, he was understandably guarded. After the obligatory small talk about where I was staying and the frustrations of Jakarta traffic, we chatted briefly about my interest in corruption issues in election campaigns. Even though I had been referred to him by a colleague, his questions betrayed an underlying suspicion about my motivations. His direct approach, asking me what I wanted from him even before I got to my list of questions, was a change from many of the interviews I had already conducted with candidates. Feeling somewhat confronted, but also acknowledging that it was good to have these things out in the open, I explained that I was interested in how anticorruption candidates campaign in an environment so dominated by money politics. Upon hearing my answer, he shook his head sadly, as if to indicate that he had often asked himself the very same question. At the same time, he seemed genuinely pleased to be identified by a colleague as such a candidate.

Following these preliminary introductions, I started the formal part of my interview by asking him why he had chosen to become a politician. For me, the question was simply background to help build an understanding of the narrative he presented about himself and his career thus far. In responding, however, Ambo launched into a preemptive explanation about why he had resigned from his previous position as a legislator representing a different party. His desire to explain his move made sense in a context where politicians are often accused of party-switching purely to improve their chances of being elected. Such moves are often criticized as being self-serving and aimed as furthering individual interests rather than better representing constituents. Positioning his decision as one based on conscience, rather than ambition, Ambo stressed that it had been a very difficult decision to make. Ultimately, he went ahead with it because he felt his previous party had not been serious about several issues, particularly around investigations into corruption in the national legislature. By moving, he sought to return with the backing of a party that he believed to be more supportive of his anticorruption agenda. While he knew he would face criticism for defecting, he felt it was a risk worth taking in order to do what he wanted to do as a legislator.

Within minutes of the interview commencing, Ambo had already begun projecting an image of himself as a politician with strong morals and integrity who had long-term political ambitions highlighting his background as an activist who had been involved in the anti-Suharto protests of the late 1990s and who had spent some years as an investigative journalist. He explained that fighting corruption had been a personal goal for many years, even before he entered politics—unlike other candidates who were primarily interested in personal gain, whether in the form of money or prestige. Furthermore, he leveraged this background—his "track record"—to lay claim to anticorruption ideals that distinguished himself from other candidates who oppose corruption "just to get votes."

Perceptions of Political Parties

Ambo linked his desire to present himself as an anticorruption candidate to his decision to join a new party that prided itself on being corruption-free. To his mind, this new party was not bound by the "bad habits" entrenched in other parties. He spoke scathingly of his previous party and the others he had worked with during his prior term in the national legislature. Joining a new party offered a chance to build something different, with a new organizational culture and a new approach to voters and elections. However, this idealism was tinged with realism as he spoke about how difficult it was to make sure that all the party cadres and candidates wanted the same thing. He seemed to believe in the opportunities that his party presented, but he also conceded that many candidates who represent a political party in Indonesia do not feel the same way. "For some people, it's just a vehicle to become a candidate and the truth is there is not much we can do about that because we do need the candidates.... We have to recruit so quickly and often we don't really know what they are like until much later," he said somewhat forlornly.

Ambo was also frank in his assessments of the broader party system. For most voters, he said, the system was confusing, and political parties often said one thing but did another. Based on this assessment, he said that voters had every right to be suspicious:

> I can tell you that there is not one single party that is steadfast in its ideology.... There are so many examples of this. Look at the national budget. The parties in the DPR [Dewan Perwakilan Rakyat (National People's Representative Council)] now all talk about equality and justice in the distribution of the budget but look at all that money that is collected here in Jakarta. It goes to Java, and what's left goes to Aceh and Papua to keep them calm. What about Sulawesi, what about the rest of the provinces? That's not justice. The parties just talk about [justice] ... but nothing changes. If the money stays in Jakarta, then it's easier for them to be corrupt.

He understood that for voters, especially in his electoral district in Sulawesi, the activities and actions of the national legislature seem both far removed and of no real benefit to them—and that political parties did little to help this perception by having representatives that appeared more interested in jockeying for power and self-enrichment, rather than actually helping their constituents.

Cognizant of the impact of the corruption scandals that had plagued the Democratic Party and PKS (Partai Keadilan Sejahtera [Prosperous Justice Party]) over the past few years, he felt a need to present his party as even more uncompromisingly against corruption than other emerging parties:

> We have to learn from other new parties in the legislature.... They have no corruption cases against them, and we can learn from that.... [But] we have to aim higher ... and be more disciplined about it.... If we fall short even once, we'll be finished. I think other parties have already felt the effect of that.

Ambo hoped his own party would genuinely advocate for corruption eradication if it got into power. But he acknowledged that this would be tough, pointing to the many candidates who had won seats in the previous election based, at least partly, on strong anticorruption rhetoric, and then done very little to stand up against corruption. Not surprisingly, he was in favor of being "merciless" (*tanpa ampun*) toward candidates within his own party who were found to engage in vote buying during the elections.

Ambo reflected on the damage that the behavior of individual candidates could do to a party's overall reputation, especially for new parties like his that were trying their utmost to project an image of change, and he mulled over the strategies his party had adopted to respond to this risk. One strategy involved the decision to offer a campaign budget to candidates who, in their assessment, had a decent chance of success. It was common for candidates to spend vast sums to both be nominated by a party and then conduct their electoral campaign. If successful, it was also normal for successful candidates to leverage their political positions to recoup some of those costs, fueling personal motivations for corruption in the legislature.[4] As part of this internal policy, the party funded the usual campaign materials (such as banners and t-shirts) but also other key expenses such as fees for "witnesses" to observe the vote counting, who could both monitor the count and ensure that the results were not tampered with. Ambo made the point that this was a helpful tool for managing the party's image but would probably not be enough to put an end to money politics. Nor would it help the party if any of their successful candidates did become embroiled in corruption scandals once they entered the national legislature.

While Ambo was open in critiquing Indonesia's political system, he also acknowledged that he benefitted greatly from his relationship to his party. Being a senior party figure and the first-ranked candidate in his district shaped Ambo's campaign in a number of ways. He was privileged to receive financial backing, which meant that he had more resources than many other candidates. Party funding paid for his campaign materials, as well as some rallies and transportation—which was particularly important because Ambo was based in Jakarta but campaigning in Sulawesi. Ambo also had access to local media outlets with connections to his party. A reporter followed him when he was in Sulawesi, and a television crew was present at several of his rallies to film his speeches. At one rally I attended, journalists interviewed locals to ask why they were supporting the candidate, with the aim of adding these local endorsements to their coverage of Ambo's campaign. While it is difficult to quantify the benefits that this media exposure brought, it was clear that it gave him a comparative advantage against others within his own party as well as candidates from rival parties with less access to the media.

Anticipated Challenges

Having run for office before, Ambo was under no illusions as to how stressful the process would be. One complicating factor was his availability for campaigning in his local electoral district. Due to his seniority in the party, he knew he would have to attend to many duties at the national level. Not only did he have commitments at the central office, but he was also required to sometimes accompany the party leader during the national campaign. He traveled extensively all over Indonesia to promote the party in the lead-up to the election. Ambo was also aware, based on his previous experience, that life on the campaign trail was exhausting. Anticipating meetings from morning to night, sometimes with people he did not particularly want to meet, he approached the campaign with something of a sense of dread. When I asked him what the worst aspect of campaigning was, expecting him to say more about money politics, he surprised me by replying, "Sometimes I would not see my children for weeks . . . and that's really hard." But he knew what it would be like and would make sure to always bring back small gifts (*oleh-oleh*) for his children after every trip "so they don't miss me so much." He knew that it would be tough, but he was prepared to do what it took to win.

Ambo was also worried that the fact that he could not spend long periods in his own electoral district might disadvantage his campaign. Campaign teams, he said, are like staff: they just do what they are told by their boss and become lazy—or even worse, do things that they are not supposed to do—if the boss is absent. Wondering where this distrust came from, I followed up by asking why he felt they were unreliable. He responded, "You have to understand that some people are here to help themselves. I know this, and so I need to be cautious. That's the reality of a campaign. If you're not careful, people will do whatever they want and it's your campaign that suffers, not them." He pointed to examples of campaign staff pocketing money for themselves or promising benefits without his knowledge as they attempted to secure votes, saying that he had seen this in other candidates' teams in his previous campaign. Ambo felt that not being able to monitor his campaign team closely made him vulnerable to these kinds of incidents, and it worried him that they could undermine his carefully cultivated image.

Being an anticorruption candidate in an electoral environment where vote buying is so prevalent also weighed heavily on Ambo's mind. He expressed his disquiet with the strategy early on and, in subsequent meetings throughout the campaign, he voiced frustration with voters who were too easily swayed by things that "did not matter," like being given small amounts of cash that "weren't even enough to buy a meal for their family." When asked about how he thought voters would respond to his anticorruption messages, he said that he understood that it would not be easy but underscored the importance of demonstrating his commitment:

> I think people are tired. Because it's confusing, disorientating . . . who should they trust? They're always being lied to. But we can't give up. We have to keep telling them that we can't let the corruptors win, we can't be

beaten by corruption. And we have to show them that every party has good people . . . some good people and some bad people. That's how it is for every party. We just have to show them that we are the good ones.

Even so, as he conceded in our first discussion, talking about corruption was a risky campaign strategy that might not appeal to voters accustomed to being wooed by candidates with "big wallets." He went on to explain that money politics was a particularly serious problem in his electoral district because many candidates did not actually live in South Sulawesi and did not want to do the hard work of visiting voters and campaigning in person. Instead, they would send emissaries out to negotiate payments in return for votes. But he also believed, somewhat optimistically, that there were still enough people who were not swayed by this. These were the people, he said, who would be more inclined to vote for somebody with a proven commitment and a strong track record. Logically, then, this was the constituency he was hoping to target with his campaign.

More vexing for Ambo was the interference run by community leaders who took advantage of the elections for their own benefit. In late 2013, he told me that he had heard from people in his electoral district that a local Islamic religious leader was promoting a particular candidate from Golkar. The candidate was an incumbent whom he knew personally from his previous term in the national legislature. Ambo made it clear that he did not have a high opinion of him. While he was reluctant to go into detail about what brought him to this conclusion—he was unsure about exactly what the religious leader had received in return for the endorsement or whether there was some familial connection—he did say that the Golkar legislator "did not care" about corruption. The main target of his annoyance, in this case, was the cleric who had chosen to promote this rival candidate. According to Ambo, he was clearly not interested in helping the people to elect a candidate based on merit. However, by virtue of his position, voters may be persuaded by him. It was terrible, said Ambo, that they would be encouraged to vote against their interests by someone in authority. He said he could not blame voters for taking their cues from people in authority—this was normal, not just in politics but in all aspects of life. And it was exactly because it was so normal that it would be difficult for him to overcome.

On the Campaign Trail

In July 2013, Ambo was headed to his electoral district to conduct some initial meetings with local party cadres and government officials. This marked the beginning of my in situ observations of his campaign, which would span three trips to South Sulawesi, interspersed with regular discussions when he was in Jakarta. Flying into Makassar with a small team, then driving out to a regional town, our first car trip was spent talking about what was happening at party headquarters as they began to ramp up the national campaign. Even though polling day was almost ten months away, the candidate was already showing signs of stress from having to juggle his Jakarta commitments and his own campaign. His hope for this visit was to organize his campaign team and to touch base with some local officials to see if they might be willing to support him. He was pessimistic about this ask, suspecting they would want something in return that he was not willing to promise, but he had a family connection to one of the officials through marriage, which he hoped would provide some leverage.

After driving for several hours, we stopped at a roadside restaurant for lunch. Upon entering, the staff greeted Ambo cheerily and the owner, sitting at a desk at the front of the restaurant, got up to give him a warm embrace. This restaurant, he told me, was owned by a family member who had helped him in his previous campaign. "What kind of help?" I asked. "He told people to vote for me." The owner joined us for a seafood lunch. He and Ambo chatted about how the restaurant was less busy these days before they began talking about the campaign. "Who's been through here?" the candidate asked, trying to ascertain which rivals had started organizing in the local area. The owner told him that, while still quiet (*masih sepi*), a few people were beginning to make a move. He said it was mostly new candidates who were starting to get organized, people who did not yet have a following (commonly referred to as *massa*, a term for a loyal group of voters). Ambo did not ask too many follow-up questions, as the discussion turned to family and food, seeming to enjoy the meal and the chance to chat.

While it is technically against the law to campaign outside of the designated campaign period—between March 16 and April 6, 2014, for the 2014 election—it is common for candidates to begin planning, holding meetings, and negotiating with voters well before those official dates. Ambo was among those looking to begin organizing early, particularly because he knew that his involvement in the national-level campaign would be time-consuming. Back in the car, he said that he was pleased to hear that most candidates had not begun electioneering in earnest. He had been concerned about rivals getting a head start. Understanding how important it was to know the lay of the land, this lunch was more than just a familial encounter; even if it had been relatively light touch, it was nevertheless an important act of intelligence gathering.

Over the course of this first trip, it became apparent that Ambo was a keen planner, who put a great deal of thought into how his campaign would be run, including his use of corruption as a key campaign issue. Visiting the district's main party office next morning, he spoke to a gathering of about ten people, telling them that he was counting on them to talk to everybody they knew and encourage them to vote for him. During the meeting he emphasized how important it was that his team relay that he was a clean candidate—one that was committed to fighting corruption and not being a part of it. To his mind, it was important that his team understood that this commitment was a crucial part of his campaign strategy. While it was not explicitly mentioned, it was clear in the meeting that he had no intention of buying votes. The attendees nodded along, and some even asked questions. This did not seem to allay his fears that they would stray from his campaign strategy, though. After the meeting, he again lamented to me that he could not be in two places at once to oversee the campaign and meet his other responsibilities in Jakarta.

That evening, we sat at a coffee shop and Ambo told me about his experience in the last campaign. He described how tiring it had been, going from village to village, talking at gatherings, and worrying about who he could trust. The logistics of running an "on the ground" campaign—which had become even more popular in 2014 because the *blusukan* strategy (which involved dropping in for informal discussions) had been popularized by then–presidential candidate Joko Widodo—were complex.[5] As the campaign progressed, I observed these challenges directly. First, Ambo needed to identify local contacts and liaise through them to set up meetings and publicize them among residents. Having a local contact made it more likely that people would attend, as they could use their community connections to encourage people to come along. Second, because Ambo's time in the district was so limited, each visit consisted of numerous outings every day, some lasting several hours. These meetings were interspersed with long periods in the car, traveling between places, while also coordinating his team, some of whom were traveling in other vehicles, in preparation for these meetings. In addition, considerations such as stopping to pray, meals, and paying for gas amplified the long days traveling between different villages, especially as the candidate was committed to keeping meticulous records of his expenditure.

While in the electoral district, I asked Ambo if it was possible for members of his campaign team to do some of this hard work while he was away. Of course, they would continue the campaign in his absence, but Ambo also explained that last time around some members of his campaign team had made problematic promises on his behalf. He was evasive when I asked him about the exact nature of those promises, but he mentioned that one team member had promised to provide cash payments for votes and the community had been annoyed when Ambo "reneged" on the promise made on his behalf. I pressed further on why he would work with people in whom he did not have confidence. He responded by saying that every candidate needed a team, and it was important to have people who he could task with activities like putting up banners or distributing t-shirts, but he still preferred to keep an eye on what they were doing and how they represented him. The only way to be sure of this, according to Ambo, was to make it known that he was keeping a keen eye on the team because it was impossible to know (*siapa tahu*) what promises they might make, or how they may describe him, when he was not there. In addition, he felt it was more useful for people to meet him personally to get a sense of how genuine he was. At the same time, he felt he could not outsource his discussions with local officials, who might be offended and not feel important if he did not meet with them in person.

Dealing with Gatekeepers

While individual voters were Ambo's main campaign target, this did not preclude him from attempting to garner support from people with influence. Early forays into the field were focused on meeting with local politicians and government officials, who acted as gatekeepers in his electoral district. The purpose of these meetings was threefold. First, it was an established campaign norm to reach out to local officials, to solicit their tacit permission to campaign in their area and to get them onside so as to campaign within their areas without too much interference. Second, he wanted to get a sense for their personal involvement in the local election and whether they themselves were the kind of corrupt officials who may take the opportunity to rent-seek from candidates. Third, he used the meetings as an opportunity to collect intelligence and to see whether any rivals already had some kind of hold over the area or not.

On the second day of our first trip, we headed out to meet the first of the three local officials Ambo planned to meet during this trip. Arriving at the first official's house at around 9 a.m., we were early enough to seemingly catch him unaware. He was not home. The candidate commented wryly to me that "this is Indonesia" (*inilah Indonesia!*). The official was at another house a few minutes away, but a quick phone call saw him return home within fifteen minutes. After an Islamic greeting and a handshake, the meeting took place over sweet tea. Ambo first reminisced about how he had come through the area a few years ago and asked about how the crops were looking at this time of year. He seemed keen to make the meeting as personal as possible and was full of smiles—a stark contrast to the pessimism he had previously expressed about the role of authority figures in elections. It was important to be charming, both to try to win the official over and to obtain as much intelligence as possible from them to help his campaign.

After some time, Ambo finally steered the conversation to the upcoming election. He spoke about his previous experience in the legislature and understanding how the government systems worked. He said that he thought that it was important for someone from the district be elected to represent the area because voters needed to have someone who would champion their needs at the national level. In essence, he made the case that he *understood* what they needed. He then asked the official about the specific issues and problems their community faced. When the official mentioned that the weather had been dry and the community was worried about a lack of water, the candidate nodded knowingly. The meeting ended over an hour later, with Ambo politely declining the offer of an early lunch. Over its course, the issue of corruption was never mentioned.

"How did that go?" I asked once we were back in the car. "I don't know," he replied. From my perspective as an outsider, the meeting seemed to have been productive, with the official showing a general interest in Ambo's campaign and answering his questions politely. But Ambo was not convinced. Apparently, this official had a reputation, something I had not been aware of before the meeting. According to Ambo, the fact that he did not ask for anything at all, even a donation to a local community group or charity, was not a good sign. I was confused—wasn't it a good thing not to be asked for money? Trying to better understand his response, I pressed him on why it was a bad thing. Ambo explained that it might mean the official was already planning to help one of his rivals. If they were open to supporting him, the official would have tested him on some terms—a conditionality, so to speak—in the meeting. Ambo had been prepared for this, but the request never came. Based on this, he decided to wait and see what his intelligence told him about this local area before deciding whether it would be worth meeting again with the official. Months later, I asked him whether he ever sought out another meeting. He replied that he had not. When I asked why, he said that he had heard the official was supporting another candidate from Golkar who had been campaigning hard in that district. He had suspected it would be a waste of time to follow up.

In two other similar meetings, the ask for financial contribution was more obvious, though wrapped up in nuanced discussions about the needs of the local community. We arrived mid-afternoon for the second meeting, to be greeted by the official and a group of about six local men, all smoking in the front room of the official's house. It was hot outside, and the small group was chatting casually. Upon our arrival, phone calls were made to summon a handful more attendees to the meeting. Here, the reception was warmer. As one of Ambo's relatives was married to the district head, a ritual discussion of family was required before Ambo could begin talking about the election. He commenced by outlining his previous experience in the national legislature. He explained that had been so disappointed with the quality of politicians that he felt he had to run again. Surveying the room, it was hard to know how much interest the audience had in this observation. At least two men were looking at their mobile phones, while others nodded, but with glazed stares. Ambo then pivoted to talk about how Sulawesi was overlooked by people in Jakarta and he wanted to "make sure that we aren't forgotten . . . [and] make sure they don't take everything from us." Impassioned, he rattled off a list of problems in the area, infrastructure being key. The audience was more interested now, as he began asking them questions about what they thought about the government. When the meeting ended, he promised to return soon to talk more about local infrastructure issues. He also gave them his phone number, saying "call me anytime if you have any problems with the government." Again, there had been no overt talk of money or corruption.

On the surface, the meeting went no better or worse than others I had attended. But the candidate was particularly pleased. These were "good people," he later told me in the car. They had not asked for money either but this time it was not a bad sign. Perplexed, I asked what made the meeting different from the other meeting where he had not been asked for anything—something he had previously identified as a bad sign. His explanation? He could tell they were open to his advances. How? Because a relative had told him that they were. It became apparent that Ambo was using his network of personal connections to gather inside information. While he did not know if they would support him in the end, he felt that he could persuade them to do so because they knew him, and he was family. This seemed a simplistic response, and I suspected there was more. Later, at a café, he explained that he could not predict if another candidate would swoop in with grand promises or money. But what he needed to know now, at this early stage of the campaign, was how to avoid wasting his time, as the election drew closer, on people who had no intention of voting for him in the first place.

Toward the end of my first trip with Ambo, I asked why he rarely spoke about corruption in these small meetings, given that it was his main campaign platform. In Jakarta, he had told me he was an "anticorruption candidate," so why not tell these people the same thing? He responded:

> It's different talking to you, you're thinking about corruption in an academic way. For the officials here, corruption doesn't matter like it matters in Jakarta. . . . Talking about corruption in Bank Century or the KPK [Komisi Pemberantasan Korupsi (Corruption Eradication Commission)] is too abstract for them. It's better if you show them that you understand their problems, that you care about the people in this area.

He also pointed out that he was aware that many of the officials he met with had probably engaged in some form of corruption during their time in government. During another campaign visit, we found ourselves in the opulent mansion of a Bupati (local district head). The house was full, with a crowd of around thirty people. Unlike most of the other campaign meetings I had attended with him, Ambo was mingling rather than addressing the group. While not privy to Ambo's conversations during the event, he was disparaging of the Bupati after we left. "Can you imagine how corrupt he must be to be able to afford that house?" he thundered. "If that was the case," I asked, "why meet him at all?" It was necessary, he explained, to neutralize another gatekeeper. If he wanted to campaign in the district without being disturbed, he needed to be on good terms with the Bupati. Asking whether he had been asked for anything in return for access, Ambo said that he had not at this stage. He suspected, though, that there may be a request later. Reflecting on this reality of campaigning, he observed: "It's a game for these officials . . . and for now I have to play along."

While he seemed resentful to be pandering to such people, he also understood it as a normal part of campaigning. Gaining access to communities was more important than condemning corruption at the early stages of the campaign. With allegiances still uncertain, speaking out passionately against corruption could do more harm than good if he was associating with someone who had engaged in the very activities he was railing against. In short, his initial strategy was more about getting the lay of the land and gaining access to gatekeepers rather than directly winning voters over.

Engaging with Voters

By the time I took my next trip to the field with Ambo, his campaign had entered its "second phase," although the official campaign period was yet to begin. As he had explained in Jakarta at a previous catch-up, his strategy had shifted gears from neutralizing gatekeepers to talking directly to voters. This strategy was more time-consuming, but he felt that if people could meet him, he would be able to win them over by demonstrating his dedication to being a good representative without having to spend lots of money. He also said that his campaign was designed to "sell who he was, not pay people to believe who he was." This, as he saw it, was a point of difference between him and other candidates, who "have to pay because they don't stand for anything." In addition to drawing on his experience in the national legislature, he also highlighted his past as an activist, assuring audiences that he would continue to press for those guilty of corruption—often referred in Indonesia as "corruptors" (*koruptor*)—to be brought to justice. His campaign rhetoric drew heavily upon his involvement in the investigations into political corruption scandals. He believed that asserting his prior commitment to fighting corruption, for which he claimed to have made career and personal sacrifices, would give him an advantage over his competitors who lacked his impressive track record.

Ambo met with voters in mosques, at people's houses, or at local *warung* (small eating places) in their local areas. These gatherings, which varied in size between fifteen and forty people, were very relaxed. Ambo stressed to me that he wanted to avoid lavish, formal events in order to promote his image as "one of the people." He also explained that he preferred informal settings because they made it easier for him to connect with voters. The events were usually set up in advance through a personal contact or by a member of his campaign team. These occasions were not only an opportunity to promote himself directly; they also provided voters with a chance to share their problems with him, which he would often relate back to wider issues of corruption. In these meetings he showcased his personal values and used the personal experiences of the attendees to try to highlight why it was important to have better politicians, like him, in power.

The first such meeting that I attended took place in the evening in a hall adjacent to the local mosque. Some of the faithful stayed behind to share a meal with the candidate after the evening prayer. Sitting together on the floor, those present explained to Ambo that a politician who had been successful in the previous election had promised to build a new washing area for the mosque, but they had never seen him again. His response to this story was rather blunt: "*Aduh*, did you really think he would help . . . he'd already gotten what he wanted from you, hadn't he?" He continued to speak plainly, explaining that it is up to voters to be smarter and more discerning in who they support. In positioning himself as offering something different, he told them:

> I could do the same thing, I could give you a small amount of money, or make promises. . . . But I won't do that because that's not good for you. What you need is to have a representative who will fight to make the system better, so you don't have to ask anymore. Those politicians in Jakarta are dirty, and they are there because people think it's normal. . . . I'm not normal, I'm not going to lie to you.

The head of the mosque responded positively to Ambo's statements but also cautioned him about the importance of being more than just a face on a banner—he needed to show people who he was if he wanted them to vote for him. Ambo agreed and outlined his plan for the next week, visiting villages in the *blusukan* style to show them who he was and to talk to them about how money was interfering with democracy. He thanked the cleric for his advice and praised him for understanding how important it was for community leaders to lead by example and show citizens how to vote "well."

This exchange provided my first glimpse of the candidate speaking out against corruption on the campaign trail. He had used the meeting to promote himself as unique in his stance, in contrast with "normal" politicians who buy votes and are simply interested in the benefits offered by public office. In an effort to appear understanding of their situation, he acknowledged that it was tempting to take money from these candidates but cautioned against letting it influence their votes. Later, in an informal chat, he elaborated further, explaining that he was not there to make people feel bad or judged but to let them know that accepting money did not mean that they no longer had the option to give their vote to someone else: "They can take the money. I don't agree with it but let them take it. But they can still vote for a good candidate. That's what I'm telling them." It seemed that speaking out directly against vote buying was not part of Ambo's campaign strategy. Instead, he wanted voters to understand that taking money was a personal choice but it did not necessarily have to drive their final decision.

Ambo's pledge to fight corruption increased in visibility during the official campaign period. He emphasized it in his campaign statements, becoming even more vocal about the need to vote out dirty officials. His reputation grew in some quarters, and people began coming to him for help or advice to address their own problems. For example, in one meeting, a villager complained that the village head had made a deal with a private company to set up an irrigation system. In return, villagers had to give 15 percent of their crops (or cash equivalent) to the company, and they were required to buy all their fertilizer from it. The company was owned by a local district legislator, who they believed was exploiting them by marking up the cost of fertilizer. Ambo responded passionately to this story, saying that it was clearly a case of corruption, even using the English term "rent-seeking." He urged the villagers to share the story with their neighbors and friends to stop the village head from being reelected. He also suggested that they document the case and share that documentation with him so that he could personally report the village head to the authorities, giving them his personal cell phone number and encouraging them to call him with updates. His response was received positively by the villagers, who were pleased that someone in power would take the time not only to listen to their complaints but also to lobby on their behalf.

In another small event about a month out from the election, Ambo met with a group near his home village. He had known some of the people in attendance growing up and was keen to reconnect with them. His first priority was, of course, to get their votes. At the same time, he seemed to have a genuine interest in how they were doing and the problems they were facing. At the meeting, he asked whether other candidates had offered them any inducements. One person spoke up, saying that he thought another candidate had made a play for votes by establishing small projects in areas where he already had support, paid for through his "aspiration fund."[6] I presumed that Ambo would rail against this behavior and encourage people to reject it, but he did not. Instead, he said, that is what the aspiration fund is for: "whether you agree with [his decision] or not, it's not corruption." He then added that, if he was returned to office, he would use his funds in a different way, traveling around the district to see what local communities really needed, regardless of whether they had voted for him. Later, he explained to me that while the aspiration funds gave incumbents an unfair advantage in elections, he was not morally opposed to the scheme. It was helpful for sitting members to have money to be able to assist poor constituents. And, as a true representative of the local area, who understood the issues there better than politicians or bureaucrats who lacked a close connection to the area, he believed he was in a position to use them well if elected. It was part of his branding to show that, having grown up there, he cared about what happened and would therefore be less likely to try to cheat local people.

While Ambo's strategy seemed to be gaining traction, it was not without its downside. Toward the end of the campaign, he spoke to me of the toll it had taken on his health. He was physically and mentally exhausted well before the official campaign period ended, not just from the extensive travel within his electoral district but also from having to manage national party affairs while on the road. He saw great benefit in talking to citizens via these intimate meetings and was convinced that his strategy was the best way forward, but he also missed his wife and children in Jakarta. Every day, at various times, I would see him on the phone to his family in Jakarta, asking his children about school or who they had played with that afternoon. Regardless, he persisted with the strategy, understanding that this was a crucial time in the campaign and his future success rested on making a good impression when he was before a crowd. For him, this was an opportunity to demonstrate to constituents that he was not only committed to standing up for what is right but also to listening to them directly, rather than simply sending his campaign team out to solicit votes for him.

At the same time, Ambo's view of voters was inconsistent, especially considering that he had placed his faith in the willingness of a core mass of voters to choose him because they believed that fighting corruption was more important than receiving some sort of payment or favor. His campaign strategy, at its heart, was built on an assumption that good people existed and, if they knew what he stood for, they would want him as their representative. At the same time, he could be disparaging of voters. Even before I first went to Sulawesi with him, he had commented on the prevalence of vote buying and how disappointing it was that so many citizens would choose a candidate based on money. While he claimed to understand why voters were suspicious of politicians and saw the activities of the national legislature as being very far removed from their daily lives, he had difficulty in accepting this as a justification for (what he considered to be) poor voting decisions. His frustration at the final results reflected a contradiction—that he had hoped his approach would appeal to large numbers of voters, but he was unsurprised that voters had lived up to the stereotype that they were more interested in money than values.

Standing Apart from the Crowd

In terms of personal campaign strategy, Ambo set out to present himself as a different type of politician. But the fact that he was a party cadre also shaped the way he presented his party within his campaign. He saw himself as a representative of the party in many ways. While he knew that he was in competition with others within his own party, he regularly asserted that the most important thing was to choose his party, even stating at several gathering that "I don't care who you vote for as long they are from [party name]." He did not enter into tandem arrangements—the common strategy of forming an alliance with other members of one's party campaigning for seats at different levels of government and sharing campaign costs—with provincial or district-level candidates. However, he did attend several rallies held by other candidates competing for seats in the provincial and local legislatures during the official campaign period to promote the party.

But while Ambo worked hard for his party and wanted it to be successful, it did not sit at the heart of his personal campaign. Because his political identity drew so heavily on his personal ideals and identity, he rarely discussed other aspects of his party's platform beyond telling voters that his party was different and committed to changing the status quo. His individual campaign was about showcasing himself as an honest candidate. He was intent on presenting himself as a friend to voters, someone who had their best interests at heart and would stand up for them against injustice. This image was one he cultivated carefully throughout the campaign. His small, informal gatherings were a means for presenting himself to voters as "one of them" and giving them an opportunity to share their concerns. In his speeches, he repeatedly discussed his experience in the national legislature, claiming that he had left his former party because, among other reasons, he did not want to betray the people. He had felt like a traitor for accepting the salary and perks of office while not being able to fight for what he believed in because of his party affiliation. Referring to himself satirically as "stupid" for foregoing the lifestyle and sizeable salary of a legislator, he said he would rather resign than be part of "a dirty [party] . . . full of corruptors and traitors." In doing so, he positioned his actions as evidence of his commitment to the people: he was so disgusted by the behavior and priorities of other legislators and could not be like them, even if it meant stepping away from all the associated benefits.

A few months in, the strategy was building momentum for Ambo's campaign. During one car ride to a night's accommodation, Ambo recalled an unsolicited phone call he had received recently. In it, a village head told him that he could make sure his village voted for him. Upon being asked about what he wanted in return, he stated that the village head had said he wanted him to "stay true to his Bugis roots." He saw the interaction as a good sign that at least some voters were responding positively to his campaign. He enjoyed being seen as a candidate who was standing up against corruption and was outspoken about doing the right thing. Moreover, he was pleased that he was being identified as a genuine local, despite being based in Jakarta. It had been part of his strategy to portray himself as "son of the region" (*putra daerah*), who spoke the local language, understood the challenges facing local people, and would fight corruption on their behalf.[7]

Ambo also demonstrated that he was not afraid to condemn money politics when he saw it in action. On one occasion, I joined him for a meeting with his campaign team in a five-star hotel in Makassar. A rival from another party was hosting a "workshop" for village heads at the conference center attached to the hotel. This rival candidate had paid for them to come to Makassar from all over his electoral district and to stay in the hotel. When Ambo discovered this, he was outraged. Expressing his frustration to his campaign team, he said that there was no need to hold the workshop in a fancy Makassar hotel if its purpose was to discuss local issues. The lavish trip was, he said, a blatant attempt to win their favor. Having recognized some of the district heads, dressed in their leisurewear and fluffy white hotel slippers, he confronted them in the hotel lobby. He told them, in full public view, that it was shameful to be accepting favors from a man who was using them just to get votes. Adding that only traitors to the nation agreed to sell themselves for money, he urged them to think about the villagers and what was best for them, not who would pay for the most nights in a fancy hotel.

Not surprisingly, this confrontation was extremely awkward, both for the targets of Ambo's ire and those milling around in the reception area. The district heads stood silently, heads bowed, and no one blustered in defense against his accusations. Instead, there were some mumbled words, followed by a hasty exit via the hotel elevator. Later, Ambo told me that it was unfortunate that more people did not openly criticize people like these village heads for taking advantage of their positions in this way. It happened all the time and, according to him, the only way to stop it would be to shame the behavior. This response reflected his frustration with the normalization of vote buying in elections and, in particular, the role that people in authority played in shaping how votes were cast. With so much confusion around what political parties and candidates stood for, people could be easily persuaded to choose candidates who were not interested in upholding values and working for the nation. It was for these reasons that he was so disappointed to see officials take advantage of their positions for "meaningless" perks like a stay at a five-star hotel.

Complaints about vote buying and political candidates, and especially about "outsiders" swooping in and paying for people's support, were a mainstay of shadowing Ambo over the course of his campaign. But this did not mean that no money was exchanged, or that he rejected campaign strategies that cost money. He did make some strategic donations but, as he stressed to me, only to local mosques. He claimed that he would not make payments to individuals (even for a charitable cause) or to village projects, because it would be too easy for individuals to pocket the funds. Fearing that he might be perceived as engaging in money politics, he diligently checked receipts for services and goods (although he dryly acknowledged that these were easily forged). Gift-giving was also a sensitive issue for Ambo, who did engage in the usual campaign activities of distributing t-shirts and other memorabilia, providing food, and organizing events—including a traditional Javanese puppet performance for Javanese migrants and a soccer clinic for young boys in his hometown.

Ambo undertook these activities reluctantly because he wanted people to vote for him based on his values, not because he hosted an event. When I asked why he engaged in these common practices, he said he did not want to lose because of a "trivial things like not giving away t-shirts." To his mind, however, there was no inconsistency between his decision to do so and his broader campaign objectives. He preferred, though, to focus his campaign on his commitment to improving the lot of ordinary people by fighting corruption in parliament. What is more, he wanted his campaign team to promote him to voters based on this commitment. In one address to a local party branch office, he berated his team for failing to "sell" him to local voters. This outburst was prompted by his annoyance at seeing members of his team simply giving out t-shirts and walking away while at a campaign rally. He expected his staffers to use their interactions with voters to promote his policies and ideas. In the same meeting, Ambo reiterated that money politics was completely against his ethos and urged his staff to report any suspicious behavior on the part of other candidates running for his party so that he could have them dismissed. He also said that if any of his team members saw violations of electoral rules by other candidates from any party—their own included—they should be reported to the Electoral Supervisory Board (Badan Pengawas Pemilu, Bawaslu).

At his last rally, organized the week before campaigning ended, Ambo took to the stage after being introduced by the master of ceremonies as a "local political warrior" (*pejuang politik lokal*). In front of a crowd of approximately five hundred people, surrounded by food vendors and party flags, he began his speech by talking about his childhood growing up in the area. At this point, he spoke for several minutes in the local language. After switching back to Indonesian, he talked about his move to Jakarta, his realization that Indonesia needed democracy, and his experience marching in the 1998 protests against Suharto. Playing upon the introduction he had been given, he positioned himself as a fighter who had worked to combat corruption in many ways, most recently as a politician. It was through this role, he said, that he came to realize the Reformasi was not complete, and that the fight needed to continue. Indonesians needed politicians who were not afraid of the rich and powerful, to speak up for the rights of everyone, not just in Java, and who would make sure that money was not lost but was spent on the people. He ended his address by saying that people needed to vote for change. If they did not want to vote for him, he said, then they should choose someone else from his party, because his party was truly committed to improving Indonesia for everyone, not just the elites in Jakarta. This final charismatic display was a chance to endear himself to voters by claiming to be different. But would his efforts be enough?

Reflections on the Campaign

Ambo was a strategist who wanted to win but sought to do so without resorting to commonplace vote-buying tactics that he so frequently condemned. His reputation was everything, and he strove to present himself as a unique and principled politician throughout his campaign. But while he was hopeful that this would be enough to secure victory, he knew that he had chosen a difficult path. Ambo's disillusionment with elections became most evident when I interviewed him after the quick count results became available. While it looked like he would succeed, he received far fewer votes than his team's polling had suggested he would in the week leading up to the election. Being a "son of the region," he was outraged that he did not receive more votes. The disappointing result was not, he maintained, a reflection of his efforts. Rather, he said, the fact that vote buying remained the norm meant that it was difficult for honest candidates to succeed. He blamed his poor numbers on the use of money politics by his rivals and those who had rewarded their behavior, claiming that "the winner of the election was money." According to him, the bribery had been "brutal," much worse than in the previous election. However, at same time, he said he was proud to have triumphed without resorting to bribery. He hoped that he could set an example for other candidates in future elections by demonstrating that they did not have to pay vast sums for votes but, instead, could win voters over through other means.

Since Ambo identified vote buying as so prevalent, and presented himself as staunchly against it, it is interesting to reflect on the boundaries he set for himself in using money to influence voters. For him, vote buying involved entering into specific arrangements where money was exchanged with voters or influential figures in exchange for an explicit or tacit undertaking that people would vote for that candidate. He distinguished this from charitable donations or activities that were framed as "giving back" to the community, through which he demonstrated his commitment to local citizens. He saw the donations he gave to local mosques and the soccer clinic he funded as acts of benevolence that portrayed him in a positive light but were not intended as bribes. He stressed that he did not ask for votes in return for these activities; they were a gesture of goodwill. But his willingness to engage in such activities as part of his election campaign could certainly be interpreted as attempts to buy votes. When asked whether he was worried about how these actions might be perceived, Ambo distinguished himself from rivals by explaining that the crucial difference lay in candidates' expectations regarding the outcomes of these actions. For him, the problem of money politics was not about spending money in and of itself but rather about the implications of exchanging money or promises in return for votes.

I asked the candidate several times throughout his campaign why it was so important to him to avoid money politics. His responses varied, depending on time and place. In the early days, he asserted not only that his commitment was informed by who he was and what he believed in but also that his campaign was "for the nation" (*untuk negara*). People needed to see that not all politicians were the same and that there were genuine people (like himself) running for office. At the same time, he often referred to himself as "not that sort of candidate." If voters did not select him based on what he stood for, then he would rather not win at all. Yet, while identifying the strategy he had adopted as being primarily a reflection of his own values, at different times he offered other, more functional justifications. At one point in the campaign, he told me that he had promised his wife he would not use their personal savings during the campaign, and so he could not afford to spend vast sums to buy votes, even if he wanted to. As the campaign continued, much closer to polling day, he offered yet another rationale for his strategy: that he could not change course now because he had already worked so hard to win votes by being an anticorruption candidate.

As the campaign progressed, it became clear to me that the anticorruptionism intersected with Ambo's personal context in very specific ways. The narrative he presented about himself, being an activist in 1998 and caring about corruption eradication as a part of a wider democratic project for Indonesia, was part of an identity-building project. Running as an anticorruption candidate was a clear extension of these personal experiences. But, while he identified and presented himself as an "anticorruption candidate," he played equally on his identity as someone who was born locally and grew up in the area. He leveraged this positionality constantly, using his familial connections to solicit meetings, transitioning from Indonesian to the local language when he addressed a crowd, sitting with groups in the local mosque, and reciting Islamic prayers. He would tell those listening, repeatedly, that he was "one of them," that he *understood* them. This both legitimized his candidacy in his own mind and became an important tool in his approach to voters. Without this background, he could have claimed none of these things. It was important to him that voters saw him as being genuinely invested in the local community, and the fact that he was highly educated, based in Jakarta, and seemingly had no intention of returning to live in Sulawesi was, to his mind, irrelevant. His day-to-day life as a politician in the capital *was* utterly different to the realities of people in his electoral district, but this never came up. Nor did he acknowledge it was relevant when I questioned him about it. To him Jakarta was simply a place he lived, albeit for over fifteen years. It was where he was *from* that was much more important.

After the final rally, we had dinner. I asked how he was feeling about his prospects. He had exuded such confidence during the event that I expected him to be positive about his chances. Instead, despite his initial optimism, Ambo had become increasingly cynical about the election as the campaign progressed. He talked about the emotional toll the campaign had taken on him, how draining it was to keep fighting for what he believed was right, while also missing his family back in Jakarta. While he spoke openly about the corrupt nature of politicians in his public appearances, in private he shared his belief that voters were equally complicit in the problem. The frustration of campaigning so hard, only to be thwarted by money politics, was all the more infuriating because so many voters were open to being bought. He blamed voters for not demanding more from their politicians. He said, at one point: "I'm from here, I care and I'm a good candidate. If people don't choose me it's not because I'm not good. It's because they don't want someone who's good."

This chapter recounts the story of a self-proclaimed "anticorruption candidate," Ambo, who saw his campaign as a reflection of his individual values and identity. Despite understanding the risks of running on an anticorruption platform, he committed to the strategy for both personal and pragmatic reasons. He played on his identity by planning a strategy that allowed him to maximize the impact of his positionality and social capital in promoting (what he believed to be) the salient issue of corruption. Ambo did not completely disregard campaign norms—he attempted to charm gatekeepers, distributed campaign trinkets, and made donations to local mosques. But his use of money was calculated and guided by parameters that he believed were acceptable, so he could rightfully call himself "clean." As a senior party figure, he was able to harness party resources to mount a substantial campaign. However, even with these benefits, Ambo was uncertain about his prospects of winning given the prevalence of money politics in South Sulawesi. Most important, he stood his ground, refusing to capitulate to mass vote-buying tactics when faced with the possibility of losing the election.

Following Ambo over an extended period revealed some of the paradoxes of his campaign strategy, as he negotiated his ongoing concerns about how to best run his campaign and how it would be received. These tensions manifested in the ways he would present himself publicly as opposed to the way he discussed the campaign behind the scenes. He asked voters to trust him to do the right thing, but he did not extend this same trust to his own campaign team. He acknowledged that voters had every right to be suspicious after being let down by previous candidates who had made grand promises, but privately criticized them for being "materialistic." While he was committed to his party and was proud to be part of a new "clean" organization, his campaign was focused primarily on promoting his own achievements and aspirations. He lived in a middle-class suburb of Jakarta, to which he privately yearned to return, while many of the people he was vying to represent still lived in small villages, working as farmers or traders. He was a *putera daerah* who had been transplanted, and thrived, elsewhere.

While Ambo may not have thought too deeply about his passing comments or the contradictions that he embodied, to me they were humanizing. The deep sense of loss he felt in winning by only a small margin was understandable, given the thousands of hours he had poured into his party and his campaign, and the sacrifices he had made—the seemingly never-ending travel, feeling forced to deal with officials who he despised, and being away from home and family. As his experience shows, while many candidates start out with the aspiration of running a clean campaign that rejects all forms of vote buying, the reality on the ground can be confronting once they begin their campaigns in earnest. It was Ambo's personal convictions that guided his campaign and helped him, more or less, stay his course. But, as we shall see in the following chapter, not all anticorruption candidates are able to carry the weight of their anticorruptionist rhetoric through to election day.

4
BOWING TO PRESSURE

Choosing to present oneself as an anticorruption candidate is a strategic decision in electoral campaigns. This choice may have its roots in a candidate's personal values, it may seem like a winning strategy, or it may be some combination of both. But what happens when a candidate who begins their campaign with the aim of appealing to voters based on an anticorruption platform finds their strategy failing? For ambitious and idealistic candidates who hope that their stand against corruption can help propel them to triumph, campaigning in an environment where vote buying has been thoroughly normalized presents a harsh reality. The pressure to engage in money politics forces these candidates to evaluate their campaign at every turn and, in some cases, to question their initial choices. The candidate must decide how they will navigate these challenges and, ultimately, whether they will make compromises.

The previous chapter presented one case study—the story of Ambo, who was largely able to reject money politics and remain with the bounds of what he deemed acceptable behavior. This chapter tells a story with a similar beginning yet a different conclusion. This is the experience of Ayu, who, like Ambo, was intent on promoting herself as a "clean" candidate but ended up engaging in the very practices she had previously condemned.[1] Campaigning in East Java, Ayu's efforts veered off course as she struggled to gain momentum through her grassroots campaign. Encouraged by her campaign team, she set her personal values aside and used commonplace vote-buying tactics in an attempt to shore up voter support. Unfortunately for Ayu, the investment did not pay off, leaving her thoroughly dejected when the results were tallied. She had made so many concessions for a chance at victory, but it had all been in vain.

The Candidate

When I first met Ayu in October 2012, she was in the early planning stages of her bid for selection, a month before the party opened nominations for candidates at the national, provincial, and district levels.[2] I had been introduced by a friend of a friend to a freelancer who had worked in her party's marketing department and, although the marketer had moved on from that position, she still knew people there. The marketer gave me a few phone numbers of people from the party with whom she was still in contact, including Ayu. Our first meeting, set up via text message, was on a weekend in a coffee shop close to her home. She arrived, wearing a batik blouse, apologizing that she was late because it had been difficult to find a parking spot. Seated next to a large family birthday gathering, with young children running between the tables, her first question to me was how I knew her "friend." She seemed satisfied with my response that we had met through a mutual acquaintance and happily began answering my background questions about how she had become involved in politics.

Ayu was from a well-off family and led a comfortable upper-middle-class lifestyle in Jakarta. Soft spoken and stylishly presented, she told me that she was the mother of two grown children who were both studying at university at the time of our meeting. With her children now older, she had found herself with more time to take on professional work and had taken an accounting position for her party at the time of its inception. She was open to working for a political party because of a family connection—she was the daughter of a previous MPR (Majelis Permusyawaratan Rakyat, People's Consultative Assembly) member, selected by former President Suharto and had been proud of her father while growing up. She said that during her time with the party she had developed a good working relationship with her colleagues at the central office, and she generally enjoyed her position. By the time we met, she was responsible for overseeing the financial reporting from local branches. She would, it turned out, also come to oversee candidate "registration" fees for the upcoming election. These were often open to negotiation with the party leadership, but it then fell to her to ensure the collection of payments. Being a loyal party cadre, her own candidacy fees were waived.

Her choice of party affiliation was no accident. She had known and respected the party founder for some time. As she explained it, she had had known him for decades, having met him through her father. Her initial motivation for joining the party was to support its founder's presidential bid. She described him as "patient and wise" and believed he could lead Indonesia "back onto the track of Reformasi." It was her support for his presidential bid, rather than a particular affinity with the party's ideology or platform, that motivated her decision to pursue a seat in the DPR. She did, however, highlight a number of elements of the party's ethos, including its stance against corruption, that she personally supported. According to Ayu, combating corruption was a party priority, both for maintaining its integrity and in presenting itself as an alternative to the current leadership. She presented this as a key stance in her own political campaign, contending that if she won, she would never be corrupt.

Ayu was not an incumbent, but she had run for office in the 2009 elections. From her brief description, although she had not entered the race expecting to win, it had been a far from pleasant experience. Although she was competing for the same party, she felt that it would be different this time. Ayu had been convinced by the party leader to try again, with the promise that she would appear first on the party list in her chosen electoral district. She had considered the offer for several weeks before agreeing to run. Ayu also knew that the party was keen to make sure they met the official gender quota, which required that women make up at least 30 percent of the candidates for each electoral district and thought she could help them meet this obligation. But it was about more than just quotas for Ayu. She talked about how being in the national legislature was a way for her to do something good for the country, decrying the current state of politics. When I asked her about her aim in for running for office, she told me, "There needs to better politicians. . . . It's like the country is being run by naughty children!"

While candidate nominations were not finalized before our first meeting, Ayu had already decided that she would compete in East Java. This was an interesting decision, given that she had spent practically her entire life in Jakarta. When I asked her why she had opted for East Java, she cited a familial connection through her parents to the area even though, in reality, she had little experience of it. She had extended family there but she preferred to stay in a local hotel rather than with relatives while traveling in the region. All her siblings lived in Jakarta, and Jakarta was where she had raised her own children. During campaign visits, her Javanese seemed stilted. While she claimed to understand it, she did not appear confident when speaking. In truth, she subsequently admitted, she chose not to run in Jakarta because it was "too competitive." When considering her other options, she preferred the idea of running in a more rural area where "people would be more open to talking." Still, she identified as Javanese and thought the local voters would be able to accept her if she could show them that she was a good, honest candidate. Moreover, her political party believed that some areas of East

Java were a potential stronghold for the leader in a potential presidential race, and she would be able to promote him to voters as a part of her campaign, imagining that this alignment would make her additionally appealing.

The Party and the Personal

This initial meeting provided much insight into the candidate who, although she had been working within the party for some time and already competed in an election, was not overtly politically ambitious. Indeed, according to Ayu's own description of her history with the party, her decision to run in 2014 was the outcome of opportunities that were presented to her by virtue of her connections to the party leader rather than a calculated drive for political office. She had not shopped around for parties, weighing her chances of success with one versus another, like many other candidates did. Nor had she even intended to launch a second campaign pitch before she was convinced to do so. Loyalty to her party persuaded her to run, a loyalty driven by a personal, rather than ideological, relationship. This is not to say that she was not keen to win—her actions clearly demonstrated that she was—but her motivations for becoming involved in politics were quite different to those of many others, including the other candidates I followed. For Ayu, running for the national legislature seemed more like a logical step for a loyal supporter of the party leader, rather than being driven by a desire for influence or a clear vision of how to effect change.

According to Ayu, many politicians become "arrogant" (*sombong*) because they believe they have been elected as an individual rather than a representative of a political party—an assumption fueled by the fact that they applied to the party without any commitment to the party's "vision and mission" (*visi dan misi*).[3] She explained that this is why it was best for her party to have candidates with strong ideals so they "don't fall into this trap of becoming corrupt," thus bringing the party into disrepute. Ayu's sense of morality informed this judgment. She described many legislative representatives who arrived in Jakarta for the first time as having "culture shock" and being swept up in the materialism of the capital, "wanting new cell phones, tablets, clothes." The problem was, she observed, that the salary of a legislator simply "isn't enough for all these fancy things, especially with the debt they probably have from their campaigns." Ayu saw herself as the type of person who would not be seduced by these things because she already "had everything she needed" and, therefore would be both a good quality candidate and politician.

While the party leader felt Ayu offered something as a candidate, there is no doubt that Ayu also believed her party offered her benefits. As a personal friend of the leader, her ties went beyond simply being a cadre and an employee. While she did not have an official position within the party leadership, she had access to the highest echelons, which gave her many advantages as a candidate. In addition to being promised the first-rank position on the party list, she was given some party funding to run her campaign. Though a modest amount in comparison to the vast amounts that candidates often feel compelled to spend, it was enough to hire a car for the duration of her campaign, pay for some prominent billboard advertisements and banners, fund some profile pieces in local media, and "sponsor" some local food stalls. It was also enough to fund a campaign team, which included hiring a "professional" research agency to help her strategize for the delivery of her campaign in the local area and a "marketing team" to help with promotion. Commissioned about seven months out from voting day, both these groups were composed of individuals who had helped candidates in previous elections, with the research agency conducting preelection surveys to ascertain local levels of support and the marketing team helping her to make local connections and strategize. She was still required to pay some expenses herself, including her core campaign team, made up of four office staff and a few people dotted throughout the constituency. Nevertheless, being granted funding that was only given to select candidates led some in the party to believe that she was the recipient of special treatment. There were even rumors among local cadres that her campaign was being personally funded by the party leader himself.

Ayu's relationship with the party leader was particularly significant because she did not have a close connection to the local branch in her electoral district. She hoped that this association would facilitate offers of assistance from local cadres but, unfortunately for her, this was not the case. This was a frustration that stayed with her throughout the campaign because, as she saw it, local party cadres were clearly more interested in helping other candidates further down the party list, rather than the "number one" candidate. For Ayu, this seemed like a betrayal of the party leadership. She reasoned that if the national leadership were supportive of her campaign, then the faithful response from cadres would be to support her wholeheartedly. Instead, she found herself having to develop a campaign with the help of hired staff. Moreover, without the option of easily tapping into existing party or personal networks, her strategy leaned heavily on in-person visits and meetings, meaning that the persuasiveness of her strategy would be even more crucial to her prospects of success.

An Anticorruption Agenda

Regardless of how Ayu came by them, she had grasped the opportunities offered to her and set about preparing for her 2014 campaign. She made the conscious decision that she would present as an anticorruption candidate, embedding this identity at the core of her campaign strategy as she began planning. She contended that the fundamental aim of the fight against corruption was to improve the lives of ordinary people, since eradicating corruption would help to alleviate poverty in Indonesia. Campaigning in primarily rural areas, she thought that this would appeal to local voters who often feel forgotten by the national government. But, in contrast to the other anticorruption candidates described in this book, Ayu's claim to an anticorruption identity did not lie in her previous track record, or in an otherwise demonstratable public commitment to the issue. To her, she simply was "clean." She had been a devoted wife, raising her children and looking after her household; she had led a good life as a Muslim who had done charity work and was concerned about people who were not as fortunate as herself. She saw herself as an embodiment of a life lived with a commitment to core values that meant she could not possibly be viewed as anything other than "anticorruption."

Consciously or unconsciously, Ayu mobilized this discourse during the early days of her campaign. She told voters that she had never been in a position to be corrupt and she had no reason to be so in any case, because she was a "good, honest, person." While I was cognizant of her upbringing, and often wondered how her father's military connections during the New Order may have contributed to her comfortable lifestyle, this was not something she even considered in view of her campaign—though nor did she mention her personal links to the military in her engagement with voters. Instead, she highlighted other credentials such as her education (she had a master's degree in economics) and her experience in accounting (so she was good with numbers), as well as her ideals for the country. The very idea that her own life was something distinctly unattainable for the voters whose support she sought to secure was summarily glossed over as she talked about her credentials for being a committed legislator.

Ayu's campaign strategy centered upon building a positive image by meeting constituents and presenting as someone committed to public welfare, while supplementing her campaign rhetoric with charitable works, such as purchasing new equipment for the community mosque, donating to local schools, and bankrolling entertainment events. She also promoted this persona in her personal meetings with voters. Like Ambo, she felt that voters would need to meet her in order to be convinced by her campaign. Her campaign philosophy, she liked to claim, was based on an Indonesian saying: "They can't love you if they don't know you" (*kalau nggak kenal, nggak sayang*). In an early discussion with her, she argued that a political party could not expect support without the trust of the people, who were responsible for giving them a "mandate" (*amanat*) to govern the country. Talking to people in person was, to her mind, the best way to build this trust. She also identified this as a point of difference between herself and other candidates—she was willing to go to villages and engage with ordinary voters directly, unlike those who were "too arrogant" (*terlalu sombong*) to do so.

Presenting as an anticorruption candidate aligned closely with the broader image that her party wanted to mobilize. At the outset of the campaign, Ayu made it clear that she believed that having an anticorruption agenda was very important for the party's campaign. Ayu was adamant that this meant—as part of her role as a loyal cadre—that she had to publicly oppose money politics and vote buying. But it was a utilitarian strategy, too. Though she did not openly admit to having engaged in vote-buying activities in 2009, she did tell me that she had learned from prior experience that vote buying was an expensive undertaking. It is possible to speculate, therefore, that she took this stance because she believed she had less funding to draw on than several of her competitors: even if she had wanted to flout the party "rules" and give out money in return for votes, she simply could not compete with wealthier candidates who had better networks in her electoral district.

However, while Ayu felt that combating corruption was both a party and personal priority, she was apprehensive about openly describing herself as an "anticorruption" candidate. During my first site visit in March 2013, she discussed at some length concerns about the terminology used in her campaign materials. Some of her campaign team members were worried about using the term anticorruption and suggested that she instead use the word clean (*bersih*). Presenting herself as clean, rather than as being "anticorruption," was preferable as it was a more encompassing term that referred not just to corruption but to her general conduct as a politician. Ayu was amenable to the idea, as it invoked a number of her self-identified characteristics, such as coming from a "good" background, being honest, and hardworking. Ayu and the team also agreed that the term "anticorruption" (*antikorupsi*) had been tainted by its use in the 2009 election, when the Democratic Party used "say no to corruption!" as its national campaign slogan. She wanted to avoid any parallels between the two campaigns, given that the Democratic Party had subsequently been hit with numerous corruption scandals. Based on these considerations, she decided to tailor her language to avoid the word corruption, instead preferring descriptors like "with integrity," "honest," and "clean."

On the Campaign Trail

In February 2013, I had tagged along with Ayu and a high-level party delegation accompanying the party leader to launch the party's campaign in Bali. Ayu was not really in campaign mode during the Bali visit. She was there simply to observe and undertake small tasks assigned to her by her boss. She had, at one stage, been asked to acquire some makeup for the leader as the television camera crew that had arrived to film him had brought none. As we rifled through her toiletry bag to find some powder to take off the shine, she humorously asked me if I thought he would need blush and lipstick as well. The Bali visit had been a three-day whirlwind, with numerous pit stops and long meetings. As we headed back to Jakarta, I asked her when she would be launching her campaign. "Next month," Ayu replied.

In March 2013, I joined her in East Java as she made her first visit to her electoral district as a prospective candidate. Arriving in the evening, I had dinner with Ayu before the activities of the next few days began. With the election so far away, I asked why she had decided to come now, over a year out from polling day. The purpose of this trip, she said, was to meet the local party officials and, more specifically, to ingratiate herself to them before the party list announcement from the central office. Though she knew some of the local cadres through their visits to party headquarters, she had not spent any time with local branches before. The local party leadership were aware that she was applying to be a candidate in their district, so her presence was unsuprising. Even if they were not familiar with her position in the Jakarta office, it was highly likely they knew of her personal relationship to the party leader. At this stage, she knew she would be given the first-rank place but, as the visit was before the finalization of candidate approval, local officials had not yet been officially informed of this fact. Ayu was not yet planning on revealing this information; rather, she wanted to build a rapport with them before her rank was confirmed.

Ayu's first meeting took place at the home of the leader of the party's local branch, who I will call Amalia. It was a large house with a big garden area at the back. Chairs were arranged in a circle, and as more people arrived more seats were added in a second layer around the inner circle. Amalia was currently a member of the local legislature; Ayu had met her during a visit to Jakarta to meet the party leader. She had a commanding presence, and when she spoke, the other cadres listened intently. This preliminary strategy discussion was an opportunity for Ayu to introduce herself to local cadres and, hopefully, establish their support for her candidacy. But while she imagined this would be an opportunity to share her own ideas and discuss how they could ensure that the electoral campaign was run in accordance with the party's charter, the meeting did not turn out to be the chance she had hoped for.

Instead, Amalia dominated the discussion and took control as she talked about how they could promote the party's "vision and mission" and discussed the branch's vote targets for the election. There was, Amalia stressed, the prospect of capitalizing on the Democratic Party's sinking reputation and perhaps stealing the seats they had won in the previous election. She emphasized that this meant their party's reputation had to be "spotless" to appeal to voters. It was also important, she said, for them to use the campaign to educate voters about the importance of choosing good candidates. Ayu nodded in agreement, speaking a few sentences to affirm what Amalia had said, adding a few moralistic comments such as "being seen as hypocritical is just as bad as being seen as corrupt." But she did not really assert herself. She seemed uncomfortable with her status as an outsider within the meeting, not knowing most of the participants, and uneasy about offering her thoughts.

Jakarta Insider, Local Outsider

When I asked Amalia after that first meeting when she would be starting her own campaign, she responded confidently, "I've been campaigning for the last five years. This is my home. . . . I show people who I am every day." It seemed a loaded comment to me, given she knew I was shadowing Ayu who, very obviously, did *not* call the area "home." Amalia's local profile was impressive, and her campaign strongly emphasized the theme of anticorruption. At a public event during the official campaign period, held outside the local legislature, Amalia signed a personal pledge to fight money politics before a large crowd that cheered as she stood to wave. But, although she clearly had a bank of supporters—evidenced by the fact that she easily won reelection—she did not go out of her way to offer Ayu help, nor did she offer to campaign with her. Despite this, Ayu and Amalia were on good terms, and Ayu considered her a friend. This was important because, she would later tell me, she did not have many friends in the local branches.

This first meeting was the start of a long journey for Ayu, campaigning in an area where many in her own party had little interest in supporting her candidacy. Disentangling complex local power plays became an important focus of her first few visits, as she met with party cadres to try and understand the situation on the ground. She was also cognizant that, as someone from party headquarters, there would be aspects of the local situation that some cadres would not want her to know about, fearing that she would report back to the party leader. Though she joked to me one point that she was a "spy" from the central office, the situation did concern her, as she realized how difficult it would be for her to overcome such conjecture when building local relationships. She lamented that local cadres were not interested in "working together to promote the party," which disappointed her, especially since it was the party that was providing them the platform to run for office in the first place.

Political in-fighting seemed to be a prominent theme among party cadres in Ayu's electoral district. During this first trip to the region, I shadowed her at five different meetings with cadres, some current and former sub-branch leaders. It was clear that these visits left her feeling overwhelmed and confused by the conflicting stories that she was being told. The branch's internal fragmentation became more evident with each meeting I observed. The day after the event at Amalia's house, we met with a sub-branch leader who openly discussed some of the local rivalries that had arisen over the past few months. A particular focus of his account was another sub-branch leader, who I will call Lestari, a local businessperson and member of the DRPD II, who had been accused of corruption. The national executive had tried to fire her but she had refused to resign, threatening to take her supporters with her to another party if she was dismissed. The sub-branch leader who Ayu met lamented the reputational damage that Lestari had wrought upon the party and asked Ayu to talk to the party leader to address the situation. Ayu responded that she would, and that if the party leader knew the full story he would "surely intervene." Ayu had her own reservations about this situation, explaining later that when she had tried to set up a meeting with Lestari, "she had made up some lies . . . to avoid meeting with me." Ayu was also confused as to why Lestari would want to represent a political party that was attempting to expel her when there were so many other options, but she reasoned that at this late stage it would be difficult to secure the endorsement of another party.

The idea that each of the sub-branches had become "little kingdoms," with cadres who acted in self-interest rather than working to promote the party as a whole, came up again in the next meeting. Ayu met another former sub-branch leader, who had resigned after the controversy involving Lestari. Because party lists for the local legislative elections are put forward by the sub-branches, these offices become sites for power struggles between cadres jockeying for position and influence. Ayu was vaguely aware of this through her position as a financial controller for the party, overseeing the payment of party dues and candidate nomination fees. But she had not understood the intensity of these rivalries until she experienced them in person. She felt torn because she herself was keen to make local connections to promote her own candidacy, and it was important to align herself with the "right" local cadres to best generate support for her campaign. Concerned about her own image, she did not want to form alliances with anyone viewed as corrupt, even if they had a strong support base. But Lestari's story was just one of many local intrigues, and it was difficult for Ayu to discern fact from fiction when deciding who she would try to enlist.

Ayu herself became a controversial figure among local cadres, which heightened antagonism toward her among some. She was very pleased to be granted the first spot on the ballot. For her, holding the highest rank on the party's candidate list for the national legislature was a badge of honor. But the announcement of the final list incensed many local party officials and cadres. Ayu had deposed a sitting legislative member who was relegated to a lower rank by decisions made by executive leaders in Jakarta. The incumbent was a prominent local businessman who had run a successful campaign in 2009 and who was popular among local party members. He also had family members representing the party in the election at other levels of government and in other electoral districts. The outcome caused great consternation, and the incumbent's allies were unhappy with the party list and Ayu's place on it. Ayu maintained that the incumbent still had a good chance of winning despite his position on the party ticket, reasoning that he did not need a high rank because he already had such a strong local profile. But this friction alienated her from some factions within the party.

In the beginning, I had not understood exactly how controversial Ayu's candidacy was. It later became clear how little support she received from the local branch over the course of her campaign. Ayu did not appear to have access to the party resources already available in the electoral district, and eventually she had to hire her own campaign team, rent her own office space, and work hard to negotiate her tandem campaign arrangements with other candidates running for seats in the local and provincial legislatures. By contrast, Ambo had these resources offered to him while Ayu had to do the extra work for her campaign. She was able to garner support from a handful of sub-branches, but others were not even interested in meeting with her because their loyalties lay elsewhere. Those who did support her did not offer much—they could put up banners and connect her to local leaders and communities. Meanwhile, candidates with better connections within the local branches were able to use the party offices to organize their campaigns and promote themselves through cadre networks.

While she was clearly an outsider in the eyes of local party cadres, Ayu imagined herself as someone with strong ties to the area. Many of Ayu's relatives had since moved to other parts of Indonesia, but she often visited one relative who was a medical doctor and had practiced locally for most of her career. Through this connection, Ayu built a small circle of trusted friends and acquaintances that she would sometimes consult to better understand local issues and people's attitudes toward various sitting politicians. She was wary of asking her paid staff such questions, a feeling that amplified as the campaign wore on. She often felt they were just telling her what they believed she wanted to hear, or worse, they were trying to persuade her to do something that was for their own benefit rather than hers. Being an outsider made the few close connections she did have all the more important, as she tried to find her footing in the local area.

Observing Ayu as she met with the members of various sub-branches of the party revealed how much more difficult it was for her to campaign as an outsider.

Ayu tried to counter her outsider status by forming "tandem" arrangements with candidates for provincial and local government from her party, people who were better connected within the voter base. While a common campaign strategy for many candidates, it was all the more important for Ayu who needed the support to establish a foothold in the electoral district. This opened some doors to her, as she attended local meetings with these other candidates and was introduced by them to power brokers. But this did not detract from the sense that she had to work overtime in order to build the key relationships that would help her win. At the same time, these tandem arrangements were a political minefield because Ayu's alliances would also influence her relationships with local cadres. Her first tandem arrangements were with an incumbent at the provincial level and one newcomer at the local level. They were the first candidates who agreed to team up with her. As the campaign continued, she realized that she has not chosen the best partners and later shifted to another tandem arrangement with a different local-level candidate. This was one of many changes Ayu made to her campaign strategy, after deciding that some of her initial decisions had been rather naïve.

Ayu's lack of a solid local support base made her a target for freelance "marketing" companies who were looking to be a part of a campaign team. During a second visit to East Java, I sat in on a meeting between Ayu and one such company, represented by two men who claimed to have helped in previous elections for district heads. Their key argument was essentially that, because most voters are not loyal party supporters, the best way to approach the campaign was to "capture" village leaders who, in turn, would convince their constituents to vote for Ayu. They promised that if she hired them, they could guarantee a large number of votes in particular areas where these men had existing relationships with the village heads. They brought with them a portfolio of charts and figures, with a breakdown of exactly how many votes they could "guarantee." I was not privy to discussions about how much these services cost, but Ayu was cautious about the prospect of paying for something that might be worth nothing. Conversely, she also recognized that she would need help to win. While she did not hire that company, she did eventually commission a different group, recommended to her by a local cadre. When I met them on a subsequent visit they seemed to present similar ideas. Ayu agreed that targeting village heads was a good strategy and one that she intended to integrate into her campaign approach.

Campaign in Action

The party was front and center in Ayu's campaign materials, which were printed in the party colors and bore the official party slogan. This was significant because candidates were given autonomy in designing all aspects of their campaigns, including their publicity materials. When I asked her about this decision, Ayu gave a number of reasons for choosing to directly align herself with national party symbols. First, she truly believed that identifying herself closely with her party and its leader would be a drawcard for voters. Unlike many other candidates, who developed their campaigns squarely based on their individual profile, she saw the party leader's presidential aspirations as a core component of her appeal. Her two large billboards along a main arterial road displayed her profile next to that of the party leader, with the party slogan splashed in bold letters underneath both of them. Second, as a candidate who was neither independently wealthy nor wishing to go into debt, she felt that aligning with the party's advertising would help her profile: "they will see me as a loyal member of [the party] . . . so if they like the party then they will like me."

Ayu took steps to physically present herself as a representative of the party in her public appearances as well. Her campaign "uniform" was a batik shirt (she had had several tailored) that she had chosen specially because it matched the official party color. For some of her later village visits, she had commissioned a local bakery to make donuts frosted with the party colors, presented in cardboard boxes with her image and a party sticker attached. Almost every campaign address she made to voters incorporated some words about the potential of the party leader to be a great president, who would steer Indonesia back on course by eradicating corruption and creating government programs to help rural and poor citizens. She would try to end her public addresses with the party's official slogan in order to underscore her relationship and commitment to the party.

Ayu did not have a particularly strong media strategy. In 2013, she purchased space in some local media outlets and organized to have positive biographical pieces published by them. Though she had been reluctant to pay for media stories about herself, she had received money from the central office specifically to do so. When she tried to make connections with local media, she found that rival candidates, even within her own party, had made deals that made it difficult for her to advertise with certain media outlets. The media outlets amenable to her were small and had low circulation. As a result, this media strategy was not overly successful. While one article went to print, another did not, as it was purchased in a magazine that went bankrupt before the election. She had managed to get her money back but resented the time and effort it had taken to organize in the first place, and she gave up on paid media after this.

Ayu also set up Facebook and Twitter accounts at the beginning of 2014. She had previously told me that she was wary of using social media as a campaign tool, but the party's central office had encouraged candidates to make use of the Internet, and it was free. Ayu was not especially technologically savvy, so her staff handled posting most of the Facebook updates, tweets, and photos. She was also unconvinced by its value, arguing that many Javanese villagers still did not use Twitter or Facebook. She later mentioned that her media strategy was a "waste of time" because most voters were not interested in following candidates on social media, especially if they did not know them personally. Instead, Ayu focused most of her energy on face-to-face meetings with voters and community leaders. Walks through local communities (*blusukan*) during which she would try to talk to people as they went about their daily business, a campaign strategy popularized by the Jakarta Governor and 2014 presidential candidate Joko Widodo (Jokowi), supplemented these meetings. She explained that she was consciously adopting Jokowi's strategy because it had contributed to his popularity. During these visits, she could present herself, answer questions, and hand out trinkets, t-shirts, or food. In August 2013, a few months into campaigning, Ayu also adopted another common campaign strategy, setting up a *posko*—akin to a campaign office—where voters could come and talk to her or to members of her team. While it became a useful meeting place for the campaign team, campaign team members did not report many drop-in visits from voters.

Early on in her campaign, Ayu was not particularly discerning about whom she met with or where the meetings were held—she simply wanted to get out and start building relationships. As the campaign progressed, however, she became more selective about whom she would meet. These visits were always set up in advance by her campaign team or through her tandem partners. Sometimes they were brief and involved no one other than village leaders. At other times, they were gatherings attended by up to fifty people. Ayu would usually begin by introducing herself, highlighting her links to the area and the fact that she had family there, and discuss her educational background. She also attempted to engage with villagers in order to learn about their "aspirations" (*aspirasi*), hoping to build trust by seeming interested in, and empathetic toward, them. In later meetings, she provided a guide on how to vote for her and her party, bringing a mock ballot paper and pointing out exactly where her name was.

Ayu also used these initial meetings with voters to express her party's official philosophy on corruption and vote buying—namely, that asking for money promotes "low-quality leaders" (*pemimpin yang kurang berkualitas*). Her argument was based on two contentions. First, if a candidate has resorted to money politics to get elected, they will need to recoup large sums once in office.[4] Second, if a candidate has bribed voters, then they owe them nothing once elected because the people who voted for them have already been compensated. Ayu advanced this idea to discourage those present from asking for or expecting money in return for their votes. It also echoed statements by the party's central leadership that played to the party's clean reputation and its purported desire to remain free from corruption. Ayu also used this argument to emphasize her loyalty to voters—the fact that she *did not* offer them cash was, she said, a demonstration of her long-term commitment because she intended to deliver benefits to them by doing a good job as a member of the national legislature. In multiple meetings she declared to the audience that "you shouldn't sell yourselves so cheaply," suggesting that an honest representative was worth "more than Rp. 20,000 or Rp. 50,000" (between USD 1.75 and 4.35).

While Ayu presented herself as being staunchly opposed to vote buying, she still attempted to use the money she did have to curry favor with voters. She worked to build an image as someone committed to public welfare through "charitable work." By the end of her campaign, Ayu had spent money on a whole range of goods and activities, such as purchasing a new sound system for one mosque, refurbishing the washing area at two others, and providing female students at a local Islamic boarding school (*pesantren*) with new headscarves. She also ran coloring-in competitions at local primary schools with small cash prizes for winners, purchased new percussion instruments for a local martial arts group, and funded a shadow puppet performance.[5] Ayu's most fruitful donation was, perhaps, to the martial arts group who she would often ask to perform at her campaign events.

Ayu considered small gifts and other gratuities as crucial to winning support. For her, this was not a form of money politics but a kind gesture that contributed to her main aim of familiarizing voters with her campaign and convincing them that she cared about their welfare. In addition to giving money to community groups, Ayu often subsidized the costs of food, tea, cigarettes, and "transport" for villagers to attend meetings (which she often referred to by the Arabic-derived term *silaturrahmi*, meaning group discussions that are intended to build fraternity or affection for a person or an idea). Payments were sometimes in-kind, and sometimes in small amounts of cash that (at least in theory) compensated people for their time and effort in attending. Again, Ayu refuted that these expenses constituted vote buying, instead framing them as normal campaign costs that were simply about demonstrating her generous nature.

While these donations were certainly attempting to win over voters, Ayu's attitude toward these costs was stoic—of course, it would be better not to have to spend the money, but it was a gesture of goodwill. In discussions she made a clear distinction between candidates who actually met with and talked to voters before giving them something, and others who simply "paid people through middlemen and never actually turned up to meet them." The latter, she believed, were simply trying to win with the money. By contrast, she saw herself as trying to win by getting to know potential voters and demonstrating, with the help of donations, that she was interested in supporting them. But wary of her budget limitations, Ayu sought to make strategic donations for maximum return. The expenses mounted as the election date drew closer, and the use of money as way of endearing herself to voters seemed to take hold as the dominant campaign strategy.

Shifting Priorities

Challenges to Ayu's campaign strategy came early as she grappled with a range of responses from potential supporters. Some comments that suggested voters were interested in choosing an anticorruption candidate heartened her. For example, during one village visit, one voter told her directly that they hoped she would not "become like Angelina Sondakh," a politician who became infamous for her involvement in a national corruption scandal. Ayu readily promised she would not. Sometimes there was encouraging dialogue with attendees, giving her a sense that they were willing to support her. However, her hope to ingratiate herself with voters by emphasizing her familial ties to the area quickly dissipated. Voters were not buying her attempts to present herself as one of them. At one meeting, a campaign staffer nudged me when she started speaking Javanese, pointing out that her language was too formal: "she sounds like a Javanese queen!" she whispered, implying that she was likely alienating the villagers she was attempting to woo. On several occasions Ayu herself sensed a general lack of enthusiasm to her campaign. However, she preferred to blame voter unresponsiveness on the fact that the village was already "bought" by another candidate rather than questioning whether she had convincingly pitched her candidacy to the audience.

More concerning to Ayu, however, were the frequent requests for money or services. Early in her campaign Ayu would delicately try to explain why she could not make a "contribution" (*kontribusi*), a euphemism often used when requesting money. She argued that doing so could be seen as a type of vote buying and, even if she could afford it, it would still be wrong. During one particular visit, when asked what her contribution to the village would be, Ayu reiterated her theory that candidates who spend lots of money on their campaigns often have to get loans and will later resort to corruption to pay their debts. The group initially welcomed this statement, but the discussion changed course when one woman asked if Ayu might consider donating money so they could purchase new uniforms for their local women's organization. Ayu deflected this request with the rationale that she was a clean, simple candidate who did not have lots of money, unlike some of her rivals. Furthermore, she argued that if she bought uniforms for one group, she would have to buy them for all groups. But, despite her chiding tone, she agreed to contribute the equivalent of around USD 45 to the local mosque at the same meeting. After leaving the village, she expressed irritation at the request, speculating that the women there would not vote for her because they had not received anything for their group.

In spite of her frustrations, Ayu continued to visit villages and meet with voters in these forum-style events. Sometimes she went to five villages in one day, targeting those in more remote areas that other candidates were less likely to visit. She also turned to gender identity as a means for attracting support. Halfway through her campaign she adopted the very deliberate strategy of seeking out meetings with women's groups. She concentrated on women for two reasons. First, she said that she sometimes found men condescending and uninterested in entertaining the possibility of a female representative. Second, she felt she could potentially draw support from women, playing on their sense of exclusion from politics. Ayu believed she could capitalize on this sentiment, positioning herself as a contrast to other candidates and promising that, unlike other politicians, she would be a political champion for women's issues. She focused particularly on gaining access to communities through two women's groups: Family Welfare Development (Pembinaan Kesejahteraan Keluarga, PKK), a locally based mothers' association that was established during the Suharto period and usually run by the wife of the village head, and Jemaah Talil, an Islamic devotional group where women gather to sing/recite passages from the Qur'an.

At these meeting, Ayu talked about the importance of having women representatives in the national legislature to ensure that the government took women's concerns seriously. In the meetings that I attended, she would use phrases like "only women can know women's struggles" to highlight the point, though she did not really elaborate on what these specific issues might be. She would emphasize "women's spirit" (*semangat perempuan*) as a reason for voting for her, arguing that women understand each other's problems and a female candidate was more likely to sympathize with their priorities. However, even these meetings would, like most others, often end in some request for a contribution. For example, during one meeting, she was asked to contribute money to a PKK branch to start a new training program. She declined, saying that she could not do this because she was afraid people would think she was buying their votes. Later, she expressed annoyance at the request as she believed that the village was fairly well off and the women did not really need training and it was simply a veiled request for cash.

Ayu had made the point early to me in her campaign that, because of her limited funds, it was important that her donations generated votes. She tried her utmost to be strategic and vet the area where she donated to assure herself that they had not already been captured by another candidate. But even these attempts to boost her profile often seemed fruitless and she felt taken advantage of. In one instance, she made a substantial donation to an Islamic boarding school (*pesantren*). However, during a later meeting with the school's leader, Ayu was disappointed to find that the school and village were flying banners and flags from another political party. The school leader explained that the village chief had a family member competing in the election and there was nothing he could do about the banners. After the meeting, Ayu expressed her frustration that her donation appeared not to have garnered the influence she had hoped for and worried that she had wasted her campaign funds. On another occasion, Ayu agreed to use her own money to finance the provision of a new irrigation system for a village. At the time, she justified the upfront donation as strategic for building trust because people were used to unfulfilled promises from politicians, but she later admitted doubts about whether this had been a good decision because her campaign team had not been able to confirm that the village was committed to her.

Despite her proclaimed rejection of vote buying as a strategy, Ayu came under increasing pressure as the election neared to give cash to villagers directly in return for their votes. This pressure came chiefly from members of her campaign team. Commissioned polling done in late 2013 suggested that her popularity was far below several rivals, including from her own party, and that she would not secure sufficient votes for a legislative seat. In response, her campaign team urged the use of cash payments, especially to village heads or respected figures (*tokoh*) who could distribute the money to citizens in return for their support.[6] All members of her team had worked on various other elections, either the 2009 national election or local elections, and the consensus was that money was the only way to secure votes in the area. Because vote buying was such a prominent strategy in East Java, they were concerned that she would have no chance of success if she refused to offer cash. The team was concerned that her public appearances and selective donations would not be enough, with one team member commenting: "it does help if people like you . . . But it will still be hard [to win] if someone else is offering them money."

But not all campaign team members agreed that using cash was a good idea. Most seemed to have no moral objections to vote buying; rather, they did not believe it would be an effective strategy for *her* because she lacked the local ties needed to win using money. In short, they felt that even if she decided to shift strategies and start offering money to people as a matter of course, she would probably still lose. Moreover, she had already told voters during meetings that asking for money reflected poorly on them and would lead to the election of leaders who did not really care about their needs. These observations concerned Ayu, who was torn between her desire to maintain her principles and keep her campaign budget to a minimum, and how best to win. While she was amenable to making "donations," she had considered direct cash payments as completely out of bounds. These discussions highlighted a tension within her campaign team that worsened as the election drew near, with some members resigning in the month leading up to ballot day.

By the beginning of 2014, Ayu had become deeply cynical about the motives of the voters in her electoral district. Being repeatedly asked for contributions, both subtly and overtly, she felt a sense of hopelessness about her campaign. She had come to the conclusion that presenting herself as a clean and honest candidate was not appealing to voters because they were more interested in the material benefits offered by other candidates. Having made this realization, she referred to the topic of corruption less and less frequently. If asked about it, she would rehash the party's slogan (which was also her own). However, she skirted the issue even when given the opportunity to talk in more depth about being clean. She reverted to simplistic explanations, saying during one visit that "our party wants honest candidates and won't tolerate members who are not honest . . . who like to play games (*main-main*)." In a different village, she vaguely referred to her party as not having candidates "who are . . . like that (*seperti gitu*)," but she provided no elaboration.

As the election date drew closer, it became evident that she was still polling poorly. Ayu talked less and less about fighting corruption or keeping things clean. The most important aspect of her meetings was now providing instructions on how to vote for her and how to avoid casting an invalid vote. She even developed a tip to help voters remember her. Since she was the first-ranked candidate for her party, she suggested that voters think of the shape of a nail, which Indonesian voters use to pierce their ballot papers, as resembling a number "1" to remind them that she was the "number 1" candidate. Her prospects of winning also prompted Ayu to review her tandem arrangements. One of her existing tandem agreements was with a lowly ranked and poorly funded candidate, and she needed to find a more lucrative tandem arrangement through which to better promote herself during the crucial last weeks of campaigning. She entered into an arrangement with a district legislative incumbent who came from a wealthy family and had a high profile in her district. Through this arrangement she was able to piggyback on a better-funded campaign but was also expected to contribute more money than she would have otherwise spent.

Conducting mass rallies came at a cost, and her new tandem partner expected her to pull her weight. In addition, their events were much more lavish than her own events had been. For one tandem arrangement, she agreed to provide two motorcycles and a refrigerator as raffle prizes during a few large rallies as a way of encouraging attendance. Each attendee got a ticket, with the prizes drawn by a local *dangdut* singer hired to entertain the crowd. She was also obliged to contribute to the cost of marching bands, dancers, singers, and other entertainment, as well as the usual payments to attendees for food and travel costs. Afterwards, she was cautiously optimistic. The crowds had been large, and attendees seemed to have enjoyed themselves. But she could not escape the sense of exasperation that it had taken so much money to get them there in the first place, and still it was not enough.

On election day, a campaign team member told me that Ayu had instructed her to withdraw Rp. 200 million from the bank the previous day and deliver it to certain members of the campaign team. While I was unable to obtain confirmation from other sources about how the money was used, the team member was sure it was for a "dawn attack" (*serangan fajar*), the practice of distributing cash to voters the night before the election with the express intent of influencing their voting decision.[7] I was uncomfortable with the idea of asking Ayu directly if she had engaged in a dawn attack, especially since I knew by then that she her loss had been all but confirmed. Instead, my post-election questions focused on how she felt her campaign had changed over time and whether she still felt strongly against vote buying. Though she did not openly discuss her actions on those final days of the campaign, she did say that Indonesia was not ready for a clean election and told me that some members of her campaign team had urged her to buy votes on the eve of the election, a practice also commonly referred to as "bombing" (*ngebom*).

Reflections on the Campaign

Ayu did acknowledge that her emphasis on being clean had diminished, as her strategies had changed over time. She gave several reasons for this. She had found that corruption was an uncomfortable issue to discuss publicly (*nggak enak dibahas*). Ayu's focus on anticorruption rhetoric decreased at the same time that her strategic donations to mosques, schools, and arts groups, as well as funding village works, increased. Members of her campaign team would scout areas to find institutions or schools that could benefit from additional funds and then negotiate with the local community leaders to arrange a donation in return for electoral support. Alternatively, they would approach local figures and ask them how she could help the village—that is, for what purpose could she donate money. Ayu was certainly uncomfortable about this shift in strategy. She had been able to justify her donations when she saw them as supplementary to her primary strategy. As time passed, though, her campaign began to heavily rely on the promise of payments.

However, while she had a defense for her actions, ready to mobilize if ever questioned, she did admit that she was worried about her campaign becoming like "everybody else's." The shift in her campaign took her well into the very territory that she had wanted to avoid. Her actions could be categorized as vote buying, in contravention of the legislation regulating election campaigns. Ayu's own shift in how she presented herself, drawing less on a clean image over time, mirrored her acknowledgment that her initial strategy was untenable given her circumstances as an outsider candidate. Reflecting on the experience, Ayu's insistence that her donations were acceptable was not out of the ordinary in the electoral context.[8] It echoed existing campaign norms that rationalized this behavior as a means to an end. More noteworthy is, perhaps, the fact that Ayu could not openly acknowledge her actions for what they were. She was concerned enough about the optics of this new approach to tone down her anticorruption rhetoric but still justified it as something she needed to do in order to win. Taking these factors into account, the possibility that she may have done something outright illegal in the final days of the campaign seems an act of desperation, rather than a suggestion that she no longer believed herself to be a clean candidate.

In the end, Ayu was tired and demoralized by her campaign experience. In comparing it to her effort in 2009, she described it as being a much more involved campaign with more "heartbreak." Evidently, her prior candidacy had not sufficiently prepared her for the 2014 campaign. She seemed particularly despondent one night, as we sat in the hotel eating takeout *nasi padang*. It had been a grueling day as we had visited multiple villages and she had just received the results of some informal polling conducted by her team. The results were not positive, and she was talking through her ideas for how to boost her numbers. At one point, she fell silent then stated simply that she felt like giving up. It was not the first time she expressed negativity about the election, but it felt to me like she was seriously considering stepping away. Her ideal of a legislative seat won on hard work and moral discourse was long gone by now—just that day she had made promises to "donate" to two separate community groups—and she had embarked on a very different route to the one she had envisaged. But, even so, she was exasperated by how the campaign had panned out. The next day, we headed out to a large rally, and she appeared to have regained her composure. The large crowd boosted her spirits slightly, albeit temporarily.

Ultimately, Ayu believed that the reason she had to expend so much money during her campaign was because voters demanded it. Moreover, she believed that this was the case because most voters actually wanted to be bribed. She worried about alienating them by talking about anticorruption issues or money politics, making them feel guilty—and her, unpopular. Ayu also argued that voters thought all politicians were corrupt in some way, and so they probably found it hard to believe that there were candidates that genuinely cared about fighting corruption. In other words, Ayu felt that talking about corruption made her seem like a hypocrite. She found that her early use of anticorruption discourse as a defensive tool against requests for "contributions" was ineffective, lamenting in her description of voter demands that "even a blind person here can still read money."

During a post-election interview, after receiving confirmation that she had lost, she observed that: "anticorruption doesn't mean anything to those people . . . they don't care." She added that, while some political parties do their utmost to avoid being corrupt, it was just an "intellectual exercise" because voters saw a market. Expectations of being paid in exchange for votes were too strong and too hard to fight in East Java. Contemplating her experiences, Ayu described the campaign as "unfair" (*nggak fair*) and "a mess" (*kacau*) because it was all about "playing games" (*main-mainan*):

> Every election is like a party (*pesta*). People want a present. The people who take the money, they aren't taking any risks . . . who's going to arrest them? It's the people who give the money who get blamed . . . the candidates.

Reflecting on her loss, Ayu opined that her electoral district did not support clean candidates and that the election had reinforced the prominence of money in politics. Commenting on the issue in general terms, she observed that the media were so focused on presenting candidates in a bad light, but they never seem to blame voters: "no one ever writes about what people demand from candidates. But it's the truth . . . why would anybody pay [for votes] if they didn't have to?"

This chapter recounts the experiences of a candidate who initially believed that she could defy the odds by marketing herself as a clean candidate, and by staying true to that identity throughout her electoral campaign. As a loyal cadre who strongly supported the presidential aspirations of her party's leader, she saw the campaign as an opportunity to help her party by staying true to its vision of having integrity and commitment to the nation. The earliest iteration of her campaign strategy was premised on the idea that she could win voters over by showing them a "different type of candidate"—one who would show kindness through charitable donations but would never stoop to the dirty tactics of her less principled rivals. But as the campaign wore on, cracks began to form in this plan, as the realities of campaigning as an outsider from Jakarta became more pronounced. In the desperation to win, her righteous stance fell away, making room for an increasing number of "donations" and expenses.

Tracking the campaign over time brought many issues to the fore, as I observed the shifting nature of the operation. Without insider knowledge, Ayu made some poor decisions. She initially formed a tandem arrangement with a candidate who did not have a solid voter base. She ended up campaigning in some areas where her rivals already had established strongholds, causing her to waste time and money. The importance of positionality—being an "insider" within the local party and having strong social ties—was seemingly magnified because Ayu had neither. Her attempts to leverage her gender as a way of forming local bonds did not generate the support she hoped for. But what was particularly striking was the way in which the distinction that Ayu made between "donations" and vote buying became increasingly blurred as she gave money to more and more people. The extent to which Ayu's campaign advisers were responsible for her decisions to spend money in ways that pushed the campaign firmly into the realm of illegality is hard to discern. Ayu certainly felt that it was voter demands that drove her to increase her expenditure, but we can also ask whether her desire to win simply overwhelmed her will to reject the very strategies that she has initially criticized. It is also not clear to me how much of her personal funds she used to finance the campaign, or whether she had, at some point, received a cash injection from an external source. However much it was, it was evident that she would not be able to recoup any personal money she had spent.

Ayu's personal response to the election was anger. She had spent so much time trying to give people what they wanted but it had all come to nothing. She described the experience of feeling pressured to go against her own values in the campaign, and still being unsuccessful in her bid for a seat, as "bitter" (*pahit*). She was adamant that this was the last time she would ever compete in an election. Her cynicism toward the electoral process, solidified during her second campaign, underscored her overall frustration that money politics still played a crucial role in the election. However, she did not reflect on the flaws in her own campaign, her inability to connect with voters, or even concede that she should have done things differently. In looking to lay blame, she was adamant that if the public had higher standards, if they understood how important it was to elect clean candidates to lead the nation, she would have had a fighting chance. We can ponder what may have happened if Ayu had been a locally embedded candidate, but this was simply not the case. However, as the next chapter shows, having strong local connections does not necessarily eliminate the likelihood of money politics in electoral campaigns.

5
EXPERIENCED AND PRAGMATIC

The previous chapters focused on candidates who characterized themselves as "anticorruption" and took this identity to heart in their campaigns, at least at the outset. They promoted a "clean" image, which they hoped to uphold through their actions over the course of their electioneering. They believed that vote buying was unethical, even as they felt forced to change their strategies under the pressure of campaigning among voters who expected inducements. In this chapter, we follow a different type of candidate who, despite presenting himself as keen to eradicate corruption, took a much more pragmatic view of money politics in the elections. This candidate, who I will call Bontor, ran in the province of North Sumatra. Because Bontor served in the national legislature for over twenty years, he had been through the campaign process many times, albeit against vastly different political backdrops.

Bontor fervently promoted himself as an "anticorruption candidate," styling his campaign pitch around his extensive experience and "track record" (*rekam jejak*) as a sitting politician. Running multiple campaigns had taught him about the value of community ties, and he drew strongly on his background of being from the area and a member of the dominant ethnic group in his electoral district. At the same time, his familiarity with campaigning had taught him that distributing money was simply a part of the game. Over the course of his campaign, he used funds to reward villages that had supported his previous election bid, as well as distributing small payments directly to voters and supporting local community groups. Bontor rejected the characterization of his actions as vote buying, while describing the distribution of money and favors as a necessity.

Conducting his campaign squarely within the bounds of electoral norms while also presenting himself as an "anticorruption candidate," Bontor's experience reflects the manifestation of the dual influence of corruption upon Indonesian elections. He both strove to portray an anticorruption image but unashamedly engaged in vote-buying behavior to increase his chances of success.

The Candidate

I first encountered Bontor by chance in April 2013. I was at the national legislature to interview another politician when a flyer for a public seminar on a proposed anti–black magic (*santet*) law, to be held later that day, caught my eye. I decided to attend, taking a seat at the back of the meeting room. There was a politician seated toward the front who had a great deal to say in opposition to the law, offering his party's view on the proposal. After the seminar concluded, I approached him to introduce myself and ask if he would be willing to be interviewed about corruption and campaigning in the upcoming elections. He agreed and we scheduled a meeting at his office a few days later.

Bontor, who is softly spoken with a calm demeanor, was reserved when I began the interview. With several years as a politician under his belt, he seemed initially cautious in his responses, keen to present his party in a positive light and reticent to talk about family and personal matters. I already knew that Bontor was originally from North Sumatra and a member of the Batak ethnic group, which is dominant in that area of the country. However, it was not until I traveled with him to his electoral district—three times between July 2013 and April 2014—that I appreciated his position and bonds within the community, which included membership in a local church network and strong kinship ties. Although he resided in Jakarta, as did most of his close relatives, Bontor had married a woman from a well-connected local family that was still based in North Sumatra. Through his political connections and his wife's familial networks they had come to own several properties and businesses in his electoral district. I suspect that Bontor became more open to my presence on the campaign trail because of my own Batak heritage, introducing me to people we met along the road using my mother's clan name. He jokingly scolded me for my unfamiliarity with Batak lineages and complicated clan relationships and would often pause a conversation about the campaign to explain certain Batak customs and kinship structures during our travels in North Sumatra. He seemed to take great pleasure in describing the ins and outs of the Batak culture, made all the more evident as he leveraged his insider status throughout his electoral campaign. His primary message seemed to be that Bataks had a different worldview that only other Bataks could truly understand.

A seasoned campaigner with significant electoral experience, Bontor had been a politician for over two decades when I met him. The 2014 election was Bontor's sixth election and his second for his current party. He had represented one of the three government-sanctioned political parties during the New Order but had since shifted his allegiances. He decided to change parties because his own political priorities had changed, and his new party was a better fit. After being approached by one of the new parties in 2008, Bontor decided to officially switch when he contested the 2009 elections, remaining with that party ever since. He was confident about being returned to the legislature but did concede that it would not be as easy to win as it had been in previous elections because there was increasing cynicism toward politicians. This cynicism he felt, were driven by prevailing stereotypes that all politicians were corrupt and self-serving. He explained that even he was once accused of corruption—not because there was evidence against him but because people refused to believe there were any clean politicians. At the same time, he accepted that voters had a right to feel angry about the high levels of corruption in the national legislature. For Bontor, showing voters that he was one of the "good guys" meant demonstrating his integrity through actions and using the resources at his disposal to illustrate that he was committed to helping people within his electoral district, by which he primarily meant fellow Batak.

When I asked Bontor which political issues he felt were most important, he first spoke about economic development, stating that "the potential of individuals is also Indonesia's potential." In deciding to shift parties, Bontor highlighted his interest in promoting economic equality within Indonesia, particularly "for the 50 percent of Indonesians who work in the agricultural sector."[1] He saw his current party as representatives of the "little people" (*rakyat kecil*), who were the backbone of the Indonesian economy, and he highlighted the importance of ensuring these people were employed and able to share in the benefits of economic growth. He raised corruption as an issue after I asked what the distinguishing features of his party were, linking both his personal reputation and that of his party to an anticorruption focus. This would end up being one of the central rhetorical platforms for his campaign as he traveled through his electoral district.

An Anticorruption Reputation

In our first interview, I asked Bontor several questions about his party's stance on corruption and his personal understanding of what it meant to be an "anticorruption" politician in the national legislature. Bontor had developed a reputation for speaking out against corruption over his previous term, something he had felt much more empowered to do after joining his new party. He publicly condemned a variety of activities in the legislature, as well as broader patterns in other parts of the government. The current crop of legislators, he said, were not well respected by the public because they were so many corruption charges and convictions. This had contributed to legislature's negative image:

> People see them become members of the national legislature and, all of a sudden, they are living these extravagant lives.... [They are] hedonistic, showing off their wealth, they like to wear fancy and expensive accessories ... so of course the public don't trust them. They give all of us in the national legislature a bad name and make it seem like we're all misusing our positions.

At the same time, he said, there was "no point" in "arguing that we're not like that ... what's important is to demonstrate that we're not like that through our actions, not words." Bontor argued that every party cadre was, without exception, obliged to uphold anticorruption values, and that any "guilty people" would be immediately expelled. The fact that his party had never had any members accused of, or arrested for, corruption was attractive to voters.

Bontor often drew attention to the fact that none of his party's legislators had been caught up in corruption cases. However, this was possibly attributable to the fact that the party was so new that opportunities for corruption had, thus far, been limited. Nevertheless, he proudly proclaimed that although 318 district heads, mayors, and governors had been accused of corruption over the last five years, not one of them had been affiliated with his party. Later, at his rallies, he would stress that there would never be a corruption conviction from within his party. "We are the cleanest [party] in Indonesia" he would say to his audiences, "and I am proud to be one of its members." He would often close his address with a statement along the lines of: "if you want to see a corruption-free Indonesia, you must ensure that there are as many representatives as possible from [the party] in the national legislature!" Whether Bontor actually believed this is less clear, but he certainly stated it repeatedly throughout his campaign, using it as a rallying call to voters: if his party could increase its presence in the legislature, it could more easily implement government-wide strategies to combat corruption.

In our interviews, Bontor outlined several ways in which his party had proven its commitment to eradicating corruption in Indonesia. He asserted that corruption led to broader problems of inequality in Indonesia and was therefore one of the most important challenges facing the country. This was why, he said, that his party was so firm in its commitment to combating corruption. According to Bontor, the public appreciated that stance:

> [The party] has taken a leading position in pushing for eradicating corruption. That's what we hope will differentiate us from other parties ... [the party] is seen as one of the cleanest parties because we don't have any cadres involved in corruption.

At the same time, he openly critiqued particular decisions among his fellow legislators, who he deemed "corrupt." To highlight his own reputation for speaking out against corruption, Bontor mentioned several activities that he had publicly condemned as money-making opportunities designed to funnel money into "politicians' pockets rather than to the people." For example, he spoke about his vocal denunciation of plans to renovate the parliament building in Jakarta just a year earlier, which he contended was merely a revenue-raising opportunity for the ruling Democratic Party. Bontor rejected the proposed renovations, alleging that the project budget had been marked up and the company awarded the project tender was linked to a Democratic Party politician, Nazaruddin.[2] In reaching this conclusion, Bontor's party had consulted with the bureaucrats tasked with building management and maintenance, who had estimated the cost of the proposed renovations to be less than half of the allocated budget. The project was slated to go ahead but was halted at the last minute due to the arrest of the construction company's director on an unrelated corruption charge. Bontor referred to this arrest as an "intervention from God," allowing protests to mount until the renovation plans were finally abandoned.

Another crusade Bontor had taken up was the use of overseas study tours by politicians, which he perceived as a gross misuse of public funding. He estimated that between fifty and sixty national legislators had gone overseas the previous year at a cost to the public of approximately USD 24.5 million. These study tours—with their business-class flights, meals, accommodation, and a generous per diem—were clearly extravagant and unnecessary. According to Bontor, however, they were of "no benefit the people of Indonesia at all." Instead, he rationalized, embassy staff should do research and report back to politicians on how things are done in other countries because "that's what they are there for ... and it's much more cost-effective." He also accused legislators who had participated in these trips of lying about their expenses to get more money from the government, a practice so common that he felt somebody had to bring it to the attention of voters. Bontor claimed that his own party had saved the government close to USD 3.5 million by refusing to engage in such trips over the past four years of government and, in rallies, would ask the audience to "imagine if all political parties agreed to this!" When he spoke to audiences, he framed the issue in absolute terms, suggesting that because other parties did not care enough to ask their members to refrain from participating in these "unnecessary" study tours, they were morally bankrupt and uninterested in saving the government money.

Bontor's mounting critiques against other politicians made him a media darling. He found that journalists sought him out for comments because they knew that he would have an opinion on the various corruption scandals faced by the government. The 2014 election, set among a bevy of political scandals and "attacks," presented an opportunity to solidify this reputation by vocally pronouncing to defend the much-loved public institution.[3] Bontor had been widely reported as defending the integrity of the KPK (Komisi Pemberantasan Korupsi, Corruption Eradication Commission) and rejecting government efforts to undermine its power. To promote himself as an anticorruption candidate, Bontor emphasized his own track record in the legislature, frequently pointing to his personal efforts to combat corrupt behavior in Indonesia's national legislature. To hammer home this persona, he distributed a thirty-six-page pocket-sized booklet at his events titled "Corruption Breeds Poverty, Fight Corruption for a Prosperous Society," which offered a compilation of his thoughts on how to improve government systems and extracts from news articles about corruption issues in which he had been identified as being firmly aligned with anticorruption ideals.

An Experienced Candidate

Bontor's 2014 electoral campaign was built on more than two and a half decades in public office and offered him advantages that Ambo and Ayu could only dream of. As an incumbent, Bontor had the weight of his reputation and track record behind him. Voters were familiar with his name and face, an important consideration when casting votes as a candidate's photo is displayed beside their name and party on the ballot paper. Not surprisingly, perhaps, he was calmer and more measured in how he planned for and managed the day-to-day pressures of the campaign trail than either of the other two candidates. He did not struggle to decipher which campaign staff were trustworthy and which were not. He knew which areas he could draw support from, had worked with many of his campaign team members before, and enjoyed a network of preexisting supporters who could feed him intelligence about what his rivals were doing. Moreover, his political leadership and connections made it easier to obtain funding for his campaign. He was open about the fact that his own campaign had cost approximately USD 328,400, but "only" around USD 82,000 of his campaign cost had come from his own pocket.[4] The remainder was provided by the party or donated by outsiders. Bontor acknowledged that this was a significant sum, but he also believed it was less than half what a newcomer candidate would need to spend to build their profile with voters. This resource base put Bontor in a strong position. With multiple seats available, he was confident that so long as he did and said the right things, victory would be his.

Bontor understood the role that money played in election campaigns and how the availability of funds determined the feasibility of different campaign strategies. Rallies and meetings were costly. A single rally with just one hundred attendees could cost up to USD 3,000, including rental costs for equipment, food, t-shirts, entertainment, and "transport money" (*uang transpor*) for the audience. Small costs added up, with Bontor saying he had distributed over 80,000 t-shirts during his 2009 campaign, in addition to other campaign paraphernalia like banners, posters, and flags. He accepted these expenses as an integral part of Indonesia's "campaign culture" (*budaya kampanye*). At the same time, Bontor took nothing for granted, even exclaiming once, "I still had to spend over Rp 4 billion on my campaign and I'm an incumbent!" Like Ayu, he lamented that even after this expenditure there was no guarantee that people would choose him. He estimated that for every rally held, a candidate might expect no more than 40 percent of the audience to vote for her or him. With these odds, he reasoned, candidates had to hold as many rallies as they could afford in order to amass a winning number of votes.

Bontor counted himself lucky that his rallies were usually held in his strongholds where he could draw on his reputation and his personal connection to the region. In his view, the money he spent on these events would go further in securing voters' backing. Due to the large size of his electoral district, Bontor acknowledged that it would be impossible to campaign across its entirety. Instead, he focused on areas where he had polled well in the past and he was most likely to win. He believed that if a candidate preserved a "good reputation" (*nama yang baik*) throughout a legislative term—which he felt he had and would certainly tell people about—people who had previously voted in favor were likely to do so again. His network of supporters was drawn from people he had known and worked with for an extended period, meaning that he felt assured of their allegiance and that, unlike other candidates, he need not worry about being duped by untrustworthy brokers who saw the campaign as a cash cow. His campaign strategy from the outset was to concentrate on retaining previous votes, which he calculated as being enough to secure victory, rather than stretching his resources to secure new supporters.

On the Campaign Trail

Our first trip to the electoral district was in July 2013. Taking an early morning flight from Jakarta to Medan, our first stop after leaving the airport was Lapas

Klas 1 prison. The prison had recently been the site of a large fire and mass breakout, resulting in the escape of around 10 percent of inmates. In explaining why we had to make this unusual pit stop, he explained that the inmates had revolted because of the dire living conditions, including no running water and electricity, and it was important to bring attention to the issue: "They are still Indonesian people, even if they committed a crime they should still be provided with water and electricity.... The truth is the prisons have the money, it's just not managed well. It's another example of corruption in the government system." Bontor had a brief discussion with the prison management, convincing them to allow the local media gathered outside to film the fire damage on the inside of the building. He later told me that it was important for the media to capture these images, otherwise the public would never know what had happened. Standing in the courtyard of the prison, surrounded by remaining inmates and few journalists and cameramen, he told the audience that he would be reporting back to the national legislature and would do what he could to bring attention to their "emergency." The prisoners cheered and sought photos with him, while prison officials came up to shake his hand.

As we were leaving, I asked what the rationale was behind this unplanned pit stop given that the prison was not even in Bontor's electoral district.[5] He said he had been asked to attend by his party and he could represent them through highlighting injustice that had occurred as a result of the government not doing its duty. It was important to position the party as a protector of ordinary people, who could be in danger as a result of the mass prison break:

> The truth is not many people will care about the prisoners [as individuals], but they will care that some of them they got loose ... they might feel scared. So, we can show that we want to protect them from danger ... that [if they elect us] we will pay more attention to these things.

Furthermore, during the visit Bontor wanted to draw attention to the reason the prison break occurred, highlighting that it was corruption within the police force that had led to gross dissatisfaction among the prisoners. As he explained later, his party was keen to talk about the failings of the justice system, which was something the government had failed to address. In the early rallies I saw he referred back to his visit to Lapas Klas 1 prison, to underscore how government failure and that corruption among people in authority can lead to real problems for local communities, connecting the case to broader corruption issues by asking his listeners to "imagine if all government money went to helping citizens, not to elites," and "how much better and stronger we would be."

The prison visit spoke to both his reputation as a politician who could draw media attention and his role within the party. As a member of the party leadership, he saw his 2014 election campaign as fulfilling two purposes. On the one hand, he was aiming to secure reelection through his own campaign activities. On the other, he was representing his party in the province of North Sumatra, providing it an important link to local communities and shifting the perceptions that it was, like other political parties, concerned mostly with political matters on Java. The party wanted to leverage his reputation, ethnic background, and ties to the region to position it as being aware and concerned with local issues. For Bontor, this dual focus meant that he was frequently required to campaign outside of his own electoral district.

From the prison we headed by car to an afternoon rally in a village, which a member of Bontor's campaign team estimated was attended by around 1,500 people. Jointly held by four candidates competing for legislative positions at various levels of government, the rally featured Bontor as the guest of honor. Exiting the car in a makeshift parking lot adjacent to a large marquee covering rows of seats, Bontor was greeted by rally organizers who scrambled to shake his hand and welcome him. He waved warmly at attendees as he was shown to his seat on a raised stage. As I took my place among the crowd, I asked the person next to me why they had decided to come to the rally. She replied that she and Bontor shared familial ties, explaining that they had common ancestors (*sama nenek*), as did many in the audience. As the proceedings began, a man stood at the stage lectern and began with a greeting in the local language.

This rally was to be my first real glimpse of Bontor, the *Batak* politician, in action, as he addressed the crowd in their language (switching back and forth to Indonesian), prayed to the Christian God with them, and spoke to them of his achievements as a politician in Jakarta. He was a compelling orator who spoke of his vision for a corruption-free Indonesia—one that he and his party would fight for. The audience was supportive and clapped when he paused. He ended his speech with the final statement that he was proud to represent the Batak community and hoped they would vote for him again so that he could continue to strive, with his party, for a better Indonesia. He followed his address by warmly inviting the next candidates to the stage for their address, switching to Batak to leave the audience with a lasting sense of his connection to the community.

Local Ties Make the Man

Capitalizing on his ethnic identity was a significant aspect of Bontor's electoral campaign. Alongside his long-term profile in politics, he used his status as a respected Batak elder to present himself as a true representative of his community in government. This status imbued him with an authority that demanded respect from other Bataks. I saw this repeatedly while with him on the campaign trail, as we went to people's homes and meetings where he was greeted like an old friend. The phrase *sama nenek* came up several times as I spoke to Bontor and audience members at rallies. It was clear that Bontor played upon kinship loyalty in order to appeal to local voters. At multiple rallies, Bontor was introduced as an "elder" (*pengetua*) of the local area and he began his address by stating how proud he was to be a representative of the Batak community in Jakarta. In other rallies, he pledged that if he was reelected he would make it a personal priority to continue to oversee the national budget for North Sumatra and "make sure that all the money goes to the people . . . and not the pockets of officials." He presented himself as a channel for communicating local interests to ensure that national decision making took the needs of the Batak community into account. Whether these needs were especially different from the needs of citizens from different ethnic groups was not clear from Bontor's rhetoric, but the crowd seemed appreciative of the sentiment, cheering supportively.

Electioneering with Bontor was more than just rallies and media appearances. We went to church services, weddings, and funerals, as well as to small meetings in coffee shops and people's homes. At one funeral, Bontor's presence was gratefully acknowledged by the family and he was asked to give a short speech, even though he had not met the deceased. After a prayer and some words of condolence, he went on to say that he hoped he would receive their votes. Unlike Ayu and Ambo, Bontor was a known entity who did not have to find ways to introduce and endear himself to local gatekeepers—they knew who he was and, if anything, they wanted his backing rather than vice versa. Each encounter was casual, resembling a get-together between old friends more than a professional meeting. They revolved mostly around how the vote collecting was progressing and whether any additional goods (such as t-shirts or business cards) or money to pay for events were required. Participants also discussed whether there were any local issues that Bontor should be aware of, especially whether his rivals were campaigning in the area and whether they presented a threat.

Bontor acknowledged that his electoral district encompassed voters from a range of different backgrounds and religions, but his own strategy focused primarily on appealing to Bataks with similar kinship and religious backgrounds to himself. He explained to me that this kind of engagement was the best use of his time and resources. This demographic had been a strong support base in previous elections, and he could use his funds to consolidate their support for him, thus ensuring his reelection. He did not completely exclude other groups from his campaign; for example, he organized a series of meals for the breaking of fast during the Islamic fasting month of Ramadan (*iftar*) for Muslims in his constituency. However, he was doubtful about whether they would support him regardless of these efforts. As a Christian, Bontor opted to concentrate his campaign activity in majority Christian areas, believing it was unlikely that Muslims would vote for a Christian candidate, regardless of whether they respected him as an anticorruption politician. More concretely, he felt that other political parties were specifically targeting this demographic and had captured much of the Muslim population in the electoral district, therefore making it even more pointless to try to win them over in his electoral campaign.[6]

Bontor's religion was in fact a crucial facet of his political identity. He described himself as a "true Christian," who regularly attended church in Jakarta and saw his faith as integral in allowing him to become a successful politician, which he did "with God's help." But it was also a useful political tool to help him appeal to voters. Several rallies commenced with Bontor praying that God would protect the local citizens and guide his electoral campaign. One of his recurring talking points was his rejection of polygamy, a controversial topic that had been in the media due to political debates about the legality of men taking multiple wives.[7] However, this was more a tactic than something grounded in actual policy. For example, at one rally he stated that his party was staunchly against polygamy and that no man who was a party member was permitted to have more than one wife, expecting this would be well-received by his female and/or Christian audience. He later conceded that his party had no decisive stance against polygamy nor any party rules about it for members, admitting that he made the statement in the hope of increasing his popularity. He had opportunistically fibbed to the audience to appeal to their Christian values, but he felt it was justified because if it was up to him "it would be a party policy . . . we just haven't discussed it yet."

Bontor also used his church connections to organize rallies, donated to several church communities, and supported local Christian youth groups and congregations. In turn, many youth group members volunteered to be part of his campaign team. When he met with one group for an organizing meeting, he asked them to make sure that all their young Christian friends were planning to vote—and for him. His appeal as someone of the same religious faith was implied, but he explicitly asked that they promote him on the grounds that had a track record as a politician and was a committed anticorruption campaigner. As he saw it, religion could be leveraged for an electoral campaign, but it was also important to him that people believed he was a good politician who was committed to improving Indonesia and being a champion for the people.

Bontor also wanted to present himself as a politician who advocated for diversity in Indonesian politics. When I questioned him about why he talked publicly about this, he replied that, as a member of a minority group himself, it was important to remind people about the importance of having diverse (and especially non-Muslim) voices in the national legislature. He understood that his own party was founded by a Javanese Muslim who was unlikely to understand the local challenges faced by Batak Christians in North Sumatra. But he could present himself as a conduit for these interests and those of other minority groups as well. In some speeches, he underscored his advocacy for minorities in politics by openly expressing support for the then-governor of Jakarta, Basuki Tjahaja Purnama (commonly known as Ahok), an ethnic Chinese politician who had been subjected to race-related criticism.[8] At the same time, he stressed that his own political party was keen to include voices from around Indonesia in its leadership, not just those reflecting Javanese interests. He also emphasized that his party's leader was greatly interested in the challenges facing the economically downtrodden, such as poor farmers, and had been advocating for the government to provide more assistance, for instance, by supplying new tractors to the local farmer cooperatives.

Even though Bontor's identity and rhetoric were a key part of how he appealed to voters, he also acknowledged the importance of demonstrating that he was able to present material gains to his constituents, both in terms of what he represented in the national legislature and what he referred to as "tangible benefits." Tangible benefits was a loose concept for Bontor, but he was keen to show that he was a man who supported his people. The distribution of cash payments at his rallies was one way to achieve this end. He also built relations with people in communities by using their services during campaigns (such as purchasing food or paying local youths to put up posters). In addition to expenditure on rallies, Bontor, like Ambo and Ayu, made donations to local causes and groups in order to curry favor with voters. Like them, also, he said that these payments demonstrated his generosity and helped to ensure that people did not forget him. There was also a cultural element to this strategy, as Bontor framed the delivery of these kinds of "benefits" within Batak discourses of gift-giving. At one point he described the provision of campaign trinkets and small cash payments as small gifts (*oleh-oleh*), which were customary tokens from someone who was returning to visit family and friends. At other times, he portrayed cash payments as recognition and an expression of gratitude for past support or a reimbursement for attending his events. Either way, they were very much an embodiment of what Bontor referred to as tangible benefits.

When asked what he deemed a reasonable amount of money to give out, Bontor replied that he would not give more than USD 1 (Rp 10,000) to any individual. He contrasted such payments with "money politics," which he argued was certainly improper behavior and would involve much larger sums of money.[9] Although Bontor never elaborated on what, exactly, constituted a "large sum of money" his rationale against so-called large payments was also pragmatic. Because he was a national legislative candidate, distributing large amounts of cash across his electoral district would be prohibitively expensive. Bontor calculated that even giving a dollar to each rally attendee added up to a significant expense, and he had to consider carefully whether it was a good use of money. Unlike Ambo and Ayu, Bontor comfortably rationalized these actions, stressing that such payments were not bribes. He vehemently rejected that this practice constituted money politics, saying that it was important to meet people's expectations. If attendees did not receive a payment, the rally could do more harm than good because the attendees could end up disgruntled and decide not to vote for him. Apart from complying with existing election norms, it was as if Bontor felt obliged to make the payments as a means of demonstrating his commitment to local people and their welfare; in not meeting this obligation, he was not fulfilling his part of the unspoken bargain he had with his constituents.

A Two-Track Campaign

As both an individual candidate and a representative of his political party, Bontor had two distinct goals in the context of his campaign: to promote himself and his party. His two-track campaign approach—in which he entwined his party's corruption eradication rhetoric with his own—seemed curated to leverage Bontor's individual success and popularity as a way of generating broader support for the party. Bontor had been a politician long before the party was created, but he now attempted to combine his messages with those of the party. By advocating for the party, and through his public appearances, he would underscore how the party aligned with his values, rather than the other way around. For new parties, a figure like Bontor was an asset who could raise awareness about not only the party but also the presidential aspirations of its leader, as well as being a safe bet for a much-coveted legislative seat.

This dual focus was apparent in many of Bontor's rallies, where he wove together narratives about his own anticorruption track record and that of his party, while also attempting to cast his party as unique and focused on the needs of the Indonesian people. Moreover, he was keen to undermine Joko Widodo, who had already put himself forward as a presidential nominee, taking aim at his meteoric rise and advising people to be wary of "the deals" he would have to make to become president. In doing so, he wanted to promote his party and its own presidential candidate as having the integrity and wisdom to run the country, without being beholden to entrenched political interests. This had the additional benefit of indirectly critiquing the PDIP (Partai Demokrasi Indonesia Perjuangan, Indonesian Democratic Party of Struggle), which Bontor saw as one of his party's main competitors in the election. Bontor often compared his own party to others in the national legislature, highlighting its comparatively prominent efforts to reduce corruption even with its small representation in the legislature.

The campaign presented an opportunity for Bontor to focus attention on the advantages of voting for a new party that was "clean" and "steadfastly against corruption." During his rallies, he presented corruption eradication as one of the main reasons that the party had been established. When I asked whether the party was, in fact, more a vehicle for a presidential bid, Bontor responded that the two objectives were complementary and voting in a president from a new party would go hand-in-hand with overhauling the systems that fostered corruption. Whether he believed this or not, he certainly presented himself as a loyal cadre and spoke glowingly of his party and wanted people to believe that it would be able to represent them, and justice, if it were brought to power. He also worked discussions of current, local events into his speeches to demonstrate that he was aware of the impact of corruption on the local community.

Bontor saw himself as a frontrunner, but this did not mean that his campaign was free from party interference. He felt pressure from his party's expectations, especially in the lead-up to election day. He said that he had been told by the central committee that he must win at least 150,000 votes in his electoral district to help secure the party's opportunity to nominate a presidential candidate. When he complained this would be extremely difficult, the central committee's response was that he should "do what is necessary"' to get the votes. Bontor's personal political identity and that of his party coalesced around the anticorruption image he presented in his public appearances. This was at odds with the party directive to win more votes at any cost, which implied a tacit instruction to buy votes if it was deemed necessary. But this notice came after much of the campaigning had already been done in North Sumatra and so it had little impact on the majority of Bontor's campaign.

The Perks of Incumbency

Bontor's many years of political experience had exposed him to voters from across his electoral district, and he felt confident that if they had agreed to meet with him they were likely already going to vote for him, if not help him with his campaign. He could also draw upon a trusted network of people who had assisted him in previous campaigns, allowing him to be more hands off than Ayu and Ambo in the hard work of meeting voters and convincing them to choose him. This was extremely helpful because he lived and worked in Jakarta but had the luxury of delegating a large part of his campaign work to others. It would be possible to classify this approach as clientelistic, not because it involved an explicit promise of cash or favors but because there was mutual benefit implied.[10] Bontor certainly used his time on the campaign trail to meet with power brokers—usually influential party or ethnic group figures or businessmen with whom he had worked in the past—and reinforced how helpful he had been to them in the past. In turn, there was a tacit expectation that they would rally votes on his behalf. Beyond the showy rallies, Bontor met with old contacts, some of whom he had known for decades, to discuss local issues and how he could help. "They come to me," he told me, "to discuss how we can help each other." In these more casual encounters, Bontor approached people with the confidence of someone already assured of success.

Another benefit of incumbency was that Bontor's profile as a long-term politician helped him attract the attention of journalists. Being a senior party member, he was often contacted by the media, especially local outlets, for comment on political issues. In return, there was a tacit agreement that they would paint him in a good light. He also had good relations with certain journalists to whom he gave money in return for favorable news stories. This was not uncommon—Ayu had done exactly the same. Bontor explained this payment was a recognition that journalists received low salaries and therefore needed additional income. He had Facebook and Twitter accounts, but these were managed by one of his assistants. Bontor admitted that he was not very good with technology but understood that his party expected candidates to make use of social media. However, he did not think that social media was particularly beneficial for a familiar politician like him, believing that it was more useful to new candidates who were trying to build their profile.

As he was a well-known figure in his district, people came to him for help. He claimed, for example, that—as a respected local authority—he had been asked to mediate in land disputes involving people who had backed his campaign, while asserting that he had never done anything beyond ensuring that the law was followed correctly. At one coffee shop meeting, the extent of Bontor's local reputation became clearer as he met with some local leaders to discuss the controversy between villagers and the owners of a nearby palm oil plantation. The area, with a large Javanese population, had not been strongly on Bontor's campaign radar, but the meeting presented an opportunity that he wanted to pursue. A land dispute had erupted, exacerbated by the palm oil company's use of local roads, which villagers contended was being damaged by the heavy vehicles traveling to and from the plantation and making it more difficult to travel to the nearest big city. Apart from asking Bontor to take up the villager's grievances, they also asked if he could lobby the government to fix the road, which had giant holes and was dangerous. He agreed that he could indeed encourage local authorities to prioritize road repairs. Buoyed by this encounter, Bontor later decided to host a campaign event close to the village to capitalize on the good publicity his intervention had given him within the community.

In addition to the personal relationships he had built up within his electoral district during his time as a politician, incumbency granted Bontor access to special funds such as "social assistance" (*bantuan sosial*, bansos) and "aspiration funds" (*dana aspirasi*), which he, as a local legislative representative, could channel toward village-level infrastructure and social development projects. Instead of funding such projects out of his own pocket, he could thus claim credit for a number of government-funded schemes. The schemes allowed him to direct funding to areas where he had support, fostering patronage relationships in which voters came to see Bontor as a reliable ally in government.[11] He had no qualms about claiming these projects, since, to his mind, he had facilitated them. Bontor said on several occasions that he had used these government funds to reward communities that had voted for him in the 2009 election and saw this as part of the tangible benefits that he could deliver to voters who had supported him in the past. However, he also noted he could never take voters for granted. In particular, he felt he needed to attend to those who he had not managed to assist through government development or infrastructure projects during his past term. To do this, he tried to ensure he held a local event in these areas so he could offer other benefits such as food, music, and a small cash payment.

Bontor's profile also attracted campaign donations, which, he claimed, were made because people "understood that campaigns cost money" and wanted to "help him win." These donations mostly came from businesspeople with whom he was on good terms. He accepted that some people may see this as buying influence but rejected that he had ever done anything illegal in return. However, this did not preclude him from helping people if he could "when they were in trouble." He gave an example of a donor to his previous campaign who had faced court and was extorted by the presiding judge, who wanted money to rule in his favor. According to Bontor, the businessman had asked him to intervene so that he could have a fair trial without having to pay. So Bontor rang a friend who worked at the court and requested he ask the judge to rescind his request for a bribe. In the end, the businessman did not have to pay the bribe and the judge still ruled in his favor. Bontor explained that these were common occurrences and were a matter of him countering illegal behavior, rather than using his position to influence decisions. This person, he claimed, was now a member of his campaign team and he could rely on them because he had helped them in the past.

Incumbency also offered Bontor a profile that other candidates wanted to attach themselves to. He had more tandem offers than he could accept. Candidates competing for provincial and local legislature seats were keen for his endorsement and would organize special rallies at which he was the guest of honor, without Bontor having to organize or fund the events. His small cash contributions seemed larger when combined with the contributions of the other candidate(s) who had invited him, boosting his image of being a generous politician. Bontor did not need these tandem arrangements, but other candidates sought him out, putting him in a strong bargaining position when it came to event format and deciding who would pay for them. He liked to give the impression that he supported all of his party's candidates and particularly those who had been long-term cadres, but his actual decisions were driven by kinship and religion. In reality, Bontor was keen to promote fellow Batak candidates and he made numerous appearances at events hosted by candidates that he knew through his church connections. Being an incumbent provided Bontor with the freedom to promote candidates at provincial and local levels to whom he had special ties to, rather than looking for those who could channel the most votes to him. Of these candidates he once said: "it's actually these [local legislators] who make decisions that affect the community, so it's important that we support the same interests." What Bontor seemed to be saying was that he wanted to assist candidates who were *like him*—interested in representing Batak interests and to ensure that his supporters had a voice at all levels of government.

Bontor appeared unflappable as the election date drew closer. Incumbency not only brought the security of local connections and profile but also a keen understanding of *how things worked*. The stress of long days on the campaign trail, traveling, and negotiating that I saw throughout Ayu's and Ambo's campaigns were a stark contrast to Bontor's relatively relaxed campaign journey. There were similarly long hours, late-night meetings, and flights to and from Jakarta, but they did not cause the same emotional strain or exhaustion that other candidates experienced. The people he worked with were trusted friends and he did not worry about being taken advantage of or needing to closely oversee their activities. This, in essence, was the true benefit of incumbency—the confidence of knowing that the votes were his to lose. Whether Bontor was ever in danger of losing his seat, we cannot know. But Bontor was confident about his chances, so long as his campaign reminded people of how good he had been to them, and this assurance allowed him to develop a strategy that worked for him and remain true to it.

Reflections on the Campaign

It was clear that Bontor's campaign centered upon appealing to Batak constituents, and he unabashedly used his status as an elder to attract voters. Kinship ties and religious identity provided a point of entry for rallies and meetings, as well as fostering personal ties that were decades old. For Bontor, his campaign was not about building a profile; unlike Ayu, he had no need to show voters how to vote for him on the ballot. His campaign was more about demonstrating that he had delivered on past promises. In the process, he had to show that he had not become "arrogant" (*sombong*) because of his political success and still cared deeply about his electoral district. This was what made the coffee shop meetings, funeral visits, and wedding cameos so important. Bontor felt that anticorruption was a solid platform for rallies, but it was these personal interactions that consolidated his appeal for many voters. A wedding was not the time to talk about corruption—it was a time to be present, speak in their local language, praise the delicious food being served, and offer up his prayers. At coffee shop meetings with associates and members of his campaign team, he did not feel the need to promote his anticorruption image as, he claimed, "they already know my name, know my work . . . they know I am a good person." Instead, he talked about local affairs and family gossip. These were opportunities to show that he was Batak and one of them.

But, still, money was important and Bontor's approach to money was confusing. On the one hand, he was discerning about how he spent his funds. He took calculated steps to deliver cash into the hands of individual voters, who he targeted based on ethnicity and the results of previous elections. During the course of his campaign, I witnessed several exchanges of money with people in return for attending rallies. At a July 2013 rally, audience members queued, while swaying along to music from a local band, to receive envelopes of cash. Bontor warned wryly that it was one envelope per person and urged attendees not to be greedy by trying to take more than one, since someone else would miss out. Standing apart from the crowd, I asked a woman who had just received her "gift" how much was inside, and she happily reported her envelope contained Rp 45,000 (approximately USD 3.70), which she took out and counted for me to see. Bontor later told me that he had contributed Rp 5,000 and his co-organizers had included Rp 10,000 each for each gift. Further payments that I observed during other rallies ranged from Rp 20,000 to Rp 30,000. Moreover, when asked about contributing to local development projects, he said that he rarely did this unless he was approached by a friend and could trust that funds would be spent appropriately.

On the other hand, Bontor was relaxed about how his campaign team spent money. He conceded that he did not keep close tabs on his campaign staff. He said it was difficult to say exactly what happened to all the money he provided to cover expenses, since his staff organized the events. For example, he did not personally select where the food was bought and agreed it was possible his staff might channel money for this purpose strategically in order to get votes on his behalf—but added that this was not a problem as long as the event ran smoothly. In essence, Bontor's delegation of planning, procurement, and payment responsibilities to his campaign team reflected a somewhat blasé attitude toward how campaign funds were spent. Unlike Ambo and Ayu, who tracked their expenses carefully, Bontor gave his campaign team autonomy in deciding how money was spent, which also allowed him plausible deniability about whether it had been channeled deliberately in return for support.

Bontor's campaign invokes many questions about what it means to present oneself as an anticorruption candidate and how this identity intersects with campaign strategies. He did not condone vote buying, but he did not necessarily condemn it either. Both Ambo and Ayu had argued that accepting payment in return for votes was immoral and would lead to poor leadership. At least at the beginning, they fashioned themselves as candidates wholly opposed to any kind of direct vote buying. By contrast, Bontor never described the practice in moral terms and did not seem to pass judgment on the practice. Vote buying was simply what many candidates had to do in order to win. His primary issue with vote buying was based on practicality; it was expensive, and money alone could not guarantee votes. He pitied candidates who spent so much money, especially those who he did not believe had a genuine chance of winning. In one discussion, Bontor gave an example of an acquaintance who was representing a party that was unlikely to pass the parliamentary threshold, commenting that he was worried about his campaign spending. Out of concern for this person he telephoned him and counseled him to stop wasting his money as his chances of gaining a seat, even if he was successful in the election, were low. The fringe benefits of costly campaigns were not lost on Bontor, though, who also joked that the period following the election was a good time to buy land because so many candidates went into debt as a result of campaign spending and were desperate for cash to pay back what they owed. Much of his land holdings, he said, had been acquired under these circumstances.

Furthermore, spending money did not always have to be a campaign sacrifice. Campaign visits were also an opportunity to generate support through personal business deals. On one visit, we took a detour to a snake fruit plantation so he could negotiate buying the land from its owner. During the negotiations, Bontor intimated semi-seriously that he would pay a higher price if the landowner promised he would tell everyone he knew to vote for him. Later, when I asked about whether he had been serious about his offer, he said that land deals like this were another facet of his campaign, as this was another way of "helping" constituents. Although Bontor did not classify this as a use of campaign funds because he was using his own money, and the assets themselves were unrelated to the campaign, the very fact that he had suggested to the landowner that offering electoral support could lead to a better deal seemed to give the interaction a political tone.

For Bontor, the need to spend money during a campaign was a simple, sometimes irritating fact, but he did not see it as a broader indictment on Indonesia's democracy. Neither did he lambast voters who chose to take money from candidates in the way that other self-styled anticorruption candidates did. In his mind, the choice to make payments to voters, provide goods, or fund projects was an easy one to make for most candidates, and he once speculated that this is probably what he would have to do to win if he was running for the first time. He could not compare, he said, the experiences of modern-day candidates to those of his first election campaign during the New Order. But he also said, "this is what elections are today. . . . [If you're] worried about spending money then you better not run." Regardless, these handouts were not a centerpiece of his campaign; if anything, they were a footnote to the passionate speeches he gave about fighting corruption and the need to vote for clean parties committed to corruption eradication.

In contrast to Ayu and Ambo, who wanted to present their electoral campaigns as clean and claimed that they would refuse to hand out cash, Bontor justified direct payments to voters as part of Indonesia's "campaign culture," especially among Bataks who had a "gift-giving culture." He made no excuses for the money he spent during his campaign, and his strategies paid off when he was reelected for another term. Instead of focusing on electoral behavior and critiquing the conduct of candidates and voters, Bontor's self-presentation as an anticorruption candidate focused more on challenging existing norms in the national legislature rather than in the elections themselves. His lobbying in parliament, rejection of study tours, and his anecdote about acting on behalf of his friend to "remind" a judge that that bribery was illegal were examples of what fighting corruption meant to Bontor. It was about what you did with the power you held as a legislator, rather than how you obtained that power in the first place, that mattered.

As a pragmatic candidate, who had weathered many past elections, Bontor's self-identification as an anticorruption candidate was juxtaposed with his relaxed approach to the use of money in electoral campaigns. He was not morally outraged by vote buying, nor did he complain about it on the campaign trail. He acknowledged that it was normal for candidates, especially newcomers, to attempt to buy their way into the legislature. His anticorruption identity, in essence, was drawn from his actions as a sitting politician and the mini campaigns he had waged against corruption during his time in public office, rather than his actions as a candidate. Bontor's approach to money politics was that it was necessary, but it did not exclude him from asserting an anticorruption identity. Indeed, his campaign represented an attempt to integrate the two campaign strategies. And it was his personal election context that allowed him to execute this strategy so successfully—a context that, as we will discuss in the next chapter, was simply not available to all candidates.

6
CAMPAIGNS, CONTEXT, AND CONSEQUENCES

When a legislative candidate first decides to run for an election, they bring with them a set of notions and ideals about what their campaign will look like. These assumptions relate both to what strategies they can use to win but also to their own sense of what actions are appropriate and what values they want to represent. Earlier chapters have explored how three self-identified anticorruption candidates navigated Indonesia's 2014 national legislative elections. The stories told in these chapters provide us with insights into how certain candidates managed their use of anticorruptionism and the assertion of a "clean" identity in the face of campaign challenges, particularly the pressure to engage in money politics. As we learned, each candidate responded very differently to those pressures. In Ambo's case, we see consistent *rejection*. By contrast, Ayu *acquiesced* to demands for money. Through Bontor's campaign, we see an experienced politician who had made peace with vote buying and generally accepted the norms of campaigning in ways that did not deter him from incorporating anticorruptionism as a key platform. As such, his campaign included an *integration* of money politics with other persuasive strategies, including a keen emphasis on his own anticorruption reputation.

In all three instances, their campaign trajectories reflected the decisions they made in attempting to inform and persuade, as well as embody their values in their campaign. Reflecting on the experiences of these candidates, this chapter addresses the question of how different contextual factors shape decisions about campaign execution and, more explicitly, how anticorruptionism and vote buying are responses to context. It also reflects on the normalization of money politics—namely vote buying but also, in Bontor's case, the use of clientelistic networks—and its impact. A cynical observer might wonder why a candidate would even bother developing a campaign platform, based on anticorruptionism or otherwise, given that vote buying through local brokers or direct cash/goods transfers and clientelistic relationships seemingly do more to shore up support than any electoral messages ever could. However, even if candidates have the money, vote buying offers no guarantees. Several studies confirm that voters do not necessarily see accepting money or goods as a commitment to voting for a specific candidate, and therefore potentially constitute a grave financial risk for candidates who rely solely on this strategy (Aspinall et al. 2017; Guardado and Wantchekon 2014; Muhtadi 2019; Vicente and Wantchekon 2009). Thus, having an effective campaign strategy—whether that be focusing on effective rhetoric, appearance, local connections, bribing voters, or some combination of these and other considerations—remains crucial. The cases of Ambo, Ayu, and Bontor suggest that while the Indonesian electoral environment places pressure on candidates to act in certain ways, the campaign outcomes of negotiating these pressures varies depending on an individual's unique operating context and the depth of commitment to their own values. In short, no two candidates can run the same campaign, as each individual context fosters different opportunities, and potential responses, to these demands.

Campaign Purposes

Candidates do not imagine their campaigns in a vacuum. They are first influenced by basic electoral parameters and the overarching institutional context, including the rules of eligibility, the geographic and temporal realms of the election, the political issues of the day, and the prevailing norms of electoral campaigning. These aspects of an electoral campaign often lie outside the candidate's control. But campaigns are also subject to personal contexts, such as resources, links to their party, personal identity, and their sense of morality. These factors guide the more intimate decisions that a candidate makes about the formulation and execution of their campaigns on a day-to-day basis. Much of the decision making that candidates undertake in relation to these different types of context stems from the various purposes of electoral campaigns. Campaigns are designed to inform and persuade, while also reflecting the character of the candidate. Although interrelated, the relative importance that a candidate places on each of these elements informs their strategy, as they strive to make a name for themselves among a discerning public, who not only need to know who they are but also what they can offer.

Campaigns as Information

Since a working democracy requires an informed citizenry, campaigns play an essential informational role (Banducci, Giebler, and Kritzinger 2017; Lau and Redlawsk 2001) by informing voters about competing political parties, who their candidates are, what issues are important, and where the party stands on these issues (Nadeau et al. 2008). From a political communication perspective, individual candidate campaigns are about raising voter awareness, with the assumption that the more information voters receive about a candidate and their stance on certain issues, the better able they are to make an informed decision about who they want to represent them in the legislature or in other realms of public office (Popkin 1991). Campaigns also offer an opportunity to educate voters about the mechanics of voting. We saw this when Ayu dedicated time in her village visits to show people how to cast a valid vote and, specifically, how to cast a vote for her by demonstrating where her political party, and her name, appeared on the large ballot sheet.

In this model, information is viewed as flowing from candidates to voters as they attempt to fill knowledge gaps among voters.[1] For the case study candidates, filling knowledge gaps during a campaign necessarily involved being seen and heard. Even where they had access to media outlets that could provide coverage and amplify their campaign, the candidates understood physical interactions with voters to be the key to success. Ambo, Ayu, and Bontor all traveled extensively around their electoral districts to do just this. They all felt that having voters recognize them and know who they were was an important prerequisite to winning their vote. Or, as Ayu put it, "if they don't know you, they can't love you." However, unable to visit every village in their constituencies, the extent to which they could outsource aspects of their campaign and rely on emissaries to inform voters about them was dependent on their ability to find trustworthy allies and campaign team members to canvass on their behalf. While Bontor was confident of his preexisting profile and the support of his informal networks in getting the word out about his bid for reelection, Ambo and Ayu were more reluctant to delegate this task. As a result, they both traveled much more frequently in their electoral districts than Bontor and spent more time monitoring their campaign staff. When briefing his team, Ambo stressed the importance of talking to voters about him, rather than simply giving them a t-shirt and walking away. Ayu also emphasized the need to engage with voters; though, for her, being seen by constituents was especially crucial as she did not wholly trust her campaign team and she knew that she was an unknown entity for most voters in her electoral district.

Using individual campaigns as an opportunity to inform voters about political parties—their platforms and priorities—is not common in Indonesia. In many cases, the party–candidate relationship is perfunctory, with candidates not ideologically bound to the party they represent. This is evidenced by the phenomenon of "party shopping" in Indonesia, where candidates apply to represent the party that they believe will offer them the best advantage in a particular election (Aspinall 2013, 40). Because the number of party members wanting to run for office often falls short of the number of seats available in any given electoral district, parties are inclined to approve candidates that are more interested in winning for themselves rather than for their party. Recruiting candidates from outside the party is even encouraged. As many parties charge a fee in return for their backing, their recruitment provides a revenue-raising opportunity (Mietzner 2013, 85). As a consequence, most candidates see national-level campaigns as "secondary to their own efforts" (Aspinall 2014a, 107). This tendency is exacerbated by the electoral contestation that occurs both between *and* within parties, shaping the way that candidates relate to their peers. While it is possible to form tandem arrangements with candidates competing at a different level of legislature, there is little incentive for candidates at the same level to work together to promote their party. In fact, candidates frequently see those from their own party as their primary competitors, giving them even less reason to focus on attacking or targeting candidates from other parties in their campaigns.

While the case study candidates all had close connections to party leadership and sought to promote their party through their campaigns, this seems an anomaly in Indonesian campaigns. They all saw themselves as party cadres with a responsibility for promoting their party. For Bontor and Ayu, this included endorsing their party's presidential candidate and discussing their leadership credentials and qualities. But even so, public mentions of their parties were generally framed to maximize benefits to their individual campaigns. Ambo, Ayu, and Bontor all felt that aligning their personal campaign with the rhetoric of their party's national campaigns—especially their stance against corruption and critiques of the current government—was beneficial in their self-portrayal as anti-corruption crusaders and in enhancing the persuasiveness of their election bids. However, this seems out of step with the broader Indonesian context.

Campaigns for Persuasion

The end goal of a campaign is not simply to give voters information; it is also to get their attention and persuade them to vote for a particular candidate (Redlawsk 2004). With a view to this imperative to convince, candidates often try to link themselves to current issues and present viewpoints that resonate with voters' preexisting assumptions on specific concerns, for example, by synchronizing their campaigns with issues that are already receiving media attention, sometimes referred to as "riding the wave" (Ansolabehere and Iyengar 1994).[2] In the lead-up to the 2014 elections, newer political parties worked to keep corruption cases in the public eye, hoping to position themselves as moral entrepreneurs in order to capitalize on the perceived flaws of the incumbent leadership. The fact that these narratives ignored the complexities and nuances of entrenched political corruption was irrelevant. The question was the extent to which these newer parties could build an anticorruption image that was more persuasive than that of other parties with the same strategy.

With these potential benefits, it makes sense that some candidates representing newer parties would gravitate to anticorruptionism in their campaigns. As we saw in chapter 2, anticorruptionism is a familiar trope in Indonesian politics. Moreover, in the lead-up to 2014, the issue was primed with extensive media coverage of corruption scandals involving political parties, members of the national legislature, and other institutions such as the Constitutional Court. In theory, at least, candidates and parties that chose to focus on this issue did not need to do the hard work of convincing voters that corruption was a significant concern. Public opinion surveys not only showed that corruption was an ongoing source of discontent but they also highlighted the suspicion with which voters viewed political parties and the government more generally. This public consensus—that corruption was a problem that needed to be addressed—meant that campaigning on anticorruption values would, candidates hoped, be appealing to voters.

History can lend significance to particular issues, but it also shapes the challenges associated with mobilizing them. Over the decades, Indonesian politicians had repeatedly promised to address corruption. Yet, it took an economic crisis and mass civil unrest to depose President Suharto and prompt reforms aimed at improving accountability in the Indonesian government. The hope that a post–New Order democracy would unravel the corrupt practices associated with Suharto's presidency remains unfulfilled. Ongoing public dissatisfaction toward corruption, steeped in decades of frustration, offered candidates a useful political issue to incorporate into their campaigns—an opportunity that Ambo, Ayu, and Bontor all took up to some extent. However, they deployed it strategically, and the veracity of messaging depended on the audience; in Ayu's case, her anticorruptionism waned significantly over time.

Tracing the use of anticorruptionism throughout a campaign speaks to candidates' perceptions of its persuasiveness. It also allows an interrogation of whether candidates view anticorruptionism as a guiding principle or a campaign tool, and how they reconciled these understandings. For Ambo, the ideology behind anticorruptionism was an integral part of how he wanted to appeal to voters and was a key value in his own political career. However, when and how it was discussed remained a strategic decision. It was not useful when talking to many gatekeepers, so Ambo did not discuss his anticorruption convictions when meeting with them. But when it was useful, he was sure to be vocal in his opposition to corruption. For Bontor, anticorruptionism was helpful, but he balanced its persuasiveness against the utility of vote buying and use of his incumbent advantage.

Campaigns as Embodiment

Campaigns are not just informational or even persuasive. They are also about individual candidates' attempts to establish an image and a reputation. As such, they become an embodiment of the appearance, personal values, and ethics of those who create them.[3] Changes in Indonesia's electoral system have privileged this aspect of campaigning by encouraging the rise of "celebrity" candidates. Gendered ideals also play a role, with the increased prevalence of beautiful female candidates (*caleg cantik*) and an emphasis on certain forms of masculinity in the presentation of male candidates (Selinaswati 2014). Furthermore, with the intensification of dynastic politics, a candidate's family pedigree can be key to capturing voter attention and influencing perceptions of who a candidate is, in addition to providing economic benefits (Kongkirati 2016; Querubin 2016). By the same token, identity is political and expressions of it are calculated decisions (Hetherington 1998). It is up to candidates to decide how much these considerations will factor into their campaign and whether appearance comes at the expense of more traditional campaign tools and strategies, such as a strong policy platform or even vote buying. Fundamentally, however, the ways that candidates conduct themselves and the actions they take reflect who they are and what they stand for. If they easily capitulate to pressure, then this certainly says something about their personal commitment to remaining "clean."

For Ambo, Ayu, and Bontor, an anticorruption reputation aligned neatly with the image that their parties were attempting to convey. But the choice to mobilize such an image remained a personal decision. Even though party leaders would no doubt have liked to present a united image across their thousands of candidates, it was unrealistic to expect homogeneity, given the autonomy that candidates have in constructing their electoral campaigns, fostered by the Indonesian electoral system. Furthermore, parties did not prioritize institutional measures to ensure the consistent adoption of official party rhetoric by candidates or, indeed, general compliance with electoral regulations. Party members found to have bought votes or to have otherwise acted illegally during the campaign were (theoretically) answerable to their party's ethics committee. But given the enormous number of candidates and the limited resources at parties' disposal—in addition to a questionable commitment to enforcing the law more generally—it was not surprising that party ethics committees were rarely called upon during the campaign period.[4]

At the same time, image was more than a campaign front for these candidates. They genuinely *believed* that their personal values made them a better option for voters. In their initial explanations to me about why they wanted to sit in the national legislature, they all asserted that they would be a *different* type of politician; Bontor and Ambo boasted they had already proven their anticorruption credentials in the legislature. But viewing their campaigns as an extension of their personal identity placed an additional burden on these candidates, as they confronted, and sometimes conceded to, voter requests for money, goods, or other forms of benefit. How they responded to these challenges offers further insight into who they were as people. Was a better chance at winning a seat in the legislature enough incentive to derail original plans? Was there a strength of conviction that allowed them to maintain the fundamental premises of their campaign strategy in the face of challenges? Exploring the answers to these questions allow us to scratch below the surface of their stated motivations and analyze how responses to campaign dilemmas are justified by a candidate when they feel pressured to do something that they would rather not.

Campaign Pressures

Discrete individual campaigns form the basis for a party's prospects of winning an election, but they occur in a very different realm from their national campaigns, which are primarily developed in, and executed from, Jakarta. This differentiation is captured in the distinction that Aspinall (2014a) draws between the "air wars" conducted across the country by political parties and the "ground wars" in which individual candidates are involved. Ambo, Ayu, and Bontor were similar insofar as they were standing for emerging, less established political parties that aspired to install a particular presidential candidate. All three candidates had personal connections to their party's leadership and were involved in the affairs of their respective national headquarters in Jakarta. Yet, they chose to compete in electoral races outside of the capital city in other parts of the country. In doing so, they faced similar institutional challenges related to voter engagement, but their ability to preempt and respond to the pressures of campaigning proved to be quite different.

Standing Out from the Crowd

In 2014, approximately 180,000 candidates competed for 19,699 seats across four levels of government. This was a very real institutional context for candidates to grapple with—the sheer volume of names and faces on the ballot papers meant that a candidate's focus was necessarily concentrated on how he or she could ensure that they stood out from the crowd. There was a heightened emphasis on crafting a strong individual profile in 2014. In 1999, the majority of Indonesians voted based on what political party they identified with rather than in support of an individual candidate (Hara 2001). Broad, though often superficial, divisions between Islamic and nationalist parties continued to echo earlier *aliran*-based voting patterns.[5] This schism presented opportunities for candidates who wished to appeal to certain subsets of the population. The identifiably Islamic parties, especially, could capitalize on different subsets of Muslim voters for support as the four major religious parties represented in the national legislature come from different roots. But, since that time, things had changed. With voters given the opportunity to select individuals directly, rather than having votes channeled through political parties, candidates could no longer depend on party identification alone to capture voter attention or support.

Ambo, Ayu, and Bontor were all first-ranked candidates for their parties. This was a matter of pride, as they saw it as an endorsement and show of faith from the party leadership. But this ranking did not necessarily offer any great advantage when it came to winning voter support. For Bontor, it crystalized his standing within the party but made little difference in how he ran his campaign. Ambo was able to use his ranking to garner support from local party cadres and generate favorable press coverage through his party's ties to media outlets, but he still knew that he had to campaign hard. In Ayu's case, top billing placed her at the center of a local power struggle. No matter how much she tried to assert that she was one of them, cadres saw Ayu as a "fly-in" candidate from Jakarta and froze her out of the local branch. Being very much a true believer in her party, the lack of backing she received from local cadres was a great disappointment for Ayu, who had entered the electoral race feeling buoyed by her first-ranked nomination.

Intraparty competition also shaped each candidate's experience. A number of scholars argue that the introduction of the open-party list correlated directly with an increase in money politics of all kinds (Aspinall 2014a; Crouch 2010; Mietzner 2015; Muhtadi 2018b; Simandjuntak 2012). Being seen to deliver "concrete benefits" through the provision of tangible goods became an increasingly popular campaign tactic, centered on attracting voters to an individual rather than a political party (Aspinall 2014a, 97) or a certain policy platform. Aspinall and Berenschot (2019, 68) argue that the 2014 elections saw a spike in cash transfers, gift giving, and the distribution of "club goods." This was a consequence of the open-party list system, as candidates scrambled to outdo one another and secure individual voter support. With multiple seats available within one electoral district contested by numerous candidates from each party, candidates ended up competing not only against rivals from other parties but with rivals from within their own party. The fact that the arena of electoral contestation exists both within *and* between parties shaped the way that they conceptualized their relationship with their parties and, in particular, with their fellow candidates. The impact of intraparty competition was most visible in Ayu's case, where decisions made by the national party office did not sit well with local party cadres. Not only was it difficult for her to attract support from branch members, but there were no systems put in place by the party to guarantee that she would get their support. As such, Ayu not only had to win over voters but also members of her own party, who could choose to throw their weight behind any of the candidates on the list.

The Importance of Resources

Electoral campaigns, if run in earnest, are expensive. And while political parties want as many of their candidates to win as many seats as possible to boost the party's power in the legislature and gain control over presidential nominations, they provide little support to ensure candidates' individual success. Some candidates did not have to pay registration fees, and even received funding for their campaigns from their parties. Ambo and Ayu were among this number. However, the majority of candidates receive nothing (Aspinall and Sukmajati 2016). Often already out-of-pocket from having to pay for their party nomination, candidates are frequently expected to source their own war chest. These costs can be significant, even if a candidate decides not to engage in money politics, since they need to pay for transportation, food, and accommodation for themselves (and sometimes members of their campaign teams), as well as for banners, advertisements, campaign paraphernalia, meetings, and rallies. A candidate's willingness to spend also factors in here. Of course, a rich candidate can also be frugal one, setting defined limits on expenditures. In such cases, resources can be considered in terms of what a candidate allows themselves to spend, rather than the sum total of their wealth.

How much money a candidate can access, either through personal wealth or donations, greatly influences the candidate's strategy and the size of their campaign. Bontor was open about this fact, stating that his own campaign had cost over USD 300,000. He noted that, although a significant sum, it was much less than a newcomer would need to spend. Of this expenditure, about USD 82,000 came from his own pocket, with the remainder provided by the party or sourced through donations. According to Bontor, these donations came mostly from businesspeople with whom he was on good terms and who wanted to support his candidacy. He did not acknowledge that these donations came with expectations, though they may well have. Ambo's party also covered most of his campaign costs. However, this is not to say that he was not mindful of campaign expenditure—indeed, the fact that he was spending party funds throughout his campaign seemed to make him even more judicious about tracking where the money went. While Ayu was less open about the source of her campaign funds or how much she had, the anxiety caused by her growing expenses implied that it was a finite amount that she could not afford to squander.

Incumbency can also be an important resource for candidates, even beyond the access to the additional funds that it bestows. Voter behavior tends to privilege established parties and incumbents rather than challengers (J. Campbell 1983; Cox and Katz 1996; Dalton and Weldon 2005). This is helpful if you happen to be an incumbent who has managed to survive a previous term without alienating your constituents. The many non-incumbents competing in any given election are likely competing against someone with whom voters are already familiar, and who has had the opportunity to channel benefits to the community (Pereira and Melo 2014). A key example in the Indonesian context is the provision of grants to communities through the aspiration fund (*dana aspirasi*) scheme introduced in 2009, which allows sitting legislators to disburse up to Rp 5 billion toward development projects within their electoral districts (Aspinall and Berenschot 2019). These funds can be used to reward local communities that supported a politician in the previous campaign or to win over communities that the candidate is hoping to capture in an upcoming election.

As the only sitting incumbent, Bontor provided a clear example of the incumbency advantage. Having directed spending from the aspiration fund, and other schemes such as social assistance (*bantuan sosial*, bansos) toward village-level infrastructure and social development, he did not need to fund such projects during his campaign. Moreover, he had consciously targeted this expenditure to areas where he had strong support as a reward to voters who had helped him win his seat in the previous legislative elections. Bontor happily took credit for these projects, even though they were funded by government-sanctioned spending programs. These programs further shaped his campaign as he steered his campaign spending to areas where he had not been able to secure other government funding for projects, to ensure that as many of his supporters as possible were able to benefit directly from voting for him.

Resources also include a candidate's social capital. For this reason, candidates carefully foster local ties, as well as presenting themselves as keen defenders of local interests, and preferably a "son of the land" (*putera daerah*). In the case of these three candidates, as for many others in Indonesia, personal connections were a factor in campaign strategy. All three candidates portrayed themselves as locals in their electoral districts, with varying degrees of success. Indeed, the depth of their local embeddedness and extent of their kinship ties were distinguishing features of their campaigns. Ambo and Bontor both drew on their local connections for insider information. For Bontor, being seen as an active member of the community through his attendance at weddings, funerals, and church services was part and parcel of this identity he cultivated. Similarly, Ambo successfully mobilized a strong local identity in his campaigning, playing on these connections to assert that he was one of them. When they addressed voters in meetings and rallies, the ability to switch between local languages and Indonesian allowed them to authentically perform, and leverage, their indigeneity. They also used their affiliations at churches and mosques, respectively, to organize meetings throughout their campaigns. Ayu tried to do the same, but she found it more difficult. Her family was from the area, but, having grown up in Jakarta, local networks were not as readily available to her. When she fronted meetings and rallies, both with members of her own party and with voters, she often felt like an outsider, needing to work much harder than other candidates to prove that she belonged. Her use of Javanese, which she hoped would ingratiate her to local voters, served to alienate her as she used a formal register that was, it seemed, construed as inappropriate for her audience. Public persona and gender may have also played some role in her struggle—she was far more softly spoken and less charismatic than Ambo and Bontor, and she often complained about how men spoke to her in meetings. But even this might have been circumvented if she had the right connections through which to appeal to a base of supporters. Strong backing from local party leadership may have also helped, but she lacked this as well.

A more effective use of brokers might have alleviated some of Ayu's difficulties in establishing trust on the ground. Campaign teams often include members hired specifically because of their influence with parts of the electoral district, assisting candidates in securing votes throughout their personal social networks (Gonzalez Ocantos, de Jonge, and Nickerson 2014). Where goods or cash are distributed to voters, brokers sometimes do so on behalf of the candidate. Brokers' own social cache adds value to the gifts, while also insulating the candidate from allegations of wrongdoing. However, their use is risky for candidates, as little can be done to guarantee that they will fulfill their promises (Stokes et al. 2013). In Indonesia, it is not uncommon for brokers to betray a candidate, for example by taking money from several candidates in one area or siphoning off funds they have been given to distribute to individual voters (Aspinall 2014b).[6] Whereas Bontor had a ready team of supporters willing to help him, and Ambo had family connections that allowed him to gather intelligence about rivals and help him set up meetings, Ayu had some close family members but they were not tuned in to the political dynamics of the region, so did not offer her much help in this regard. Instead, she turned to "professional" brokers to help her make community connections, distribute money, and/or organize community projects. Without a strong trust relationship, she was paradoxically left wondering how committed they were to her campaign while also relying heavily on their advice.

Engaging Voters

In political landscapes where the citizens feel alienated from political decision making, candidates need to find ways to make their campaign relevant to voters against a backdrop of apathy or even cynicism. This is no easy task, especially where politicians' reputation for corruption departs significantly from the democratic ideal. Studies have shown that most voters wish to make "good decisions" with minimal effort (Redlawsk 2004). These decisions are often based on "information shortcuts" that allow them to make assumptions about politicians based on cursory information (Capelos 2010; Edelman 1964). Where voters have little faith or interest in political processes, the temptation exists to forfeit their vote as a form of protest—a practice commonly referred to in Indonesia as belonging to the "white group" (*golongan putih*, or *golput*).[7] In 2014, there was much speculation that the number of *golput* voters would increase as a result of growing disillusionment with the government, especially in relation to ongoing corruption scandals (I. Wilson 2014). A *golput* vote could be a protest against the existing voting system, a rejection of the available options, or to make some other political point. Regardless of its motivation, the outcome of a *golput* is the same for candidates, namely a vote lost.

A candidate's capacity to communicate directly with voters constitutes a crucial difference between national and individual campaigns. There is often an assumption that campaign communication is a one-way street, whereby candidates provide information to voters. Moreover, much of the academic literature tends to focus on the use of non-relational forms of communication (such as posters, online posts, media coverage, and even campaign speeches).[8] However, the reality is much more complex. In Indonesia, many candidates share information primarily through face-to-face interactions with voters or through emissaries who represented them in meetings with voters. These direct channels of communication close the "feedback loop" between candidates and voters.[9] Candidates hope that voter responses will be positive. But the responses can also be challenging, especially in a context where money politics is the norm. Ambo, Ayu, and Bontor all reported that they had been asked for goods, services, and/or money during meetings with voters. Faced with this information—which national party campaigns will never access due to the nature of non-relational campaigns—candidates may feel forced to reevaluate their chances of winning if they do not accede to voters' demands.

The need to engage effectively with voters forces many candidates to confront challenging electoral norms. Not every candidate will attempt to win voters over with goods, cash, promises, and/or services, and not every voter is amenable to such enticements. But, as long as vote buying remains an established campaign norm in Indonesia, expectations of politicians as gift-givers and heads of patronage networks will remain embedded in candidate–voter relationships (Aspinall and Sukmajati 2016; Simandjuntak 2012). The three candidates certainly found that voter expectations of vote buying remain common, although each responded in different ways. Bontor incorporated this aspect of electioneering into his campaign from the very beginning, rationalizing it as a normal part of campaigning and of Batak culture, which did not negate his anticorruption stance. By contrast, Ambo, and initially Ayu, hoped to circumvent this norm. However, as the campaign continued, Ayu changed her approach to vote buying, based partly on the inputs she received directly from voters. By contrast, Ambo intensified his anti-money politics rhetoric, becoming even more vocal about corruption.

Campaign Decision Making

At the beginning of the campaign, Ambo, Ayu, and Bontor all believed that portraying themselves as an anticorruption candidate would give them an advantage. Anticorruptionism seemed a useful strategy, given the popular outcry against corruption. But the motivation for an anticorruption identity cannot be solely explained by perceived advantage—at least not at the outset. Corruption was certainly a salient issue, but it was not the only concern to which candidates could attach themselves. A better explanation for these candidates' decisions to incorporate anticorruptionism into their campaigns is that the issue fell neatly at the nexus of campaign purposes: it allowed them to inform voters about their party's stance on a prominent issue, it had persuasive value, *and* the candidates felt it reflected their personal values. They all felt comfortable with projecting themselves as anticorruption candidates because it highlighted the best in them: that they were honest, ethical, and committed to improving Indonesia.

But although they felt this way at the beginning of their campaigns, these candidates faced multiple challenges in promoting themselves as clean amidst an electoral environment where vote buying was normalized and money politics rife. Exploring a candidate's "power of agency"—which C. Campbell (2009, 407) defines as an actor's "ability to initiate and maintain a program of action" based on a range of options—is a useful lens for understanding how candidates respond to such conundrums. Cook and Emerson (1978) suggest that this power can be expressed in the ability to explore alternative options, compare these options, and the opportunity to accept the best offer or hold out for a better offer within an exchange network. At the same time, path dependency—defined as "an ideological commitment or political, institutional and social legacies" (G. Wilson 2014, 5)—and the extent to which vote buying and using money to persuade voters is embedded in local understandings of how elections should work also influence the decision-making process, possibly even circumventing rational decision making.

In truth, all three candidates had access to money and could have embarked on a money politics–focused strategy from the very beginning if they so desired. Ambo and Ayu chose not to, both because they did not want to and because they believed they could win without doing so. They were hopeful that their anticorruptionism would be persuasive. Ayu's shift toward acquiescence came as she saw diminishing returns in her initial strategy. Bontor anchored his campaign decisions in his previous experiences, leading him to believe that a successful campaign could incorporate anticorruptionism and vote-buying strategies. To this end, the way that the candidates made their decisions can be seen through the actions they take to "derive advantage from situations" (Swartz 1997, 67). Drawing on Bourdieu, Swartz (1997, 71) argues that how actors view "advantage" depends on a number of factors, including the actor's own definition of what is in their interest. At the same time, the decision cannot be divorced from the ethical predicament that it created for candidates and the emotional toll of acting against their own sense of right and wrong. In drawing distinctions between the three candidates, we see quite different responses to this negotiation between the sense of morality that these candidates held and how best to derive "advantage" during a campaign.

Rejection

Ambo was a local man who was born in and had grown up in his electoral district. While he had relocated to Jakarta for work, he still had a house, family networks, and friends in the district and could use these to pull votes. Such capital, embedded in personal identity, allowed him to trade on his identity as a local and as representing constituents' interests. A skilled orator with a commanding presence, he wove this into his anticorruption image effectively, using not only large-scale rallies but also small meetings to reinforce his persona. For example, he promised to use his influence to personally defend local farmers from price gouging by following up on a case of rent-seeking where the village head was conspiring with a local district legislator to sell marked-up fertilizer in the area. Such undertakings served to amplify the anticorruption image he projected through his public appearances and the media coverage he received.

Ambo's strategy, which he maintained throughout the campaign, entailed the mobilization of a strong anticorruption identity and a firm repudiation of those who asked for something in return for their votes. He was angered by requests for goods and money, and he incorporated his rejection of them into his own campaign rhetoric. However, this rejection of vote-buying strategies was not wholesale; Ambo still gave charitable donations, held rallies, bought food, and gave out clothing, all measures that require funds. Ambo expressed annoyance at having to worry about such things when he would have preferred to discuss political issues, but he also conceded that he would hate to lose because of a "little thing, like not giving away t-shirts." Despite these annoyances, he did not shy away from his initial strategy when unofficial polling numbers showed some of his rivals, who he believed to be running a more "traditional" campaign, as doing well. Instead of reassessing his approach, he seemed to ramp-up his use of anticorruption messaging while calling out these practices.

A strong sense of morality drove Ambo's campaign decisions. He knew that the strategy was risky but persisted because he could not bring himself to campaign in any other way. Understanding this, he tried to turn his anticorruption stance to his advantage by being even more vocal about who he was and what he stood for, a position that was enabled by his positionality, both within his party and in the community. As a member of the party's leadership, he had media resources to promote his campaign and boost his name recognition, as well as the support of local party branches. As a member of the community, he had the connections to help him meet with the right people, and this social capital offered a basis to foster trust with voters. Ambo railed against the electoral norms and, more or less, maintained his values in the process. But without party support, local connections, and his personal profile, he may well have acquiesced or integrated money politics strategies into his campaign.

Acquiescence

In Ayu's experience in East Java, we see an example of acquiescence—where the candidate made significant changes to her campaign strategy because of the consistent requests for money, particularly during village visits, and because of advice she received from her campaign team. Although she began her campaign accepting that she would have to distribute some money, she imagined that she could do so in a way that accorded with her sense of being a good person, namely through charitable donations to mosques and community groups. After months of campaigning visits and meetings, she felt worn down by direct requests for goods, money, and other favors. Feeling that her attempts to win support through building an anticorruption image was failing, Ayu changed tack. While she maintained that she was completely against individual payments for votes, she began funding some small-scale infrastructure works, made donations to Islamic boarding schools, and even contributed to a local martial arts group. Later, she began distributing money to local leaders under the thinly veiled language of "donations." She claimed this was the fault of the voters, who demanded "gifts."

In the end, Ayu could not imagine a successful outcome by simply continuing in her efforts to appeal to people's desire to see an Indonesia free of corruption. With her sense of agency slipping away, her campaign team recruited a small group of local brokers who received a payment in return for promising to source votes. On numerous occasions, she expressed a fear that she would be betrayed by those who were supposed to be helping her. In the absence of strong local networks to inform her about the lay of the land, Ayu was reliant on advice from her campaign team, who convinced her to engage in vote buying in the later stages of her campaign. She had never before run a successful electoral campaign, and she deferred often to this team for advice. In the end, Ayu used brokers to distribute money to voters because she did not believe she could win any other way. After the election was over, she was disappointed that the votes she thought she had secured did not materialize.

In her ongoing search for "advantage," Ayu not only increased upon the amount she planned to distribute but also made a last-minute decision to change tandem partners. She perceived her earlier choices of campaign partnerships as a poor choice and shifted to align herself with more endowed candidates competing for provincial and local legislatures. But even this put additional strain on her campaign, as she was asked to contribute to large, festival-like rallies and pay for expensive door prizes like motorcycles. She couched her decision to compromise and partake in activities that she had initially rejected as inevitable, and she genuinely saw no other way to win. Despite almost eighteen months of planning, traveling through the electoral district, and speaking to countless groups, she ultimately handed large sums of cash to various brokers, with the implication that the money was to be distributed directly to voters. However, the deep frustration and disappointment that plagued Ayu when she lost did not come from spending this money (although this did not help) but rather from the fact that her campaign strategy had turned into something that no longer aligned with her sense of self. And while she acknowledged that her choices were her own, she blamed voters for forcing her into an untenable position.

Integration

By the time the 2014 elections came around, Bontor was a seasoned politician. He had run for office before and understood what it entailed. He had seen rivals win and lose and had determined, based on past experience, a reliable path to success. Bontor was a self-identified anticorruption candidate, but he also accepted that the distribution of money was a normal campaign activity. He did not have a strong moral objection to cash payments to voters, arguing that the "end" of his anticorruption work in the legislature justified these cash payments as a "means." Vote buying was one aspect of his campaign strategy, which sat alongside his attempts to shore up support in his strongholds by solidifying his reputation as a caring member of the local community—and someone who was always willing to help a friend. Bontor's campaign approached voters from different angles, aimed at deriving advantage through every means he saw available. As the most experienced of the three candidates, he had spent so long in politics that he had rationalized his choices to the point that he felt relaxed about his strategy, even though, to an outside observer, it seemed somewhat paradoxical to present as a corruption-fighter while handing out cash at rallies.

Bontor felt he could rely on his voter base not only because they had voted for him in previous elections but because he had worked hard to convince them that he cared about them during his successive terms in office. As an incumbent, he could tout the benefits he had brought to his constituency over years of being a national legislator, channeling local projects to their areas, and keeping a national focus on their local needs. For Bontor, these projects offered additional leverage to his claims for reelection, establishing him as a patron and fostering what seemed to be patronage ties within his electoral district. But this alone, to his mind, was not enough to ensure success. For those who had not been convinced by these efforts, there was cash to sweeten the deal. With this in mind, Bontor's campaign had an embedded duality from the very beginning. On the one hand, speaking out against corruption was an important element of his personal brand. But at the same time, he was a pragmatic campaigner who understood the importance of distributing money. He rationalized this primarily as a reward to his loyal base of voters, many of whom were linked by ethnic Batak kinship ties. He would distribute gifts during rallies, while also speaking to the gathered crowd about the need to vote for candidates who would not steal money from the country. When asked about this dissonance, Bontor argued that it was not hypocritical to do both: he was a good legislator, who did what was best for the people, even though he had seen fellow legislators repeatedly do the wrong thing. If he wanted to be generous and use some of his money to throw a party or give small gifts to his constituents, then that was his prerogative.

Bontor's case also reflects the clearest example of clientelism within the three election campaigns. But, although he spoke frequently about his connections in the community, people he had done (legal) favors for, and his channeling of government funding to his strongholds, it is evident that he did not categorize these activities as undesirable, let alone as immoral. Thus, the integration of this strategy with anticorruptionism was not problematic for Bontor. In fact, in not attempting to rationalize this behavior at all, I sensed that Bontor saw it as simply part of his job. In contrast to cash payments, which he justified in terms of gift-giving and Batak culture, he framed the delivery of patronage to areas of support as part of his responsibility as a conscientious local representative. These benefits could be leveraged for support, but the (stated) justification *for* them was not to develop or maintain support but to serve his community. With his unproblematic approach to the inherent ethics of using government resources to address community concerns, it was easy for Bontor to maintain an integrated campaign. Although an outsider might have concerns about the hypocrisy of presenting as an anticorruption candidate while undertaking strategies that funneled government funding in beneficial ways, this simply did not appear to cross Bontor's mind.

Bontor's comparatively lighthearted approach to the campaign also reflected the benefits of incumbency and his long history in government. I do not believe that Bontor ever thought losing was possible, though he left nothing to chance. More votes were more votes, and the more he got, the more confident he could be of his place in the party and of his own appeal. But with his local reputation relatively secure, he was able to the assert an anticorruption identity that was more intimately tied to his persona as a national legislator than as a campaigner. For Bontor, these were different realms with different rules. Campaigns demanded one set of behavior, where money was a legitimate means of persuasion, while his role in the national legislature demanded that he behave another way and vehemently eschew expenses that he characterized as being contrary to the public interest. His profile in Jakarta circles, and among his party leadership, was built on his image as a corruption fighter. And if he had conducted himself well in politics, well, why not use that reputation in his campaign? He had earned the reputation and it was his to use.

Negotiating the Dilemma

Money politics, and vote buying more specifically, is considered part and parcel of elections in Indonesia. The experience of the three candidates described in this book demonstrate that this was indeed the case in the regions where they were campaigning, and that it forced each of them to make judgments about how money politics would influence their strategies for success. At the outset of their campaigns, all three were committed to presenting themselves as antitheses to the stereotype of the corrupt politician, interested only in furthering their own power—and wealth and that of their associates—drawing on anticorruptionism as a means for presenting this image. Although they were well-connected within their parties, each candidate's initial decision to present themselves as clean was ultimately an individual one because their parties did not police what they (or any other candidates, for that matter) said and did during their campaigns. Drawing on anticorruptionism was a response to their context; having considered myriad factors, they believed this strategy would help them win. Each happened to be aligned with their party's national campaign messaging, but this was the case because these *individual candidates* decided it should be so.

For Ayu and Ambo, this idealized vision was tested as the campaign progressed. Bontor's campaign strategy had been constructed quite differently, as he accepted early on that vote buying was "just the way things are." Nevertheless, the dilemma for all three candidates lay in how they perceived and negotiated two different functions of campaigns—persuading voters versus embodying their persona—and how they responded to challenges that forced them to decide which one is more important. Here lies the crux of the conundrum for genuine anticorruption candidates: is it more important to uphold one's values and self-identification as clean or to capitulate to electoral norms that hold vote buying as the essential "entry ticket" needed to be competitive?[10] This is never a black-and-white decision, and there may also be an ongoing negotiation and process of rationalization where context becomes crucial—could there be an effective way to do both?

Assertions that money politics is a reflection of society, or even cultural norms that have crossed over to become electoral norms, is something to consider when assessing these responses. All three candidates conceded that money politics was ubiquitous. They also, at various points, described it as something that "voters want," suggesting that they believed money politics was indeed "demand driven."[11] Ambo and Ayu even branded the requests from voters as irrational and against voters' best interests if they wanted an Indonesia free of corruption. Of course, these perspectives were self-serving insofar that they allowed the candidates to invoke narratives of victimhood without considering how voters construe their interests and the role of national legislators in realizing those interests. But, regardless of how the rationality of money politics was understood, these candidates certainly felt the pressure to adopt the practice. In terms of decision-making agency, this left them with three choices: either attempt to integrate vote buying while maintaining anticorruptionism, acquiesce to these commonly held electoral norms and relinquish the use of anticorruptionism, or reject these demands altogether. These candidates had money and could, and did, use it in their campaigns—meaning that, unlike candidates without enough funds to even consider a vote-buying strategy, they faced a genuine choice. The decisions they made reflected their operating context and their sense of power (or powerlessness) in eschewing vote buying as a strategy.

Determining how important it was to buy votes, and how it was construed within the bounds of campaign norms, depended on the candidate. The ability to maintain a particular course of action in the face of resistance also shifted during the campaign. Bontor's campaign was the most stable. From the beginning, he imagined a multifaceted campaign, which amalgamated anticorruption rhetoric, channeled his aspiration funds, and distributed cash. He was pragmatic about these tactics, having long decided that vote buying was a necessary component of election campaigns. His previous experience, local networks, and confidence in his reputation as a legislator shielded him from self-doubt, allowing him to maintain his initial campaign strategy to the end. He did not problematize his behavior and voters seemed to respond positively to his campaign, additionally shielding him from introspection that might lead him to doubt his approach.

Likewise, Ambo had local ties and enough self-assurance to believe that an anticorruption-centered campaign could win him a seat in the legislature. His open disdain for local leaders who accepted money or favors from politicians was evident throughout his campaign, only intensifying in response to the corrupt behavior of his rivals. Unlike Bontor, he was a relative newcomer to politics with a somewhat radical, unyielding approach. Yet while his personal commitment to the anticorruption issue was a key driver for his strategy, without the other aspects of his positionality the pressure to acquiesce to vote buying would surely have been more intense. It would be interesting to see how Ambo would have negotiated his campaign if he had been an incumbent like Bontor and whether he would have used his incumbency to develop patronage ties within the community. But, having spent time with Ambo in the field, it is hard for me to imagine him compromising on this front since it was so closely tied to his own self of sense and his political identity was so closely linked to his personal history as a long-term corruption fighter. He was his campaign, and his campaign was him. He would rather present himself as a crusader and lose than to compromise his values in order to win.

The election game was quite different for Ayu, whose case is illustrative of the potential for asserting pressure on candidates who feel anxious about their prospects and are not fixed in their ideology. Ayu came across as staunch in her initial musings about being an anticorruption champion in the legislature and running a clean campaign, especially as it matched so neatly within her party's official stance on the issue. Her eventual decisions, however, reflected a recalculation about the utility of maintaining this strategy. Even before she overtly bought votes, she was already trying to curry favor with voters by providing targeted funding to various community groups. Being in the public eye and asking that voters choose them over numerous other options makes candidates vulnerable to all kinds of pressures and demands. Ayu could have continued on her initial path but came to believe that this would certainly result in failure—something she was not willing to accept. As she saw it, the alternative was to align more with the very campaign norms she had originally disparaged. Had Ayu been fortunate enough to have the local connections that Bontor and Ambo enjoyed, this choice may not have been so stark. But as an outsider candidate in a realm where connections meant so much and without much support from her own party cadres, she felt she had no real choice. As an observer, watching her campaign change in this way was jarring. With her sense of agency slipping away, Ayu went from a candidate who "didn't want to win [using money politics]" to one who gave her campaign team permission to actively seek out brokers and approach communities with promises of funds or small-scale projects.

The contrasts between these candidates' experiences are both confronting and informative. Each candidate followed a different path, subjected to a multitude of factors that influenced the ease with which they could access and appeal to voters. The observable variances between the experiences reflect the importance of context in shaping the way that electoral candidates engage with their campaigns. None of these factors can be used in isolation to explain why certain candidates decide to use anticorruptionism as a campaign strategy or what allows them to maintain it as a strategy throughout their campaign. It is the way that different dynamics interacted, and how candidates interpreted them, that ultimately influenced the resulting campaign and the candidates' responses to the dilemma they faced.

Law No. 10/2008 on the General Election of Members for the DPR, DPD, and DPRD clearly forbids the use of any incentives to gain votes. The fact that this behavior is common campaign practice means that candidates must decide how to confront the challenges this posed. If we consider a literal reading of the legislative rules surrounding electoral campaigns, all three candidates, to some extent, broke the law. But if we gauge their actions against the backdrop of campaign norms, their responses can be seen as walking a line between illegal yet licit practices. Where this line fell in each case was mostly determined by each candidate's ability to rationalize their actions in the face of their personal values and the external pressures they confronted. The process and outcomes of this rationalization varied significantly because the candidates were operating in vastly different contexts, especially in terms of their social capital and community ties, and the way they could leverage their prior experience—as in Bontor's case, using his incumbency—to pave the way for their campaign.

Campaigns, in their early stages, draw from the candidate's imagined ideas of what voters want and what they will respond to, and how this intersects with the image that they would like to present. However, the reality of voter attitudes can challenge a candidate's initial strategy. And, once campaigns have begun in earnest, candidates find themselves looking for ways to ingratiate themselves with voters. These pressures necessarily become more pronounced as election day draws closer. In exploring these candidates' actions in the face of these pressures, this chapter has offered a brief typology of possible responses to the negotiation between asserting an anticorruption identity and engaging in money politics: a strong rejection of money politics, an acquiescence to voter demands during the course of the campaign, and an integration of vote buying with other strategies. For Bontor (despite his close community ties and connections), and eventually for Ayu, the opportunity cost of not engaging in money politics was perceived as being too high. But for Ambo it was not high enough.

As the chapter has shown, the (varying) ability of the three candidates to maintain their initial strategy was closely tied to their positionality, values, and agency in being able to derive advantage from their situation. These insights help us better understand the pressures associated with money politics, and how they manifest within an individual's campaign. However, they also have wider implications. What does it say when electoral candidates who *want* to win citizens over by presenting themselves as clean feel pressure to capitulate to the very practices they claim to oppose? What might foster the juxtaposition of anticorruptionism and the normalization of illegal campaign behavior? With elections forming the basis for political power in government, better understanding why candidates behave in the way they do can help shine a light on what it might take to disrupt the ubiquity of money politics in Indonesia and elsewhere.

CONCLUSION

Understanding what influences electoral campaigns and campaign creation provides insight into how parties and politicians leverage the electoral process to legitimize their claims to power. At the same time, a deeper inspection of how campaigns manifest and shift reveals what influences the decisions behind them. Electoral campaigns are much more than slogans, speeches, and rallies; they are an incarnation of the contexts that produce them. Context underpins every decision in electoral campaigns and the mobilization of anticorruptionism, and the consistency (or lack thereof) in its use by the candidates whose stories feature in this book is a visible manifestation of context. Context is layered, ranging from the broad and macro to the nuanced and micro, and from the universal to the deeply personal. Institutions and political history create a canvas, but candidates hold the paintbrush and decide what picture they will paint. As they do so, they draw upon what I call "imaginaries" to plan their campaign approach. They imagine what it will take to win—who they will have to win over and how to do this—and they plan a campaign that aligns with this imaginary. This imaginary draws from extant institutions, salient contemporary issues, understandings of campaign norms, and assumptions about voters.

It would be trite to simply assert that context matters—of course it does. Instead, this book moves beyond this assertion to describe how, and in what ways, context influences the development of individual electoral campaigns. Here, context extends beyond macro influences, such as electoral regulations, issue salience, and far-reaching campaign norms to include micro influences specific to the candidates themselves. Strategy is then further shaped by what resources the candidate has access to, be they financial or social, and how they can muster them. Finally, it is about their values—about how far they are willing to push their personal boundaries and make compromises in order to be successful. In this way, candidates interpret their environments through an individual lens, generating unique responses to what is happening around them. Interrogating the dilemma that self-proclaimed "anticorruption candidates" face when their imagined self-image is confronted by the realities of electioneering allows us to unravel the motivations, intentions, and tensions behind selecting particular strategies, in these cases, the rationalizations behind the use or rejection, or something in between, of money politics as a strategy for electoral success.

Unpacking the Dilemma

A careful consideration of Indonesia's broad political landscape provides some rationale as to why anticorruptionism has come to be such a prevalent, almost "safe" platform for new parties, and such a risky strategy for older parties. Corruption is a constant theme in Indonesia's post-colonial history. It was especially salient in the 2014 elections, which were preceded by a raft of high-profile corruption scandals linked to politicians and former politicians associated with a number of political parties. The fallout from these scandals demonstrated that there can be consequences for parties that use anticorruptionism to appeal to voters but then fail to live up to their promises. The Democratic Party, for example, had declared "say no to corruption" in the 2009 general election. In subsequent years, several of its members were involved in corruption scandals, which garnered extensive media coverage. The party's electoral standing declined significantly in 2014, when it gained less than half the number of national legislative seats it had received in 2009. This steep decline in votes may be partially attributable to the presidential term limit, which meant the party could no longer leverage Yudhoyono's personal appeal in its campaign. But, although the success of the Democratic Party was closely tied to Yudhoyono's persona, past events had confirmed the party was imbued with clientelistic interests. The additional negative public attention also served to severely undermine its popularity (Hamayotsu 2015). Similarly, PKS—a party that appealed to Islamic piety and morality, and which had portrayed itself as a bastion against corruption—suffered allegations of hypocrisy after its leader and a national legislator from the party were arrested and convicted of graft. PKS lost seventeen seats in the national legislature in 2014. Thus, while adoption of an anticorruption platform may have been tempting, given the scope of the problem and dissatisfaction with the status quo, it also carried the risk of backlash when parties or politicians failed to live up to their promises.

The public backlash against these parties and their scandals fueled anticorruption candidates' assumptions that there would be a critical mass of voters who would be swayed by a stated commitment to fighting corruption. These candidates imagined their campaigns in terms of "oppositional actions," taking their resistance of norms and weaponizing them to attack—either overtly or subtly—those who are a part of the status quo.[1] At the same time, they imagined themselves as being able to own this discourse and present it convincingly to voters. However, upon closer inspection, when and how this oppositional sentiment extended to the campaign, and how it interacted with decisions to participate in vote buying, were complicated. This was not a zero-sum game for anticorruption candidates. It was possible to comfortably reconcile both anticorruptionism and illegal money politics practices within one campaign, as Bontor's experience shows. Here, the candidate viewed the two strategies as divorced from one another, not necessarily identifying a paradox in using both simultaneously. Protecting the nation from the self-interest of politicians was his responsibility as a legislator, and he saw himself as having lived up to that responsibility. At the same time, his campaign practices were framed in terms of what would appeal to voters and what they wanted. In these explanations, discussion of the law and the legality of these practices was noticeably absent. His arguments against vote buying were primarily put forth in terms of it being a waste of money for those candidates who did not have the networks or the name recognition to make the expenditure worthwhile. It is possible that Bontor was being disingenuous in framing his cash exchanges and gifts in cultural terms or describing his channeling of *dana aspirasi*, or aspiration funds, to his strongholds as simply fulfilling his duty as a local representative. But if this is the case, it means that he felt the need to create and offer logical mechanisms to justify his actions, not only to me but to himself.

For Ayu and Ambo, the dilemma was much more pronounced. They had, early on, identified a relationship between rejecting vote-buying practices and broader anticorruption ideals. In this conceptualization of the problem, money politics—at least, explicit exchanges of money or goods in return for votes—was irreconcilable with presenting as an anticorruption candidate. Here, contextual factors also played a role in how the dilemma ultimately impacted their campaigns. As Ayu struggled, her campaign shifted. The donations she had made early on in her campaign were easily explained as acts of benevolence that built her profile, but this became more difficult as her campaign progressed, and she increasingly came to rely on transactions. This raises questions of how committed she was to anticorruption ideals in the first place and whether it was nothing more than self-serving rhetoric. I believe Ayu felt genuinely conflicted about how to progress her campaign and that she was uncomfortable with the path she ended up taking. But while she lay the blame for this on voters, it also says much about her own values and what she was willing to give up to have a chance at winning. After all, her party was not holding her to account for her strategy and the likelihood of facing criminal charges was remote. When she shifted to incorporate more explicit vote-buying practices into her campaign, her use of anticorruptionism visibly diminished as she felt she could no longer lay claim to that identity. She felt the tension of the dilemma acutely and without other resources to allay her fear of failure she chose a path justified by the end goal: a better opportunity of winning.

Ambo's response to the dilemma was also nuanced, even though he maintained a steady rejection of vote buying. He drew a correlation between vote buying in elections and the ubiquity of corruption in Indonesia. But he was not immune to spending money and giving charitable donations which, like Ayu, he explained with discourses of benevolence and profile raising. Unlike Ayu, though, his use of anticorruptionism intensified as he learned more about his rivals' campaign strategies. His concern that he might lose because others were buying votes did not result in him following suit; instead, it reinforced his commitment to his initial course of action—to present himself to voters as a genuine anticorruption candidate. To understand this decision, we need to consider Ambo's circumstances, which were very different to Ayu's. But beyond all the contextual factors that played into Ambo's favor was his conviction that he would rather lose than do something he could not countenance morally.

At its core, the dilemma that these candidates faced is a manifestation of the tension between an election's "official" and "unofficial" rules. The official rules dictate that using money to influence voters is illegal. The unofficial rules suggest that if you *don't* offer financial incentives to voters then you will not stand a chance. The pressure to conform to norms can be "near-magnetic . . . compelling [people] . . . to fit in or risk censure [or] condemnation" (Bobel and Kwan 2011, 1). To resist money politics in an environment where it has become normalized is an act of rebellion. In a way, candidates who genuinely want to challenge the electoral norms of money politics are embodiments of resistance. Breaking from norms and integrating a rejection of money politics into a campaign strategy amounts to a refusal to "play by the rules." But all acts of resistance have uncertain outcomes. Plans may follow their initial trajectory, or they may veer off course; resistance may succeed or fail. The outcomes of resistance represent the tension between compliance and self-determination. At the same time, dissecting individual cases compels us to move beyond this dichotomy and explore the nuances of decision making. Compromises occur in degrees, and their nature and scope are driven by the context in which an individual candidate operates.

Decisions in Context

Running for election in a democratic system necessarily involves some level of competition. During the New Order, elections were primarily an exercise to legitimize Suharto's regime. Elections in the post-1998 period have proven to be far more intense contests. The national legislative elections allow political parties to assert power over the enactment of laws and budgetary decisions, as well as determining their influence in presidential nominations. For individual candidates, elections are hotly contested and nothing is a foregone conclusion. At the same time, the emotional toll of these negotiations may wane over time, and experienced incumbents may be more attuned to and accepting of campaign norms. But although incumbency may offer some advantage, it does not negate the need to campaign effectively and persuasively appeal to citizens' interests—whatever these may be.

Against this overarching backdrop, individuals weigh their unique contexts and make decisions about whether anticorruptionism is a strategy worth mobilizing. Many choose not to, heeding the potential risks and considering their own personal histories, values, and resources. Some, however, decide that an anticorruption identity is desirable, appropriate, and achievable. Although there are observable patterns that explain why some adopt anticorruptionism while others do not, the precise reasons for that decision are unique to each candidate. Some might see anticorruptionism as an important personal value. Others may simply lack the money to buy votes. But, whatever the motivation, candidates who wish to present themselves as clean may find themselves in a precarious position. In some situations, they find that their anticorruption rhetoric simply does not resonate; voters are either not interested in it, or in them. In other cases, voters ask candidates directly for money. Many candidate–voter interactions fall somewhere in between, replete with hints that donations or other benefits will be paid for in votes. The direction that individual campaigns take in response to these interactions depends heavily on how far candidates are willing to compromise on their anticorruption ideals. While some crumble, others withstand the pressure to varying degrees.

In the Introduction, I presented a generalized decision–outcome model for anticorruption candidates' responses to money politics, which takes into account the candidates' inherent commitment to anticorruptionism, but also its perceived utility in the context of their individual campaign. This model delineates four possible outcomes of the decision-making process: acceptance, integration, acquiescence, and rejection. These broad categories capture the different outcomes of candidates' engagement with the dilemma they face. Candidates' perception of the utility of an anticorruption identity is, in turn, driven by their context. In particular, their social networks and their ability to amass support without resorting to vote buying are key. At the same time, a candidate's definition of what it means to be against corruption and the mobilization of this identity in a campaign varies from individual to individual, as is evident in the campaigns of Ambo, Ayu, and Bontor.

The matrix on decision-making outcomes, as outlined in the Introduction, can be used as a basis for categorizing candidate responses but also to interrogate what it takes to change the course of a campaign. Of the three candidates in this study, Ayu shifted furthest in her campaign strategy, moving from an initial rejection of money politics (as she defined it) to acquiescing to the practice while simultaneously erasing anticorruptionism as part of her campaign messaging. Ayu's decisions offer the most depressing insight into how pressure to engage in money politics can affect candidates. Her case also crystalizes the importance of an individual's personal context in shaping their decisions. Had she lacked the money to engage in direct vote buying, she would not have had the option to engage in money politics, and so would have had no choice but to reject it. If she had run in an electoral district where she had strong community ties, like Ambo, would she have reacted differently? Possibly. What if she had felt better supported by her political party and received more backing from local cadres? This may have helped negate the sense of hopelessness she experienced. All of these conditionalities and possibilities highlight the deeply individual nature of campaigns.

By contrast, Ambo's strong local ties and reputation gave him reason to hope that voters would choose him regardless of whether he gave them something directly in return during the campaign. In other words, his rejection of money politics occurred in a situation where he believed he could win without it. Equally salient, however, was the fact that he was not open to changing his tactics. Ultimately, this was what led him to maintain a steady course throughout his campaign. Bontor's case is, meanwhile, different again. His campaign course, the result of years of experience, started with a strategy that integrated both anticorruptionism and money politics. The way he conceptualized himself as an anticorruption candidate did not require him to choose between these two campaign strategies, and so he was able to marry both. It is unclear whether Bontor really thought he would lose if he did not offer small cash payments but, clearly, he was not willing to risk it. At the same time, he was confident that his track record spoke for itself. He *was* an anticorruption fighter; his actions in the legislature were proof of this. Bontor's unique position gave him the opportunity to integrate money politics into his broader anticorruption campaign—a path that would certainly not be available to many other candidates.

The cases examined in this book demonstrate that the decisions facing anticorruption candidates, and their engagement with vote buying, are not straightforward. Even more striking are the inner negotiations in which anticorruption candidates must engage to rationalize their decisions. Although Ambo, Ayu, and Bontor could easily reconcile the need to hand out t-shirts and food, engagement in any more serious forms of money politics was not necessarily a given. In reflecting on their experiences, some candidate stereotypes were challenged while others were validated. But, more important, these stories underscore the value of the individual perspective when trying to understand candidate behavior. They also encourage us to consider these dilemmas and the outcomes as reactions to multiple factors, interpreted through a deeply personal lens. Candidates do not simply fall into specific behavioral patterns. More accurately, campaigns are a series of decisions, sometimes made under immense pressure, that capture the essence of what a candidate wants to achieve and what they are willing to do to achieve it, within the parameters of their personal context.

Beyond the Case Studies

The focus of this study has been on elections in Indonesia and the experiences of three "anticorruption" candidates against the landscape of the 2014 national legislative elections. However, the implications of this study are far reaching. First, it offers lessons for political scientists who might hope to conduct similar studies in other parts of Indonesia or the world. By conceptualizing the campaign context in holistic terms and inviting analysis that considers both overarching national and local factors as well as individual circumstances, it invites researchers to move beyond one- or two-dimensional explanations for campaign behavior. Further, in beginning the process by exploring the political history of elections and of corruption as a political issue, then shifting to the personal stories of candidates, it elucidates the importance of broadly considering context from a macro and micro perspective, following the model proposed in chapter 1. This approach encourages us to consider the nuances of campaigns, highlighting the influence of their dynamic nature on when and why a candidate will make a particular decision. It also brings into focus why considering decisions against the backdrop of context can help to explain shifts, or indeed the steadfastness, of some campaign strategies.

Second, the study demonstrates the value of the extended case study in understanding why candidates make the decisions they make over time. If I had only interviewed Ayu at the beginning or end of her campaign, I would have had a very different understanding of her experience. At the beginning, I would have heard from an idealistic candidate who was determined to do whatever she could to remain as clean as possible. At the end, I would have encountered a disheartened candidate who had spent money trying to induce voters, without the desired result. The value of long-term ethnography is apparent in that, without it, I could never have tracked, let alone witnessed, the morphing of her campaign. Similarly, speaking to Ambo as he felt dejected, even though his bid for public office was successful, could only make sense with the knowledge of how consistently he had tried to maintain his rejection of money politics, as best he could, throughout his campaign. This book highlights the benefits of this methodological approach, which combines deep country knowledge with extensive field-based research, and how it can complement other forms of research on electoral campaigns.

There are two questions that a researcher should take to heart if considering replicating this study elsewhere: what are the external contexts that shape the candidate's campaign landscape and what are the internal (personal) contexts that cause a candidate to either accept, integrate, acquiesce to, or reject certain electoral norms? The approach used by this study, where the researcher engages in "dialogues" with participants, local processes and forces, and theory, makes it possible to provide nuanced answers to these questions. As such, it presents a potential way forward for researchers looking to explore the contexts and motivations behind campaign decisions more generally. In essence, this work offers a model for study and analysis that combines deep country knowledge with extensive field-based research to better understand why candidates make the decisions that they do. For researchers looking to apply this research to other case studies in Indonesia or further afield, it demonstrates a way for combining three different lenses—using dialogue with candidates, local forces and processes, and theory—to untangle the relationship between individuals and context as the candidates plan and execute their campaigns.

Prospects for Democracy

This study has demonstrated how the contest for power and the influence of money play out against this national backdrop in more localized environments. The way in which a candidate navigates their local environment depends on who they are. It is not simply about money, because—as Ambo's experience has shown—it is possible to win without a heavy reliance on money politics. Conversely, as Ayu's experience demonstrates, money offers no guarantees. There is more at play here: connections, community embeddedness, and local profile are important factors. But this, too, points to underlying inequalities in the way elections are run. Local elites (financial and social) rarely stumble into these positions; they are frequently born out of privilege offered by inherited wealth or social standing. The wealthy businessman is more likely than his poorer counterpart to have connections across his electoral district and opportunities to develop patronage ties that he can capitalize on in the course of an election. A woman from a prominent local family, widely respected in the community, will have name recognition that other candidates do not. Incumbents, in particular, often have advantages on multiple fronts. But again, these are circumstances that must be leveraged for votes. They do not guarantee success in and of themselves.

In focusing on the decision-making dilemmas of certain individuals, this book has highlighted the challenges faced by candidates who proclaim themselves to be against corruption. As it has shown, the choice to run on an anticorruption platform is frequently a moral decision in an environment where competition is fierce and those who engage in money politics are unlikely to be punished. Anticorruption candidates choose to adopt this strategy because they cannot, or do not want to, engage in money politics, not because they fear the penalty for doing so. But campaigns also have to resonate with voters in order for them to win. As Aspinall and Berenschot (2019) contend, political parties and the national legislature seem far removed from the realities of day-to-day life. Most voters perceive the benefits that flow from Jakarta to their communities as being channeled through bureaucrats, rather than politicians. As a result, the impact of national legislators on a voter's lived reality is rarely visible. Voter demands for money or goods may present a challenge to candidates, but these demands are understandable if citizens cannot connect the work of national legislative members to their own lives.

Ideally, voters are adequately informed about their options and have a deep understanding of the consequences of their decisions, and the majority of candidates would act with integrity in their campaigns. But in Indonesia, as in many other countries, these ideal conditions are absent. This assessment brings the role of candidates to the fore in questions of how to improve the electoral system and the quality of democracy in Indonesia. When Indonesia began a democratization process following over thirty years under the New Order regime, many were hopeful that this would change the nature of government. But the democratization process remains "incomplete."[2] As Fish, Wittenberg, and Jakli (2018) observe, Indonesia could be classified as a "tenuous democratizer," based on Freedom House measures that found the nature of the country's democracy was neither robust nor had failed. In examining who is responsible for the state of democracy, they suggest that there are five key "agents of democratic failures"—the masses, insurgents, meddling foreign powers, power-seeking armed forces, and despotic chief executives (Fish et al. 2018, 279). Neglected in this assessment, but demanding consideration, is the electoral candidate. Most candidates fail in their responsibility to enact their campaigns legally, especially with the onus to self-regulate, in the absence of official checks and balances.

If contests for power are held under conditions that encourage rather than dissuade illegal practices, the question then becomes, what, if anything, can be done to move closer to a better quality of democracy? Outcomes of democratic elections have a profound effect on the trajectory of a state—its priorities, processes, and engagement with citizens. The circumstances under which candidates become members of the legislature sets the tone for their behavior in office. Dispensing large sums of money in order to be elected provides sitting legislators with a motivation to engage in activities that help them, and their parties, to recoup funds used during campaigns. Furthermore, elites and oligarchic actors continue to enjoy an advantage in electoral contests by virtue of their power and deep pockets, and their interests continue to dominate the political sphere. This situation is not unique to Indonesia—even in contexts where vote buying is negligible, electoral campaigns often incorporate fundraising efforts to raise the money needed to cover costs associated with electioneering. While having more money cannot guarantee victory, it can certainly make inroads to purchasing advertising space, holding rallies, paying campaign consultants, and funding the myriad activities that are part and parcel of a campaign.

Furthermore, the study confirms previous insights that the rule of law is poorly enforced and candidates are largely left to their own devices. Indonesia has a law regulating the use of money in electoral campaigns, but it is frequently ignored. Candidates who attempt to act "morally"—following the rules, acting with integrity, and rejecting widely accepted electoral norms—do not necessarily reap the rewards of their efforts. It is also clear that presuming candidates will police their own campaigns has failed as a strategy for ensuring that most campaigns run in accordance with the law. Furthermore, as this study has shown, candidates who want to do the right thing are confronted by many obstacles in their efforts to win office on the back of a clean campaign. And, if the majority of legislature is elected thanks to money politics, what incentive exists to better regulate elections? There is much to gain in the maintenance of the status quo for those embedded in the system. But if these are also the very people with the power to increase electoral oversight, who can publicly call on bureaucrats and law enforcement agencies to better monitor and sanction undemocratic activity, then it seems unlikely that the pattern of money politics will diminish. A circuit breaker is needed—though pondering, in detail, what form(s) this may take is a question for a different study.

At this point, it is worth returning to the debate over the role of voters in vote buying/vote selling. My interpretation of the campaigns I studied is that, on the one hand, voters in some places have been conditioned by previous elections to believe that serious candidates will agree to provide incentives—money, goods, services, or promises—in return for support. Therefore, they do not see an issue for asking for such things and often do so before candidates offer any such incentives. This understanding is predicated on past experiences that affirm that it is both normal and acceptable to do so. On the other hand, some candidates feel pressure to capitulate to these requests because they worry about their ability to win without resorting to vote buying. Insofar as there is scope for blame, it is ultimately the candidates who decide whether to engage in the practice. This also is where the legislation guiding election campaigns places culpability—on candidates. But this situation cannot be divorced from context. If the post-1998 process of democratization had given rise to a different set of electoral norms, then candidates would no doubt be grappling with those instead. It is not necessarily the fault of today's candidates that they are held to expectations that developed through voters' lived experiences of previous elections.

Ultimately, the dichotomy of blame that the "vote buying versus vote selling debate" feels unhelpful in its implication that if one side is at fault then the other must be innocent. My research supports the notion that the phenomenon, as it existed for the case study candidates, resembles a feedback loop rather than a linear process. The loop has its roots in electoral history and the voter expectations that previous experiences have generated, while there is also pressure on candidates to comply with these expectations. The initial causes of this loop first manifested many elections ago. Since the behavior has become embedded, and there are potential advantages and disadvantages on both sides of the equation, overcoming this specific form of money politics requires breaking the circuit. Legislative efforts to criminalize vote buying have clearly failed—though this seems more a consequence of lack of implementation rather than a problem of the law itself. Conversely, efforts to discourage voters to engage in this practice have not fostered the kind of large-scale rejection of money politics required to prevent masses of voters from opting to accept economic incentives to channel their votes to specific candidates. There is work to be done on both sides.

What does all this mean for future campaigns and elections in Indonesia? First, we know that the government has failed to hold candidates accountable for breaches of the law. Second, attempts to discourage voters from requesting or accepting inducements for their votes are wanting. The transfer of money and goods is likely to continue in the absence of a more comprehensive understanding of the role played by politicians in shaping citizens' lives and the detrimental effects that vote buying can have beyond the election itself. This suggests that money politics will continue to play an important role in future elections. Indeed, reporting on the 2019 elections showed no signs of a reduction in its prevalence (Hadiz 2019).[3] Electoral institutions that aspire to support a better quality of democracy should do something to level the playing field for candidates. Observing how institutional factors influence individual campaigns underscores that the government has some way to go in improving the quality of elections. In particular, it highlights that institutions need to be sensitive to the unintended consequences of the electoral rules enacted and responsive to problems that might arise. For example, when the Constitutional Court ruled on the open-party list in 2009, the justification given was that a closed-party list "motivated candidates to prioritize close relations with the central party leadership" rather than the citizens they were supposed to represent (Butt 2015a, 156). But this ruling opened a floodgate, intensifying competition—and money politics—in elections. More tellingly, the government has not prioritized efforts to counter these unintended consequences. Perhaps there are concerns that every court in Indonesia will be flooded with defendants if the law against money politics were to be applied more strictly, putting excessive strain on the judicial system. More likely is that decision-makers worry about their own careers and that of their friends and fellow politicians if the full force of the law is brought to bear on those who flout the electoral rules.

Regardless of the institutional barriers to reform, this study should be of interest to reformers and advisers, in that it draws attention to broader electoral issues in Indonesia and highlights the need for intervention. The prevalence of vote buying is widely acknowledged, but sharing stories of how self-styled anti-corruption candidates make decisions in reaction to this prevalence further elucidates the scope and nature of the issue. That it takes a particular set of contexts and attitudes, ones not shared by many candidates, to maintain a rejection of vote buying during a campaign is telling. This invokes several questions that can be used to guide interventions, such as: What can be done to more systematically encourage stricter adherence to electoral regulations? Mietzner's (2015) call for a more generous and robust system of public subsidies for political parties, tied to better incentives to police candidate behavior, may be one potential policy response, but there would have to be others. What can be done to discourage voters from requesting/accepting financial incentives during an election? Apart from criminalizing the acceptance of money/goods or other promises—an approach that would, admittedly, be even more unwieldy to implement than prosecuting vote-buying candidates—there is some evidence that higher levels of education correlate with negative attitudes toward vote buying in Indonesia (Tawakkal et al. 2017). And how can candidates who want to reject vote buying be better supported? While reforming electoral practices is a long path, and one that may not be a priority for many in government, these initial questions may form the basis for developing new strategies to eventually undermine the prevalence of these practices.

In the meantime, addressing the challenges that anticorruption candidates face—and supporting candidates to win without resorting to illegal behavior—may be a task for smaller scale, nongovernmental actors, or even local communities, to find ways to assist these candidates to stay their course. There is existing evidence that this may work in certain circumstances in Indonesia. Caraway and Ford (2020), in their research on the electoral campaigns of labor union–backed candidates in 2014, found that some candidates were successful without resorting to vote buying. Research from further afield, such as Uganda, also suggests that civil society organizations have had success in shifting electoral norms by encouraging voters to abandon patterns of reciprocity, thus diminishing the returns for candidates who engage in vote buying (Blattman et al. 2019). Efforts such as these should be encouraged in Indonesia, but whether the context allows for comparable results will have to be tested.

Most important, this study has demonstrated that understanding candidate experiences, in an in-depth and nuanced way, matters. Just as they can be agents of democratic failure, they can also be agents for change. Candidates who reject vote buying require support from political parties, encouragement from voters, and, ultimately, need to see a benefit to their strategy to feel confident in their decisions to run counter to electoral norms. The circumstances that would broadly foster this approach, and boost confidence in the utility of presenting and conducting oneself as a clean candidate, do not yet exist in Indonesia. However, if the general dissatisfaction that citizens hold toward politicians and their parties is leveraged to help genuine anticorruption candidates win, then, perhaps, there is hope. The more of these candidates there are in the legislature, the more opportunity there will be to shape the institutions that encourage money politics in elections. But, in the absence of a sweeping, systemic overhaul of the political system, it may fall to citizens' movements to throw their support behind such candidates and give them a reason to stay their course.

Notes

INTRODUCTION

1. What is regarded as corruption under the law may clash with social norms, for example, what King (2000, 618) describes as rifts between legal norms and "folk norms," such as social networks, kinship ties, friendships, patron–client relations, and family loyalty.

2. The edited collection *Checkbook Elections? Political Finance in Comparative Perspective* (Norris and Van Es 2016) offers an excellent range of case studies exploring the role of money in politics in a variety of election case studies from around the globe.

3. Examples of studies from other regions include Africa (Cheeseman 2010; Ferree and Long 2016; Kramon 2018; Van de Walle 2014; Wantchekon 2003), for instance, Ghana (Baidoo, Dankwa, and Eshun 2018), Nigeria (Olaniyan 2020; Sule and Tal 2018), and Zimbabwe (Ndakaripa 2020), and Latin America (Carreras and İrepoğlu 2013; Gonzalez Ocantos, de Jonge, and Nickerson 2014), including Argentina (Brusco, Nazareno, and Stokes 2004) and Brazil (Avelino and Fisch 2019; Samuels 2001). A key study on vote buying in India was conducted by Vaishnav (2017).

4. This figure comes from the Lowy Institute (Bland 2019).

5. Law No. 10/2008 states in article 87(1) that candidates will be sanctioned if it is proven that a campaigner has promised or given money or other goods, directly or indirectly, in return for participants to (a) not use their right to vote, (b) use their right to vote in a way that invalidates their vote, (c) vote for a specific political party participating in the election, (d) select a specific candidate for DPR, DPRD I, or DPRD II or (e) select a specific candidate for the DPD.

6. While political observers agree that money politics is a serious electoral issue in Indonesia, it is difficult to quantify its prevalence. Muhtadi's study (2019, 47) aimed to do this through analyzing survey data, finding that between 25 and 35 percent of voters had received some form of inducement to vote for one or more candidates in the 2014 general election. Although this may seem low, it is both comparatively high by international standards and likely a conservative estimate insofar that survey respondents may have been unwilling to admit to participating in illegal activity.

7. Chen and Weiss (2019) describe anticorruption efforts as political projects. They propose three lenses for understanding the politics of anticorruption efforts, looking at them as driven by private interests, party loyalty, and political institutionalization.

8. I have used pseudonyms and deliberately obscured identities to guard the candidates' privacy and comply with the ethical parameters of the study.

1. COMPETITIVE ELECTIONS AND CAMPAIGN BEHAVIOR

1. Indonesian elections are generally classified as "competitive" but are often described as existing against the backdrop of party "cartelization" (Ambardi 2008; Slater 2004). At the same time, there are debates about how competitive elections can be if the results are heavily influenced by money politics (Hadiz 2004).

2. This rule compels parties to field at least one female candidate to every two male candidates on their party list in every electorate; parties that do not comply are not permitted to compete (Shair-Rosenfield 2012). However, although the gender quota has

shifted the nomination practices of parties, it provides no assurances regarding the final outcome of the election or the gender composition in parliament. The representation of women in Indonesia's legislative assembly remains below both world and regional averages (Prihatini 2019).

3. The circumstances behind the regime change in 1965–1966 and the respective roles of Suharto, members of the military, and the Indonesian Communist Party are far too complex to go into here, but there are several excellent books that discuss this further, including *The Indonesian Killings 1965–1966: Studies from Java and Bali* (Cribb 1990) and *The Army and the Indonesian Genocide: Mechanics of Mass Murder* (Melvin 2018).

4. These functional groups were intended to represent the interests of subsections of society that played an integral role in the "whole," such as women and workers. Under the New Order, the interests of these groups were formally represented in the parliament through Golkar, a political organization that competed in the elections, alongside state-appointed representatives from each of these groups who were also members of the People's Consultative Assembly (Bourchier 2014; Reeve 1985).

5. This particular form of "guided democracy" was presented by the regime as a reflection of the uniqueness of Indonesian society (Anderson 1990, 114; Lev 1966). "Guided Democracy" was a term coined by President Sukarno, Indonesia's first president. With the parliament in disarray and in-fighting among major political players, Sukarno sought to establish a government that balanced his own power with that of the army and the Communist Party. More on the provenance of the term and what it entails can be found in Lev (1966).

6. Pancasila—the national ideology introduced in the 1950s and still in use today—consists of five pillars: belief in one God, a just and civilized humanity, a united Indonesia, leadership through the wisdom of representative parliamentary consensus and social justice for all citizens.

7. *Aliran* was a term coined by anthropologist Clifford Geertz (1976) to describe the different socioreligious clusters that formed 1950s Indonesia to represent the interests of various Islamic subgroups in politics.

8. Golongan Karya (Golkar) was establish by Suharto and presented as a "catch-all" political vehicle that would represent the interests of the broad cross-section of social groups that contributed to Indonesia's social and political well-being (Bourchier 2014). The other two state-sanctioned political parties of the New Order were the United Development Party (Partai Persatuan Pembangunan, PPP) and the Indonesian Democratic Party (Partai Demokrasi Indonesia, PDI). These parties were artificial coalitions created in 1973 when the government consolidated nine existing political parties into two. The PDI was made up of the old Protestant and Catholic parties, two small secular parties, and the remnants of Sukarno's once-grand PNI (the Partai Nasionalis Indonesia, or Indonesian Nationalist Party), while PPP consolidated a range of Islamic political parties under one banner (Hein 1982).

9. While it is difficult to discern the extent that party ideology drove party affiliation among voters, it is clear that Golkar maintained the lion's share of votes throughout the New Order. Golkar consistently obtained over 60 percent of votes, reaching 73.2 percent of votes in 1987 (Liddle 1988). In the 1992 general election, Golkar secured 68 percent of votes (MacIntyre 1993) and 74.5 percent of votes in 1997 (Bird 1998).

10. The decentralization of Indonesia's political system led to an increase in the contests for power at the local level. For examples of more in-depth explanations of the consequences of this on legislative elections and campaigns, see Aspinall and Fealy's edited

collection, *Local Power and Politics in Indonesia* (2003), as well as Törnquist (2006) and Tomsa (2014).

11. The military was excluded completely from 2000. For a comprehensive summary of the debates surrounding the proposed changes to democratic representatives in government that occurred in 1998 see Crouch (2010).

12. The DPR now has 560 seats and the DPD has 132 seats. Candidates for the DPR must be nominated by an approved political party, while candidates for the DPD compete as individuals (though many are unofficially affiliated with a political party).

13. See Shair-Rosenfield (2019) for an in-depth analysis of elite motivations in reforming the electoral system in Indonesia.

14. These thresholds do not apply to local elections, and all eligible parties may take up the seats that they win in the local legislatures, regardless of their performance nationally.

15. Though Hanura contested elections from 2009–2019, it did not pass the national vote threshold in 2019 and was therefore unable to take up any seats in national parliament.

16. Further discussion about the gendered nature of this situation can be found in Coles (2018) and Sugiana and Putri (2018).

17. In response to the court ruling, the national legislature decided that the results of the preceding 2014 legislative elections would guide eligibility to nominate a presidential candidate in 2019, further cementing the significance of legislative election results for the presidency and the role of established political parties as gatekeepers.

18. Under 2014 regulations, candidates had to meet eligibility criteria relating to age, educational qualifications, and "loyalty" to the Pancasila doctrine and the 1945 Indonesian Constitution. They must also not have been convicted of a crime that held a sentence of five or more years.

19. These criteria were debated and influenced by party interests during Megawati's presidency (Crouch 2010, 66). As Crouch explains, Golkar was keen to restrict eligibility to candidates who had graduated from university, which would have barred Megawati Sukarnoputri as a candidate. Meanwhile, PDIP lobbied to prevent anyone either charged or convicted of a crime carrying a penalty of at least five years' incarceration, which was squarely targeted at Golkar's chairman Akbar Tandjung, who was in the midst of a very public legal appeal against a corruption conviction. The provision for physical and mental "fitness" tests were seen as a targeted attack on Abdurrahman Wahid, who was functionally blind, should he attempt to return to politics. The 2008 regulations incorporated some compromises, with educational requirements lowered to high school or equivalent, and the law slightly amended to exclude anyone who had served a prison sentence of five years or more. Meanwhile the physical and psychological fitness requirements for the presidency remained in place. See Butt (2015a) for further details.

20. Details of the Freedom House current assessment of democracy in Indonesia can be found on their website (https://freedomhouse.org/country/indonesia/freedom-world/2020).

21. See chapter 2 for details.

22. "Track record" encompasses a number of experiences that candidates can use to present themselves as committed to particular topics. This can include political record if they are an incumbent, or more personal aspects of their persona such as religiosity (Aspinall, Dettman, and Warburton 2011) or business successes (Choi 2007). However, the degree to which the Indonesian public are concerned about a candidate's track record is generally held to be low (Buehler 2003).

23. For examples of studies on brokers in Indonesian elections, see Aspinall (2014b), Aspinall, Rohman et al. (2017) and Muhtadi (2019).

2. CORRUPTION AND LEVERAGING ANTICORRUPTIONISM

1. For an extensive outline of such corruption accusations and how they contributed to the downfall of Indonesia's constitutional democracy in the 1950s see Feith (1962).

2. For example, in the lead-up to the elections of September 1955, the newspaper *Pedoman* published a scathing, anonymous letter to the editor claiming that Sukarno was a lackey of the "Co-operative Organization for Corruption," the Masyumi-PSI nickname for those who supported the first Ali Sastroamidjojo cabinet (Feith 1962, 427).

3. Before this, corruption arrests had been facilitated by a military mandate to act in the interests of the people (Crouch 1980, 40).

4. For further details of Sukarno's economic mismanagement and its impact on political stability in the 1960s, see Schwarz (2004) and chapter 1 in Subritzky (2016).

5. The circumstances behind the regime change in 1965–1966 and the respective roles of Suharto, members of the military, and the Indonesian Communist Party are far too complex to go into here, but there are several excellent books that discuss this further, including the book *The Indonesian Killings of 1965–1966: Studies from Java and Bali* edited by Cribb (1990), as well as works by McGregor (2007) and Melvin (2018).

6. In another example, Suharto highlighted corruption again in his Independence Day speech of August 1970, asserting that "there should no longer be any doubts about it. I myself will lead the fight against corruption" (cited in Elson 2001, 196).

7. The involvement of Suharto and his family in corruption has been explored in various studies including Erikson (2004) and Vatikiotis (1993).

8. In the political sphere, the PDI and the People's Democratic Party (Partai Rakyat Demokratis, PRD), formed from radical elements of the student activist movement, also became more outspoken in their reproaches of the regime.

9. Particularly, public criticism came from members of parliament from the PDI. For example, one of the party's outspoken politicians, Kwik Kian Gie, released a report in 1991 claiming there was an "alarming mental and moral erosion in almost all of the nation's elite circles," and in 1992 he presented draft legislation for a new economic competition law promoting transparency and a review on monopoly rights. However, no other faction in parliament supported the bill and it was never formally introduced (Eklöf 2003, 121).

10. For example, it published statistics to show that it was making a concerted attempt to squash corrupt practices in the bureaucracy. In the first nine months of the 1994–1995 fiscal year, for instance, the attorney-general's office also claimed to have prosecuted 358 cases of corruption that had "resulted in significant cost to the nation" (Erikson 2004, 116).

11. For example, the government conspired to undermine Megawati Soekarnoputri, daughter of the former president and an outspoken critic of the Suharto regime, in her nomination for chairperson of PDI in 1996. The government supported former PDI chairperson Soerjadi for the position, intimidating party members and using fraud to secure his nomination and subsequent appointment at an extraordinary party congress in Medan in June 1996. Meanwhile, Megawati supporters held a pro-democracy demonstration in Jakarta that ended with government troops assaulting protestors. More than one hundred people were injured and over fifty people were detained, sparking more protests throughout the country (Aspinall 2005b).

12. These early attempts to combat corruption were met with resistance, particularly as members of the judiciary were a primary target of the TGPTPK. Those seeking to uncover the corrupt activities of the elite were often met with counterclaims of defamation

by those they had accused (Butt and Lindsay 2011). For example, the case of women's rights activist, Yeni Roslaini, who, after providing legal assistance to a victim of rape, was prosecuted for libel by the accused. During the case, Roslaini contended that the trial had been unfair, and the defense had bribed the judges for a favorable ruling. In another example, Endin Wahyudin was sentenced to three months in prison and six months' probation in 2003 after reporting bribery involving three judges in Malang. The judges, who were found not guilty, later sued Wahyudin for defamation (Butt and Lindsay 2011).

13. Crouch (2010, 30) describes Wahid's use of funding as "casual" and the use of his personal masseuse as a go-between with the State Logistics Agency (Badan Urusan Logistik, Bulog) as "bizarre." However, despite being impeached, he was not prosecuted for these allegations.

14. Yudhoyono had stabilized the nation's economy after several years of poor economic growth, and Indonesia escaped the worst of the global financial crisis in 2008 (Aspinall 2010; Sukma 2009). Meanwhile, his deputy, Golkar's Jusuf Kalla, had brokered a peace agreement in Aceh province after decades of civil unrest dating back to the Darul Islam rebellion of the 1950s, which had aimed to create an autonomous Aceh within a Federal Islamic Indonesian state. For an overview of the long-standing conflict between Acehnese separatists and the Indonesian government, which effectively ended with the signing of the Helsinki Memorandum of Understanding in 2005, see Aspinall (2009).

15. Angelina's case attracted renewed interest in November 2013 when, on appeal, the Supreme Court increased her sentence to twelve years and her fine almost USD 2.4 million, far more than the original punishment sought by prosecutors. The increase was significant because in several other cases Tipikor judges had been condemned for handing down light sentences for those found guilty of corruption. The harsher Supreme Court sentence was possibly a response to public demands that those guilty of corruption face tougher punishment (*Tribbunews*, November 22, 2013).

16. For a comprehensive overview of Golkar in the Reformasi period, see Tomsa (2008) and Fionna (2016).

17. Established in 2003, the Constitutional Court was mandated under article 24C of constitutional amendments passed in 2001. It rules on matters related to the Constitution, the power of state institutions, the dissolution of political parties, and disputes over electoral outcomes. For further details, see Mahkamah Konstitusi (2014).

18. This case was also damaging for Yudhoyono because one of his explicitly stated aims during his second term was to combat the "judicial mafia" (*Suara Pembaruan*, October 26, 2011).

19. A number of institutions were engaged in public surveys of this nature in 2013–2014 in the lead-up to the 2014 general election. The main institutions conducting the surveys were Biro Pusat Statistik, Centre for Strategic and International Studies, Indonesia (CSIS), Founding Father House (FFH), Indonesian Network Election Survey (INES), *Lembaga Survei Indonesia* (LSI), Lembaga Survei Nasional (LSN), Lingkaran Survei Indonesia, Political Weather Station, Pusat Data Bersatu, Saiful Mujani Research and Consulting (SMRC), Soegeng Sarjadi School of Government (SSSG), SPACE, Transparency International Indonesia (TII), and Universitas Gadjah Mada Pusat Kajian Anti-Korupsi (UGM PUKAT).

20. The studies included in the table below are sourced from: *Detik.com* (Dhurandara 2012), the *Wall Street Journal* (Ismar and Husna 2013), *Republika* (Rini 2013), *Kompas* (Gatra 2013), *Lembaga Survei Indonesia* (2012), *Tempo* (Purnomo 2013), and *Jakarta Globe* (Setuningsih 2013). No surveys conducted between January and April 2014 were found to ask targeted questions about the existing government's anticorruption efforts.

21. The survey asked respondents what they felt were the most important candidate qualities. Thirty-six percent identified being honest and corruption-free as most important, followed by "caring about the people" (18 percent), "personality" (12 percent), and "leadership qualities" (5 percent) (*Lembaga Survei Indonesia* 2013).

22. Numerous informal conversations with staff in political party head offices suggest that it is difficult to determine the reliability of political surveys done in Indonesia, primarily because political parties sometimes commission surveys to suit their own agendas. A common modus operandi for political parties that wish to receive positive media coverage is to commission a survey with favorable outcomes, which is then released to the press as an independent study. Nevertheless, there is an evident trend across the surveys, supported by historical context and media reports, illustrating that ongoing corruption contributed to public disenfranchisement with the government.

23. The decline of party loyalty—although a phenomenon that existed before 2014— represented a stark contrast to the party alignments that were prominent during the Old and New Orders (Ufen 2008).

24. Yet, even when facing allegations of corruption, parties continued to use corruption scandals involving their rivals to their political advantage. Several members of the political elite owned media franchises (Tapsell 2010), which they used to deride political opponents and underscore the government's lack of progress in eradicating corruption.

25. PDIP officially gained 18.95 percent of votes, which was far less than its target of 27.02 percent. The result was surprising to many observers (Sadikin 2014). For example, prominent Indonesia political analyst Wimar Witoelar (2014) stated, "I was wrong. The media was wrong. The polls were wrong.... Predictions that PDIP would capture 35 per cent or more in the legislative elections proved to be grossly illusory as they got less than 20 per cent, just a few more percentage points more than Golkar, Gerindra and even the Democrat Party."

26. While survey results in Indonesia cannot always be taken at face value, the overwhelming trend reflected declining support for the Democratic Party. In a March 2013 survey, the National Survey Institute (Lembaga Survei Nasional, LSN) found that 40.4 percent of respondents saw the Democratic Party as the most corrupt party in Indonesia. Its electability also fell, with only 4.3 percent of respondents selecting them as their preferred party (Ledysia 2013). A survey published by Transparency International Indonesia in April 2013 found the Democratic Party to be the least transparent party in parliament in relation to its funding and party budget (along with Golkar and PKS, who were also defined as "not transparent") (*BBC Indonesia*, April 16, 2013). Polling by the United Data Centre (Pusat Data Bersatu, PDB) released in July 2013 found that only 9.4 percent would vote for the Democratic Party, compared to 26.43 percent of votes attained in 2009. An Indikator survey report released on April 4, 2014, found only 7.2 percent of those surveyed planned to vote for the Democratic Party (*Indikator* 2014). The Democratic Party gained 10.19 percent of the official vote (Pemilu 2014), slightly higher than most predictions.

3. STANDING HIS GROUND

1. This is a pseudonym.

2. In Indonesia, members of the national legislature are considered representatives of their party and if they resign from their party they must also step down as a member of the DPR.

3. "*Tim sukses*," which literally translates to "success team," has also been translated as "campaign team" in the work of scholars such as Aspinall (2014b) and Mietzner (2013).

4. Corruption in the national legislature is often linked to politicians hoping to recoup the costs of their individual campaign (Ganie-Rochman and Achwan 2016; Mi-

etzner 2015). While it is not the only reason for endemic corruption among legislators, it has been widely identified as a contributing factor.

5. For more on the popularization of *blusukan* as a campaign strategy, see Zulkarnain and Harris (2017).

6. The aspiration funds (*dana aspirasi*) scheme was introduced in 2009 and allows sitting legislators to disburse up to 5 billion rupiah (USD 440,000) toward development projects within their electorates (Aspinall and Berenschot 2019).

7. The "son of the region" phenomenon, sometimes referred to as "son of the soil" or "local son," captures the idea of a candidate who is from the region, is part of the dominant religious group, and attuned to the various sociocultural norms of the area (Aspinall 2011; Xue 2018).

4. BOWING TO PRESSURE

1. This is a pseudonym.

2. The final candidate lists submitted to the General Election Commission (Komisi Pemilihan Umum, KPU) in March 2013. The KPU was then responsible for ensuring that candidates met all the necessary eligibility criteria for participation in the 2014 election. It released its confirmed list of approved candidates in May 2013.

3. The term "vision and mission" (*visi dan misi*) is commonly used as shorthand to describe the platform of the party as a codification of what they hope to achieve in government. These are often presented to voters as means for distinguishing parties but, in reality, there is often little to distinguish the platforms of Indonesian political parties (Choi 2004).

4. That elections are costly and successful candidates then, in turn, use their positions to recoup their costs is a common rationalization given for high levels of corruption among legislators in Indonesia across all levels of government (Hidayat 2009; Hofman, Kaiser, and Schulze 2009; Tomsa 2015).

5. Aspinall (2014a) found that there were a number of commonly distributed gifts during campaigns, ranging from tokens bearing the party logo and the candidate's picture, religious gifts such as prayer mats or headscarves to basic foodstuffs, which were commonly delivered by the candidate's campaign team rather than the candidates themselves. While Ayu preferred to distribute gifts herself, there were times when her campaign team were charged with this task.

6. People capable of rallying votes are sometimes referred to as "brokers." The campaign team is usually comprised of at least some vote brokers—people of influence who would be able to persuade others to vote for a particular candidate. The phenomenon of using brokers was widespread in 2014, and brokers wielded significant influence over campaigns and their successful outcomes (Aspinall 2014b).

7. The prevalence of the "dawn attack" as a campaign vote-buying strategy has been discussed in Aspinall, Rohman et al. (2017); Aspinall and Mietzner (2014); Muhtadi (2019) and Ratnawaty Chotim (2019).

8. Further academic discussion of how "gifts" are understood and conceptualized can be found in Aspinall and Sukmajati (2016) and Simandjuntak (2012).

5. EXPERIENCED AND PRAGMATIC

1. This was the figure that Bontor quoted. Recent statistics from the Food and Agriculture Organization (FAO) estimated that 33 percent of Indonesia's population are agriculturalists (FAO 2015).

2. As discussed in chapter 2, Nazaruddin became infamous after being arrested for corruption in 2011.

3. Attacks on the credibility of the KPK were common among certain political parties and figures. More details on what these attacks constituted can be found in Butt (2011a), Hamayotsu and Nataatmadja (2016), Kramer (2019), and Schütte (2016).

4. Bontor's estimates of his campaign expenditure did vary. At another point, he told me he thought the campaign had cost closer to USD 300,000.

5. Prisoners serving sentences of less than five years are eligible to vote in Indonesia according to the Law No. 2012/8 on the Election of Members of the National, Provincial and Local Legislatures. While the aim of the visit was not to generate personal votes for the candidate, the appeal to inmates may still have reaped some electoral benefit for his party.

6. While PKS was predicted to do poorly in the 2014 general election due to the corruption scandals it had faced, it not only survived but achieved a higher proportion of the vote that had been expected (Kramer 2014).

7. The debate over whether to legalize polygamy in Indonesia is controversial, with proponents on both sides. For more information about the history of this debate, see Butt (1999), Mutaqin (2018), and Nurhidayatuloh et al. (2018).

8. For a comprehensive overview of the Ahok trial and its implications, see Peterson (2020).

9. For smaller meetings, he said he would not give them any money but would provide food and drinks.

10. For more on theories of how brokers operate, see Stokes et al. (2013) and their influential study on the topic.

11. Bontor's longevity as a legislator allowed him to develop longstanding networks of support, which are described as rarer in Indonesia than in other clientelistic democracies, such as the Philippines (Hutchcroft 2000). In Indonesia, there is a tendency toward "short-term, largely transactional clientelism," in which brokers are unsure they will be rewarded for their loyalty (Aspinall and Hicken 2020, 138).

6. CAMPAIGNS, CONTEXT, AND CONSEQUENCES

1. There is extensive literature on voter responses to campaigns, with summaries of literature in Bennett (2006) and Freeder, Lenz, and Turney (2019). Studies on the voter "knowledge gap" tend to concur that voters who are already "well-informed" and those who are "poorly-informed" or "under-informed" as less likely to respond to campaigns than those who are "moderately informed" (Nadeau et al. 2008) and that voters from different demographic backgrounds also respond differently to campaigns (Hansen and Pedersen 2014; Jerit and Barabas 2017).

2. Additional discussion of "issue-based campaigns" from a political party and candidate perspective can be found in Druckman, Jacobs, and Ostermeier (2004); Green and Hobolt (2008); Tomz and Van Houweling (2008); van der Brug (2004); and Walgrave, Lefevere, and Nuytemans (2009).

3. There have been a number of studies that assess the importance of a candidate's appearance, and their charisma in influencing voter decisions. For examples of studies on the influence of candidate appearance on voters, see R. Campbell and Cowley (2013) and Rosenberg et al. (1991). For some discussions on the influence of charisma, see Grabo, Spisak, and van Vugt (2017), Sheafer (2008), and van der Brug and Mughan (2007).

4. For a more nuanced discussion on party fragmentation and the implementation of "ethics" protocols within political parties, see Tomsa (2014) and James (2017).

5. Indonesian parties generally fall somewhere within the "religious–nationalist" spectrum, with Islamic parties at one end and "nationalist" (i.e., not aligned with a particular religion) at the other. Although Islamic parties have not been able to outperform their secular–nationalist rivals in elections (Nastiti and Ratri 2018), they stand as identity mark-

ers for voters who wish to see a religious influence in national politics (Tanuwidjaja 2010). Parties that have their roots in the New Order—PDIP, PPP, and Golkar—also continue to benefit from old *aliran* sentiments, though there are continuing debates of how much this advantage has declined in the post-Suharto era (Ufen 2008, Fossati, Aspinall, and Muhtadi 2020).

6. Betrayal by brokers reflect broader discussions of how brokers perceive benefit during an election period. As Aspinall and Berenschot (2019, 97) write: "If a candidate loses the election, his or her *tim sukses* members cannot expect to be rewarded at all. Their chances of future reward are tied to the success of a single politician. This all-or-nothing logic increases the likelihood of defection and misuse of campaign funds."

7. This phrase originates from the fact that voters chose not to vote for any party, thus leaving their ballot "white." The meaning has also been extended to include people who also do not physically vote, either as a political statement or out of apathy. Official estimates in 2014 showed that voter turnout was approximately 75.11 percent, an increase of 4.12 percent from 2009, while 7.86 percent of those votes were deemed spoilt or null (Pemilu 2014).

8. The concept of diffusion was adopted by social scientists during the 1990s to understand how ideas spread within, and between, social movements (Chabot and Duyvendak 2002). Classical diffusion theory holds that ideas can travel through relational, non-relational, or mediated channels (Givan, Roberts, and Soule 2010; Tarrow 2011). Relational channels rely on direct contact between people, most often those who trust each other. Non-relational diffusion occurs directly between people who do not have a relationship or indirectly through the sharing of ideas via the media.

9. Norris (2002) identifies four basic elements to campaigns: the messages that the party or candidate wishes to communicate, the channel(s) of communication employed to relay these messages, the impact of these messages upon target audiences, and the feedback loop from the audience back to the campaigning organization.

10. This "entry ticket" terminology is attributed to Thomas Power in Aspinall and Berenschot (2019).

11. Whether vote buying is motivated by voter requests ("demand driven") or by candidates' own desires to gain a competitive advantage over rivals has been debated in a number of academic publications including Allen (2015), Aspinall, Rohman et al. (2017), Muhtadi (2019), and Pradhanawati, Tawakkal, and Garner (2018).

CONCLUSION

1. Hollander and Einwohner (2004) provide a typology of resistance. In these cases, resistance may be "overt" in that it is intended by candidates and recognized by both voters and observers. If it fails to be recognized or persuasive to voters, then it may be categorized as "attempted resistance."

2. For examples of discussions about the progress of democratization in Indonesia, see Aspinall et al. (2015); Hadiz and Robison (2013); and Winters (2013).

3. Some examples of reporting include Allard and Damiana (2019), Salna and Singgih (2019), and *Straits Times* (2019).

References

Abraham, Itty, and Willem van Schendel. 2005. "Introduction: The Making of Illicitness." In *Illicit Flows and Criminal Things: States, Borders, and the Other Side of Globalization*, edited by Itty Abraham and Willem van Schendel, 1–37. Bloomington: Indiana University Press.

Ahmad, Nyarwi. 2020. "Celebrification of Politics: Understanding Migration of Celebrities into Politics Celebrification of Celebrity Politicians in the Emerging Democracy of Indonesia." *East Asia* 37: 1–17. https://doi.org/10.1007/s12140-020-09332-z.

Akuntono, Indra. 2013. "SBY, Kunci Demokrat Menangi Pemilu 2014." *Kompas*. June 29. https://nasional.kompas.com/read/2013/06/29/1743270/SBY.Kunci.Demokrat.Menangi.Pemilu.2014.

Alford, Peter. 2013. "Jakarta Rocked by Justice Chief Akil Mochtar's Arrest for Bribery." *The Australian*, October 24.

Allard, Tom, and Jessica Damiana. 2019. "Pushing the Envelope: Money Politics Mars Indonesian Poll." *Reuters*. April 11. https://www.reuters.com/article/us-indonesia-election-corruption-idUSKCN1RN06T.

Allen, Nathan W. 2015. "Clientelism and the Personal Vote in Indonesia." *Electoral Studies* 37: 73–85. https://doi.org/http://dx.doi.org/10.1016/j.electstud.2014.10.005.

Ambardi, Kuskridho. 2008. "The Making of the Indonesian Multiparty System: A Cartelized Party System and Its Origin." Doctor of Philosophy, Department of Political Science, Ohio State University.

Amelia, Rizky. 2013. "KPK Periksa Istri Akil Mochtar." *Berita Satu*. October 22. https://www.beritasatu.com/nasional/145839/kpk-periksa-istri-akil-mochtar.

Ananta, Aris, Evi Nurvidya Arifin, and Leo Suryadinata. 2005. *Emerging Democracy in Indonesia*. Singapore: ISEAS.

Anderson, Benedict R. O'G. 1990. *Language and Power: Exploring Political Cultures in Indonesia*. Ithaca, NY: Cornell University Press.

Anderson, Benedict R. O'G., and Ruth T. McVey. 1971. *A Preliminary Analysis of the October 1, 1965 Coup in Indonesia*. Ithaca, NY: Cornell Southeast Asia Program.

Ansolabehere, Stephen, and Shanto Iyengar. 1994. "Riding the Wave and Claiming Ownership Over Issues: The Joint Effects of Advertising and News Coverage in Campaigns." *Public Opinion Quarterly* 58 (3): 335–357. https://doi.org/10.1086/269431.

Aspinall, Edward. 1995. "Students and the Military: Regime Friction and Civilian Dissent in the Late Suharto Period." *Indonesia* 59 (April): 21–44. http://www.jstor.org/stable/3351126.

———. 2005a. "Elections and the Normalization of Politics in Indonesia." *South East Asia Research* 13 (2): 117–156. https://doi.org/10.5367/0000000054604515.

———. 2005b. *Opposing Suharto: Compromise, Resistance and Regime Change in Indonesia*. Palo Alto, CA: Stanford University Press.

———. 2009. *Islam and Nation: Separatist Rebellion in Aceh, Indonesia*. Palo Alto, CA: Stanford University Press.

———. 2010. "Indonesia in 2009: Democratic Triumphs and Trials." *Southeast Asian Affairs* 2010 (1): 103–125. http://muse.jhu.edu/journals/southeast_asian_affairs/v2010/2010.aspinall.html.

———. 2011. "Democratization and Ethnic Politics in Indonesia: Nine Theses." *Journal of East Asian Studies* 11 (2): 289–319. https://doi.org/10.1017/S1598240800007190.

———. 2013. "A Nation in Fragments." *Critical Asian Studies* 45 (1): 27–54. https://doi.org/10.1080/14672715.2013.758820.

———. 2014a. "Parliament and Patronage." *Journal of Democracy* 25 (4): 96–110. http://muse.jhu.edu/journals/journal_of_democracy/v025/25.4.aspinall.html.

———. 2014b. "When Brokers Betray: Clientelism, Social Networks, and Electoral Politics in Indonesia." *Critical Asian Studies* 46 (4): 545–570. https://doi.org/10.1080/14672715.2014.960706.

———. 2015. "The Yudhoyono Legacy." *The Strategist*. August 7. https://www.aspistrategist.org.au/the-yudhoyono-legacy/.

———. 2019. "Fighting Corruption When Corruption Is Pervasive: The Case of Indonesia." In *The Political Logics of Anticorruption Efforts in Asia*, edited by Cheng Chen and Meredith Weiss, 49–75. Albany: State University of New York Press.

Aspinall, Edward, and Ward Berenschot. 2019. *Democracy for Sale: Elections, Clientelism, and the State in Indonesia*. Ithaca, NY: Cornell University Press.

Aspinall, Edward, Michael Davidson, Allen Hicken, and Meredith Weiss. 2015. "Inducement or Entry Ticket? Broker Networks and Vote Buying in Indonesia." American Political Science Association Conference. San Francisco, CA.

Aspinall, Edward, Sebastian Dettman, and Eve Warburton. 2011. "When Religion Trumps Ethnicity: A Regional Election Case Study from Indonesia." *South East Asia Research* 19 (1): 27–58. https://doi.org/10.5367/sear.2011.0034.

Aspinall, Edward, and Greg Fealy. 2003. *Local Power & Politics in Indonesia*. Singapore: ISEAS.

Aspinall, Edward, and Allen Hicken. 2020. "Guns for Hire and Enduring Machines: Clientelism Beyond Parties in Indonesia and the Philippines." *Democratization* 27 (1): 137–156. https://doi.org/10.1080/13510347.2019.1590816.

Aspinall, Edward, and Marcus Mietzner. 2014. "Indonesian Politics in 2014: Democracy's Close Call." *Bulletin of Indonesian Economic Studies* 50 (3): 347–369. https://doi.org/10.1080/00074918.2014.980375.

Aspinall, Edward, Marcus Mietzner, and Dirk Tomsa. 2015. *The Yudhoyono Presidency: Indonesia's Decade of Stability and Stagnation*. Singapore: ISEAS.

Aspinall, Edward, Noor Rohman, Ahmad Zainul Hamdi, and Zusiana Elly Triantini. 2017. "Vote Buying in Indonesia: Candidate Strategies, Market Logic and Effectiveness." *Journal of East Asian Studies* 17 (1): 1–27. https://doi.org/10.1017/jea.2016.31.

Aspinall, Edward, and Made Sukmajati, eds. 2016. *Electoral Dynamics in Indonesia: Money Politics, Patronage and Clientelism at the Grassroots*. Singapore: NUS Press.

Avelino, George, and Arthur Fisch. 2019. "Money, Elections, and Candidates." In *Routledge Handbook of Brazilian Politics*, edited by Barry Ames, 161–174. London: Routledge.

Baidoo, Frank Lord, Shirley Dankwa, and Isaac Eshun. 2018. "Culture of Vote Buying and Its Implications: Range of Incentives and Conditions Politicians Offer to Electorates." *International Journal of Developing and Emerging Economies* 6 (2): 1–20.

Baiocchi, Gianpaolo, and Brian T. Connor. 2008. "The Ethnos in the Polis: Political Ethnography as a Mode of Inquiry." *Sociology Compass* 2 (1): 139–155.

Banducci, Susan, Heiko Giebler, and Sylvia Kritzinger. 2017. "Knowing More from Less: How the Information Environment Increases Knowledge of Party Positions." *British Journal of Political Science* 47 (3): 571–588. https://doi.org/10.1017/S0007123415000204.

Barton, Greg. 2006. *Gus Dur: The Authorized Biography of Abdurrahman Wahid*. Jakarta: Equinox Publishing.
Bélanger, Éric, and Bonnie M. Meguid. 2008. "Issue Salience, Issue Ownership, and Issue-Based Vote Choice." *Electoral Studies* 27 (3): 477–491. https://doi.org/10.1016/j.electstud.2008.01.001.
Bennett, Stephen Earl. 2006. "Democratic Competence, Before Converse and After." *Critical Review* 18 (1–3): 105–141. https://doi.org/10.1080/08913810608443652.
Berenschot, Ward, and Edward Aspinall. 2020. "How Clientelism Varies: Comparing Patronage Democracies." *Democratization* 27 (1): 1–19. https://doi.org/10.1080/13510347.2019.1645129.
Bertrand, Jacques. 1996. "False Starts, Succession Crises, and Regime Transition: Flirting with Openness in Indonesia." *Pacific Affairs* 69 (3): 319–340.
Bird, Judith. 1998. "Indonesia in 1997: The Tinderbox Year." *Asian Survey* 38 (2): 168–176. http://www.jstor.org/stable/2645675.
———. 1999. "Indonesia in 1998: The Pot Boils Over." *Asian Survey* 39 (1): 27–37. http://www.jstor.org/stable/2645591.
Bland, Ben. 2019. "Indonesia's Incredible Elections." Lowy Institute. https://interactives.lowyinstitute.org/features/indonesia-votes-2019/.
Blattman, Christopher, Horacio Larreguy, Benjamin Marx, and Otis R. Reid. 2019. *Eat Widely, Vote Wisely? Lessons from a Campaign Against Vote Buying in Uganda*. Cambridge: National Bureau of Economic Research.
Blunt, Peter, Mark Turner, and Henrik Lindroth. 2012. "Patronage's Progress in Post-Soeharto Indonesia." *Public Administration and Development* 32 (1): 64–81. http://dx.doi.org/10.1002/pad.617.
Bobel, Chris, and Samantha Kwan. 2011. "Introduction." In *Embodied Resistance: Challenging the Norms, Breaking the Rules*, edited by Chris Bobel and Samantha Kwan, 1–12. Nashville, TN: Vanderbilt University Press.
Bourchier, David. 2014. *Illiberal Democracy in Indonesia: The Ideology of the Family State*. New York: Routledge.
Bourchier, David, and Vedi Hadiz. 2003. *Indonesian Politics and Society*. London: Routledge.
Bourdieu, Pierre. 1996. "Physical Space, Social Space and Habitus." *Vilhelm Aubert Memorial Lecture Report* 10. Oslo: University of Oslo.
Bowler, Shaun, and David M. Farrell. 1992. "The Study of Election Campaigning." In *Electoral Strategies and Political Marketing*, edited by Shaun Bowler and David M. Farrell, 1–23. London: St. Martin's.
Brown, Colin. 2003. *A Short History of Indonesia: The Unlikely Nation?* Sydney: Allen and Unwin.
Brusco, Valeria, Marcelo Nazareno, and Susan C. Stokes. 2004. "Vote Buying in Argentina." *Latin American Research Review* 39 (2): 66–88. http://www.jstor.org/stable/1555401.
Buehler, Michael. 2003. "The Rising Importance of Personal Networks in Indonesian Local Politics." In *Deepening Democracy in Indonesia? Direct Elections for Local Leaders*, edited by Maribeth Erb and Priyambudi Sulistiyanto. Singapore: ISEAS.
Burawoy, Michael. 1998. "The Extended Case Method." *Sociological Theory* 16 (1): 4–33. https://doi.org/https://doi.org/10.1111/0735-2751.00040.
Butt, Simon. 1999. "Polygamy and Mixed Marriage in Indonesia." In *Indonesia: Law and Society*, edited by T. Lindsay, 122–144. Sydney: The Federation Press.
———. 2011a. "Anti-Corruption Reform in Indonesia: An Obituary?" *Bulletin of Indonesian Economic Studies* 47 (3): 381–394. https://doi.org/10.1080/00074918.2011.619051.

———. 2011b. *Corruption and Law in Indonesia*. London: Routledge.
———. 2015a. *The Constitutional Court and Democracy in Indonesia*. Leiden: Brill.
———. 2015b. "The Rule of Law and Anti-Corruption Reforms Under Yudhoyono: The Rise of the KPK and the Constitutional Court." In *The Yudhoyono Presidency: Indonesia's Decade of Stability and Stagnation*, edited by Edward Aspinall, Marcus Mietzner, and Dirk Tomsa, 175–198. Singapore: ISEAS.
Butt, Simon, and Tim Lindsay. 2011. "Judicial Mafia: The Courts and State Illegality in Indonesia." In *The State and Illegality in Indonesia*, edited by Edward Aspinall and Gerry van Klinken, 189–216. Leiden: KITLV Press.
Callahan, William A. 2005. "Social Capital and Corruption: Vote Buying and the Politics of Reform in Thailand." *Perspectives on Politics* 3 (3): 495–508. www.jstor.org/stable/3689020.
Campbell, Colin. 2009. "Distinguishing the Power of Agency from Agentic Power: A Note on Weber and the 'Black Box' of Personal Agency." *Sociological Theory* 27 (4): 407–418. https://doi.org/10.1111/j.1467-9558.2009.01355.x.
Campbell, James E. 1983. "The Return of the Incumbents: The Nature of the Incumbency Advantage." *The Western Political Quarterly* 36 (3): 434–444. https://doi.org/10.2307/448401. http://www.jstor.org/stable/448401.
Campbell, Rosie, and Philip Cowley. 2013. "What Voters Want: Reactions to Candidate Characteristics in a Survey Experiment." *Political Studies* 62 (4): 745–765. https://doi.org/10.1111/1467-9248.12048.
Canare, Tristan A., Ronald U. Mendoza, and Mario Antonio Lopez. 2018. "An Empirical Analysis of Vote Buying Among the Poor." *South East Asia Research* 26 (1): 58–84. https://doi.org/10.1177/0967828X17753420.
Capelos, Tereza. 2010. "Feeling the Issue: How Citizens' Affective Reactions and Leadership Perceptions Shape Policy Evaluations." *Journal of Political Marketing* 9 (1–2): 9–33. https://doi.org/10.1080/15377850903583038.
Caraway, Terri L., and Michele Ford. 2020. *Labor and Politics in Indonesia*. Cambridge: Cambridge University Press.
Carreras, Miguel, and Yasemin İrepoğlu. 2013. "Trust in Elections, Vote Buying, and Turnout in Latin America." *Electoral Studies* 32 (4): 609–619. https://doi.org/https://doi.org/10.1016/j.electstud.2013.07.012.
Chabot, S., and J. W. Duyvendak. 2002. "Globalization and Transnational Diffusion between Social Movements: Reconceptualizing the Dissemination of the Gandhian Repertoire and the 'Coming Out' Routine." *Theory and Society* 31 (6): 697–740.
Chang, Eric C. C. 2005. "Electoral Incentives for Political Corruption under Open-List Proportional Representation." *The Journal of Politics* 67 (3): 716–730. https://doi.org/10.1111/j.1468-2508.2005.00336.x.
Cheeseman, Nic. 2010. "African Elections as Vehicles for Change." *Journal of Democracy* 21 (4): 139–153. https://muse.jhu.edu/article/398739.
Chen, Cheng, and Meredith L. Weiss. 2019. "Theorizing Anticorruption as a Political Project." In *The Political Logics of Anticorruption Efforts in Asia*, edited by Cheng Chen and Meredith L. Weiss. Albany: State University of New York Press.
Cheng, Christine S., and Dominik Zaum. 2008. "Introduction: Key Themes in Peacebuilding and Corruption." *International Peacekeeping* 15 (3): 301–309. http://www.informaworld.com/10.1080/13533310802058752.
Chiang, Chun-Fang, and Brian Knight. 2011. "Media Bias and Influence: Evidence from Newspaper Endorsements." *The Review of Economic Studies* 78 (3): 795–820.
Choi, Nankyung. 2004. "Local Elections and Party Politics in Post-Reformasi Indonesia: A View from Yogyakarta." *Journal of Contemporary Southeast Asia* 26 (2): 280–301.

———. 2007. "Local Elections and Democracy in Indonesia: The Riau Archipelago." *Journal of Contemporary Asia* 37 (3): 326–345. https://doi.org/10.1080/00472330701408650.
Clarke, Nick, Will Jennings, Jonathan Moss, and Gerry Stoker. 2018. *The Good Politician: Folk Theories, Political Interaction, and the Rise of Anti-Politics*. Cambridge: Cambridge University Press.
Cochrane, Joe. 2013. "'Beef-Gate' Transfixes Scandal-Prone Indonesia." *The New York Times*, May 16. http://www.nytimes.com/2013/05/17/world/asia/beefgate-transfixes-scandal-prone-indonesia.html?pagewanted=all&_r=0.
Coles, Gregory. 2018. "'What Do I Lack as a Woman?' The Rhetoric of Megawati Sukarnoputri." *Rhetorica: A Journal of the History of Rhetoric* 36 (1): 58–91.
Collins, Paul D. 2012. "Introduction to the Special Issue: The Global Anti-Corruption Discourse—Towards Integrity Management?" *Public Administration and Development* 32 (1): 1–10. https://doi.org/10.1002/pad.618.
Colmenares, Neri Javier. 2017. "Political Corruption in Philippine Elections: Money Politics through the Pork Barrel System." *Australian Journal of Asian Law* 18 (2): 1–17. https://papers.ssrn.com/sol3/papers.cfm?abstract_id=3144932.
Cook, Karen S., and Richard M. Emerson. 1978. "Power, Equity and Commitment in Exchange Networks." *American Sociological Review* 43 (5): 721–739. https://www.jstor.org/stable/2094546?seq=1#metadata_info_tab_contents.
Cottrell, David, Michael C. Herron, and Sean J. Westwood. 2018. "An Exploration of Donald Trump's Allegations of Massive Voter Fraud in the 2016 General Election." *Electoral Studies* 51: 123–142. https://doi.org/https://doi.org/10.1016/j.electstud.2017.09.002.
Cox, Gary W., and Jonathan N. Katz. 1996. "Why Did the Incumbency Advantage in U.S. House Elections Grow?" *American Journal of Political Science* 40 (2): 478–497. https://doi.org/10.2307/2111633. www.jstor.org/stable/2111633.
Cribb, Robert. 1990. *The Indonesian Killings of 1965–1966: Studies from Java and Bali*. Melbourne: Centre of Southeast Asian Studies, Monash University.
Cribb, Robert, and Colin Brown. 1995. *Modern Indonesia: A History Since 1945*. New York: Longman.
Crouch, Harold. 1980. *The Army and Politics in Indonesia*. Rev. ed., edited by George M. Kahin. Ithaca, NY: Cornell University. 1978.
———. 2010. *Political Reform in Indonesia after Soeharto*. Singapore: ISEAS.
Cushion, Stephen, and Richard Thomas. 2018. *Reporting Elections: Rethinking the Logic of Campaign Coverage*. New York: John Wiley & Sons.
Dahm, Berhard. 1971. *History of Indonesia in the Twentieth Century*. London: Pall Mall Press.
Dalton, Russell J., and Steven A. Weldon. 2005. "Public Images of Political Parties: A Necessary Evil?" *West European Politics* 28 (5): 931–951. https://doi.org/10.1080/01402380500310527.
Dhurandara. 2012. Survei CSIS: Mayoritas Pejabat Pemerintah Dinilai Korup. *Detik.com*.
Dibley, Thushara, and Michele. Ford, eds. 2019. *Activists in Transition: Contentious Politics in the New Indonesia*. Ithaca, NY: Cornell University Press.
Dibley, Thushara, and Antoni Tsaputra. 2019. "Changing laws, changing attitudes: the place of people with disability in Indonesia." In *Contentious Belonging*, edited by Greg Fealy and Ronit Ricci, 77–94. Singapore: ISEAS Publishing. https://doi.org/10.1355/9789814843478-009.
Dick, Howard, and Jeremy Mulholland. 2016. "The Politics of Corruption in Indonesia." *Georgetown Journal of International Affairs* 17 (1): 43–47.

Dirks, Nicholas B., Geoff Eley, and Sherry B. Ortner. 1994. "Introduction." In *Culture/Power/History: A Reader in Contemporary Social Theory*, edited by Nicholas B. Dirks, Geoff Eley, and Sherry B. Ortner, 3–46. Princeton, NJ: Princeton University Press.

Downs, Anthony. 1957. *An Economic Theory of Democracy*. New York: Harper & Row.

Druckman, James N., Lawrence R. Jacobs, and Eric Ostermeier. 2004. "Candidate Strategies to Prime Issues and Image." *Journal of Politics* 66 (4): 1180–1202. https://doi.org/10.1111/j.0022-3816.2004.00295.x.

Edelman, Murray. 1964. *The Symbolic Uses of Politics*. Chicago: University of Illinois Press.

———. 1988. *Constructing the Political Spectacle*. Chicago: University of Chicago Press.

Eklöf, Stefan. 1999. *Indonesian Politics in Crisis: The Long Fall of Suharto, 1996–1998*. Vol. 1. Copenhagen: NIAS Press.

———. 2003. *Power and Culture in Suharto's Indonesia: The Indonesian Democratic Party (PDI) and the Decline of the New Order*. Copenhagen: NIAS Press.

Elson, Robert E. 2001. *Suharto: A Political Biography*. Cambridge: Cambridge University Press.

Ely, John Hart. 1998. "Gerrymanders: The Good, the Bad, and the Ugly." *Stanford Law Review* 50 (3): 607–641.

Erikson, Ross. 2004. "Corruption and Regime Legitimacy: A Study of Suharto's New Order Authoritarian Regime." MPhil Masters, Department of Chinese and Southeast Asian Studies, University of Sydney.

Farrell, David M., and Rüdiger Schmitt-Beck. 2003. *Do Political Campaigns Matter? Campaign Effects in Elections and Referendums*. London: Routledge.

Farrell, David M., and Paul Webb. 2000. "Political Parties as Campaign Organizations." In *Parties without Partisans: Political Change in Advanced Industrial Democracies*, edited by Russell J. Dalton and Martin P. Wattenberg, 102–128. Oxford: Oxford University Press.

Fealy, Greg. 2011. "Indonesian Politics in 2011: Democratic Regression and Yudhoyono's Regal Incumbency." *Bulletin of Indonesian Economic Studies* 47 (3): 333–353. https://doi.org/10.1080/00074918.2011.619050.

———. 2013. "Indonesian Politics in 2012: Graft, Intolerance, and Hope of Change in the Late Yudhoyono Period." *Southeast Asian Affairs* 2013: 101–120.

Feith, Herbert. 1962. *The Decline of Constitutional Democracy in Indonesia*. Ithaca, NY. Cornell University Press.

———. 1994. "Constitutional Democracy: How Well Did It Function?" In *Democracy in Indonesia: 1950s and 1990s*, edited by David Bourchier and John Legge, 16–25. Melbourne: Monash University.

Ferree, Karen E., and James D. Long. 2016. "Gift, Threats, and Perceptions of Ballot Secrecy in African Elections." *African Affairs* 115 (461): 621–645. https://doi.org/10.1093/afraf/adw049%J African Affairs.

Fionna, Ulla. 2014. *The Institutionalisation of Political Parties in Post-authoritarian Indonesia: From the Grass-roots Up*. Amsterdam: Amsterdam University Press.

———. 2016. "Indonesian Parties in a Deep Dilemma: The Case of Golkar." *ISEAS Perspective* 35 (2016): 1–7.

Firmansyah, Joni. 2017. "Electability of Indonesian Celebrities Candidates on National Legislative Election in 2014." 14th International Conference on Social Science and Humanities (ICSSH). Seoul.

Fish, M., J. Wittenberg, and L. Jakli. 2018. "A Decade of Democratic Decline and Stagnation." In *Democratization*, edited by Christian W. Haerpfer, Patrick Bernhagen, Christian Welzel, and Ronald F. Inglehart. Oxford: Oxford University Press.

Food and Agriculture Organization (FAO). 2015. *Small Family Farms Country Factsheet*. Food and Agriculture Organization of the United Nations (Rome). http://www.fao.org/3/i8881en/I8881EN.pdf.

Fossati, Diego, Edward Aspinall, Burhanuddin Muhtadi, and Eve Warburton. 2020. "Ideological Representation in Clientelistic Democracies: The Indonesian Case." *Electoral Studies* 63: 102–111.

Fox, Richard L., and Jennifer L. Lawless. 2005. "To Run or Not to Run for Office: Explaining Nascent Political Ambition." *American Journal of Political Science* 49 (3): 642–659. https://doi.org/10.1111/j.1540-5907.2005.00147.x.

Freeder, Sean, Gabriel S. Lenz, and Shad Turney. 2019. "The Importance of Knowing 'What Goes with What': Reinterpreting the Evidence on Policy Attitude Stability." *The Journal of Politics* 81 (1): 274–290. https://doi.org/10.1086/700005.

Ganie-Rochman, Meuthia, and Rochman Achwan. 2016. "Corruption in Indonesia's Emerging Democracy." *Journal of Developing Societies* 32 (2): 159–177.

Garrett, Geoffrey. 1998. "Global Markets and National Politics: Collision Course or Virtuous Circle?" *International Organization* 52 (4): 787–824.

Gatra, Sandro. 2013. "Survei INES: Kinerja Pemerintahan SBY Tak Memuaskan." *Kompas*. September 5, 2013. https://nasional.kompas.com/read/2013/09/05/1638409/Survei.INES.Kinerja.Pemerintahan.SBY.Tak.Memuaskan.

Geertz, Clifford. 1976. *The Religion of Java*. Chicago: University of Chicago Press.

Givan, Rebecca K., Kenneth Roberts, and Sarah A. Soule. 2010. *The Diffusion of Social Movements: Actors, Mechanisms, and Political Effects*. Cambridge: Cambridge University Press.

Gonzalez Ocantos, Ezequiel, Chad Kiewiet de Jonge, and David W. Nickerson. 2014. "The Conditionality of Vote-Buying Norms: Experimental Evidence from Latin America." *American Journal of Political Science* 58 (1): 197–211. https://doi.org/10.1111/ajps.12047.

Grabo, Allen, Brian R. Spisak, and Mark van Vugt. 2017. "Charisma as Signal: An Evolutionary Perspective on Charismatic Leadership." *The Leadership Quarterly* 28 (4): 473–485.

Green, Jane, and Sara B. Hobolt. 2008. "Owning the Issue Agenda: Party Strategies and Vote Choices in British Elections." *Electoral Studies* 27 (3): 460–476. https://doi.org/http://dx.doi.org/10.1016/j.electstud.2008.02.003.

Guardado, Jenny, and Leonard Wantchekon. 2014. *Do Electoral Handouts Affect Voter Behavior*. New York: Columbia-NYU African Political Economic Research Seminar.

Gunn, Geoffrey C. 2019. "Indonesia in 2018." *Asian Survey* 59 (1): 156. https://doi.org/10.1525/as.2019.59.1.156.

Hadiz, Vedi R. 2000. "Retrieving the Past for the Future? Indonesia and the New Order Legacy." *Southeast Asian Journal of Social Science* 28 (2): 11–33. https://doi.org/10.1163/030382400X00037.

——. 2003. "Reorganizing Political Power in Indonesia: A Reconsideration of So-Called 'Democratic Transitions.'" *The Pacific Review* 16 (4): 591–611.

——. 2004. "Indonesian Local Party Politics." *Critical Asian Studies* 36 (4): 615–636. https://doi.org/10.1080/1467271042000273275.

——. 2019. "Oligarchs, Money and Religion: Indonesia's Election." *Indonesia at Melbourne*. April 2. https://electionwatch.unimelb.edu.au/articles/oligarchs,-money-and-religion-indonesias-election.

Hadiz, Vedi R., and Richard Robison. 2013. "The Political Economy of Oligarchy and the Reorganization of Power in Indonesia." *Indonesia* (96): 35–57.

Hainsworth, Geoffrey. 2007. "Rule of Law, Anti-Corruption, Anti-Terrorism and Militant Islam: Coping with Threats to Democratic Pluralism and National Unity in

Indonesia." *Asia Pacific Viewpoint* 48 (1): 128–144. https://doi.org/10.1111/j.1467-8373.2007.00335.x.

Hall, Peter M. 1972. "A Symbolic Interactionist Analysis of Politics." *Sociological Inquiry* 42 (3–4): 35–75. https://doi.org/10.1111/j.1475-682X.1972.tb00229.x.

Hamayotsu, Kikue. 2015. "Indonesia in 2014: The Year of Electing the 'People's President.'" *Asian Survey* 55 (1): 174–183. https://doi.org/10.1525/as.2015.55.1.174.

Hamayotsu, Kikue, and Ronnie Nataatmadja. 2016. "Indonesia in 2015: The People's President's Rocky Road and Hazy Outlooks in Democratic Consolidation." *Asian Survey* 56 (1): 129–137. https://doi.org/10.1525/as.2016.56.1.129.

Hamid, Sandra. 2014. "Jokowi's Party Takes Lead in Indonesia's Elections, But Steep Road Ahead." *Asia Foundation*. April 9. https://asiafoundation.org/2014/04/09/jokowis-party-takes-lead-in-indonesias-elections-but-steep-road-ahead/.

Hamilton-Hart, Natasha. 2001. "Anti-Corruption Strategies in Indonesia." *Bulletin of Indonesian Economic Studies* 37 (1): 65–82.

Hansen, Kasper M., and Rasmus Tue Pedersen. 2014. "Campaigns Matter: How Voters Become Knowledgeable and Efficacious During Election Campaigns." *Political Communication* 31 (2): 303–324.

Hara, A. E. 2001. "The Difficult Journey of Democratization in Indonesia." *Contemporary Southeast Asia* 23 (2): 307–326.

Haris, Syamsuddin. 2004. "General Elections Under the New Order." In *Elections in Indonesia: The New Order and Beyond*, edited by Hans Antlov and Sven Cederroth, 18–37. London: Routledge.

Hein, Gordon R. 1982. "Indonesia in 1981: Countdown to the General Elections." *Asian Survey* 22 (2): 200–211. http://www.jstor.org/stable/2643947.

Hetherington, Kevin. 1998. *Expressions of Identity: Space, Performance, Politics*. London: Sage.

Heywood, Paul M. 2017. "Rethinking Corruption: Hocus-Pocus, Locus and Focus." *Slavonic & Eastern European Review* 95 (1): 21–48.

Hicken, Allen. 2007. "How Do Rules and Institutions Encourage Vote Buying?" In *Elections for Sale*, edited by Frederic Charles Schaffer, 47–60. Quezon City, Philippines: Ateneo De Manila University Press.

——. 2011. "Clientelism." *Annual Review of Political Science* 14 (1): 289–310. https://doi.org/doi:10.1146/annurev.polisci.031908.220508.

Hicken, Allen, Paul Hutchcroft, Edward Aspinall, and Meredith Weiss. 2019. "Introduction: The Local Dynamics of the National Election in the Philippines." In *Electoral Dynamics in the Philippines: Money Politics, Patronage and Clientelism at the Grassroots*, edited by Allen Hicken, Edward Aspinall, and Meredith Weiss, 1–42. Singapore: NUS Press.

Hidayat, Syarif. 2009. "Pilkada, Money Politics and the Dangers of 'Informal Governance' Practices." In *Deepening Democracy in Indonesia?: Direct Elections for Local Leaders*, edited by Maribeth Erb and Priyambudi Sulistiyanto, 125–146. Singapore: ISEAS.

Hill, Hal, and Takashi Shiraishi. 2007. "Indonesia After the Asian Crisis." *Asian Economic Policy Review* 2 (1): 123–141. https://doi.org/10.1111/j.1748-3131.2007.00058.x.

Hofman, Bert, Kai Kaiser, and Günther Schulze. 2009. "Corruption and Decentralization." In *Decentralization and Regional Autonomy in Indonesia*, edited by Coen Holtzappel and Martin Ramstedt, 99–113. Singapore: ISEAS.

Hollander, Jocelyn A., and Rachel L. Einwohner. 2004. "Conceptualizing Resistance." *Sociological Forum* 19 (4): 533–554.

Honna, Jun. 2012. "Inside the Democrat Party: Power, Politics and Conflict in Indonesia's Presidential Party." *South East Asia Research* 20 (4): 473–489. https://doi.org/10.5367/sear.2012.0125.

Hutchcroft, Paul D. 2000. "Politics and Privilege in the Philippines." In *Rents, Rent-Seeking and Economic Development: Theory and Evidence in Asia*, edited by Mustaq H. Khan and K. S. Jomo, 207–247. Cambridge: Cambridge University Press.

——. 2014. "Linking Capital and Countryside: Patronage and Clientelism in Japan, Thailand, and the Philippines." In *Clientelism, Social Policy, and the Quality of Democracy*, edited by Diego Abente Brun and Larry Diamond, 174–203. Baltimore, MD: Johns Hopkins University Press.

Indikator. 2014. "Laporan Efek Kampanye Versus Efek Jokowi: Elektabilitas Partai-Partai Jelang Pemilu Legislatif 2014." April 4. https://indikator.co.id/laporan-efek-kampanye-versus-efek-jokowi-elektabilitas-partai-partai-jelang-pemilu-legislatif-2014/.

Indrayana, Denny. 2017. "Money Politics in a More Democratic Indonesia: An Overview." *Australian Journal of Asian Law* 18 (2): 1–15.

Ismar, A., and F. Husna. 2013. "Survei Korupsi: Suap Hal Biasa." *Wall Street Journal*. January 3. http://indo.wsj.com/posts/2013/01/03/survei-korupsi-suap-hal-biasa/.

James, Owen. 2017. "Discipline and Institutionalisation: A Comparative Study of Internal Party Discipline Systems in Golkar and NasDem." Honours, Department of Indonesian Studies, University of Sydney.

Jerit, Jennifer, and Jason Barabas. 2017. "Revisiting the Gender Gap in Political Knowledge." *Political Behavior* 39 (4): 817–838.

Johnson Tan, Paige. 2012. "Reining in the Reign of the Parties: Political Parties in Contemporary Indonesia." *Asian Journal of Political Science* 20 (2): 154–179. https://doi.org/10.1080/02185377.2012.714132.

Johnston, Michael. 1996. "The Search for Definitions: The Vitality of Politics and the Issue of Corruption." *International Social Science Journal* 48 (149): 321–335. https://doi.org/10.1111/1468-2451.00035.

——. 2005. *Syndromes of Corruption: Wealth, Power and Democracy*. Cambridge: Cambridge University Press.

Jungherr, Andreas. 2016. "Twitter Use in Election Campaigns: A Systematic Literature Review." *Journal of Information Technology & Politics* 13 (1): 72–91.

Juwono, Vishnu. 2016. "Berantas Korupsi: A Political History of Governance Reform and Anti-Corruption Initiatives in Indonesia 1945–2014." PhD, International History, The London School of Economics and Political Science (LSE). http://etheses.lse.ac.uk/id/eprint/3381.

Kahin, George McTurnan. 2003. *Nationalism and Revolution in Indonesia*. Ithaca, NY: Cornell Southeast Asia Program.

Keefer, Philip, and Razvan Vlaicu. 2017. "Vote Buying and Campaign Promises." *Journal of Comparative Economics* 45 (4): 773–792. https://doi.org/https://doi.org/10.1016/j.jce.2017.07.001.

Khan, Mushtaq H. 1998. "Patron-Client Networks and the Economic Effects of Corruption in Asia." *The European Journal of Development Research* 10 (1): 15–39. http://www.informaworld.com/10.1080/09578819808426700.

King, Dwight Y. 2000. "Corruption in Indonesia: A Curable Cancer?" *Journal of International Affairs* 53 (2): 603–625.

Kleinman, Arthur. 1999. "Experience and Its Moral Modes: Culture, Human Conditions, and Disorder." *Tanner Lectures on Human Values* 20: 355–420.

Kongkirati, Prajak. 2016. "Evolving Power of Provincial Political Families in Thailand: Dynastic Power, Party Machine and Ideological Politics." *South East Asia Research* 24 (3): 386–406. https://doi.org/10.1177/0967828X16659570.

Kramer, Elisabeth. 2013. "When News Becomes Entertainment: Representations of Corruption in Indonesia's Media and the Implication of Scandal." *Media Asia* 40 (1): 60–72.

——. 2014. "A Fall from Grace? 'Beef-Gate' and the Case of Indonesia's Prosperous Justice Party." *Asian Politics and Policy* 6 (4): 555–576.
——. 2015. "What's in a Symbol? Emerging Parties and Anti-Corruption Symbols in Indonesia's 2014 National Legislative Election Campaigns." Doctoral Dissertation PhD, Department of Indonesian Studies, University of Sydney.
——. 2019. "Democratization and Indonesia's Anticorruption Movement." In *Activists in Transition: Progressive Politics in Democratic Indonesia*, edited by Thushara Dibley and Michele Ford. Ithaca, NY: Cornell University Press.
Kramon, Eric. 2018. *Money for Votes: The Causes and Consequences of Electoral Clientelism in Africa*. Cambridge: Cambridge University Press.
Kubik, Jan. 2013. "Ethnography of Politics: Foundations, Applications, Prospects." In *Political Ethnography: What Immersion Contributes to the Study of Power*, edited by Edward Schatz, 25–42. Chicago: University of Chicago Press.
Lau, Richard, and David Redlawsk. 2001. "Advantages and Disadvantages of Cognitive Heuristics in Political Decision Making." *American Journal of Political Science* 45 (4): 951–971.
Ledysia, Septiana. 2013. "Survei LSN: PD Paling Korup, Disusul Golkar dan PKS." *Detiknews*, March 24. http://news.detik.com/read/2013/03/24/144044/2202190/10/survei-lsn-pd-paling-korup-disusul-golkar-dan-pks.
Lembaga Survei Indonesia. 2011. "Pemilih mengambang dan prospek perubahan kekuatan partai politik" (Report). http://www.lsi.or.id/riset/403/Rilis%20LSI%20 29%20Mei%202011 (site discontinued).
——. 2012. "Kepercayaan Publik Pada Pemberantasan Korupsi." http://www.lsi.or.id/riset/409/Rilis_LSI_Korupsi (site discontinued).
——. 2013. *Pendapat Masyarakat Indonesia Tahun 2013*. http://www.lsi.or.id/riset/433/Opini_Publik_thdp_penyelenggara_PEMILU (site discontinued).
Lev, Daniel S. 1966. *The Transition to Guided Democracy: Indonesian Politics, 1957–1959*. Ithaca, NY: Cornell University. Modern Indonesia Project. Monograph series.
Lewis, Blane D., and Adrianus Hendrawan. 2019. "The Impact of Majority Coalitions on Local Government Spending, Service Delivery, and Corruption in Indonesia." *European Journal of Political Economy* 58: 178–191.
Leys, Colin. 1990. "What Is the Problem about Corruption?" In *Political Corruption: A Handbook*, edited by Arnold J. Heidenheimer, Michael Johnston, and Victor T. Le Vine, 51–66. New Brunswick: Traction Publishers. Original edition, 1965.
Liddle, R. William. 1988. "Indonesia in 1987: The New Order at the Height of Its Power." *Asian Survey* 28 (2): 180–191. https://doi.org/10.2307/2644819.
——. 1996. *Leadership and Culture in Indonesian Politics*, edited by Asian Studies Association of Australia. Sydney: Allen and Unwin.
——. 2000. "Indonesia in 1999: Democracy Restored." *Asian Survey* 40 (1): 32–42. https://doi.org/10.2307/3021218.
——. 2001. "Indonesia in 2000: A Shaky Start for Democracy." *Asian Survey* 41 (1): 208–220. https://doi.org/10.1525/as.2001.41.1.208.
Liddle, R. W., and S. Mujani. 2005. "Indonesia in 2004: The Rise of Susilo Bambang Yudhoyono." *Asian Survey* 45 (1): 119–126.
Lukman, Enricko. 2014. "Twitter Has Close to 20 Million Active Users in Indonesia." In *Tech in Asia*. June 4. https://www.techinasia.com/twitter-close-20-million-active-users-indonesia.
MacIntyre, Andrew. 1993. "Indonesia in 1992: Coming to Terms with the Outside World." *Asian Survey* 33 (2): 204–210. https://doi.org/10.2307/2645331.
Mackie, J.A.C. 1970. "The Commission of Four Report on Corruption." *Bulletin of Indonesian Economic Studies* 6 (3): 87–101.

MacKinnon, Danny. 2011. "Reconstructing Scale: Towards a New Scalar Politics." *Progress in Human Geography* 35 (1): 21–36. https://doi.org/10.1177/0309132510367841.
MacLaren, Laurel. 2013. "Beleaguered by Graft, Indonesians Shocked by High Court Corruption." *Asia Foundation.* October 9. https://asiafoundation.org/2013/10/09/beleaguered-by-graft-indonesians-shocked-by-high-court-corruption/.
Mahi, B. Raksaka, and Suahasil Nazara. 2012. "Survey of Recent Developments." *Bulletin of Indonesian Economic Studies* 48 (1): 7–31. https://doi.org/10.1080/00074918.2012.654482.
Mahkamah Konstitusi. 2014. *Sejarah Pembentukan Mahkamah Konstitusi.* Jakarta: Government of the Republic of Indonesia. http://www.mahkamahkonstitusi.go.id/index.php?page=web.ProfilMK&id=1.
Mahler, Matthew. 2006. "Politics as Vocation: Notes Towards a Sensualist Understanding of Political Engagement." *Qualitative Sociology* 2006 (29): 281–300.
Mallarangeng, Rizal, and R. William Liddle. 1996. "Indonesia in 1995: The Struggle for Power and Policy." *Asian Survey* 36 (2): 109–116. https://doi.org/10.2307/2645806.
Marcus, George. 1995. "Ethnography in/of the World System: The Emergence of Multi-Sited Ethnography." *Annual Review of Anthropology* 24 (1995): 95–117. https://www.annualreviews.org/doi/10.1146/annurev.an.24.100195.000523.
Marquette, Heather. 2012. "'Finding God' or 'Moral Disengagement' in the Fight Against Corruption in Developing Countries? Evidence from India and Nigeria." *Public Administration and Development* 32 (1): 11–26. https://doi.org/10.1002/pad.1605.
Masduki, Masduki. 2018. "Strategi Pemulihan Citra Partai Politik: Kasus Partai Demokrat." *Jurnal Ilmu-Ilmu Sosial* 36 (81). https://journal.uii.ac.id/Unisia/article/view/10479.
McCann, James A., and Jorge I. Domínguez. 1998. "Mexicans React to Electoral Fraud and Political Corruption: An Assessment of Public Opinion and Voting Behavior." *Electoral Studies* 17 (4): 483–503. https://doi.org/http://dx.doi.org/10.1016/S0261-3794(98)00026-2.
McGibbon, R. 2006. "Indonesian Politics in 2006: Stability, Compromise and Shifting Contests Over Ideology." *Bulletin of Indonesian Economic Studies* 42 (3): 321–340.
McGregor, Katharine E. 2007. *History in Uniform: Military Ideology and the Construction of Indonesia's Past.* Singapore: NUS Press.
Melvin, Jess. 2018. *The Army and the Indonesian Genocide: Mechanics of Mass Murder.* London: Routledge.
Mietzner, Marcus. 2013. *Money, Power, and Ideology: Political Parties in Post-Authoritarian Indonesia.* Singapore: NUS Press.
———. 2015. "Dysfunction by Design: Political Finance and Corruption in Indonesia." *Critical Asian Studies* 47 (4): 587–610. https://doi.org/10.1080/14672715.2015.1079991.
Mitchell, J. Clyde. 1983. "Case and Situation Analysis." *The Sociological Review* 31 (2): 187–211. https://doi.org/10.1111/j.1467-954X.1983.tb00387.x.
Moon, Woojin. 2004. "Party Activists, Campaign Resources and Candidate Position Taking: Theory, Tests and Applications." *British Journal of Political Science* 34 (4): 611–633. https://doi.org/10.1017/S0007123404000213.
Morgenbesser, Lee, and Thomas B. Pepinsky. 2019. "Elections as Causes of Democratization: Southeast Asia in Comparative Perspective." *Comparative Political Studies* 52 (1): 3–35. https://doi.org/10.1177/0010414018758763.
Muhtadi, Burhanuddin. 2018a. "Buying Votes in Indonesia: Partisans, Personal Networks, and Winning Margins." Doctor of Philosophy, Department of Political and Social Change, Australian National University.
———. 2018b. "A Third of Indonesian Voters Bribed During Election: How and Why." *The Conversation.* July 20, 2018. https://theconversation.com/a-third-of-indonesian-voters-bribed-during-election-how-and-why-100166.

———. 2019. *Vote Buying in Indonesia: The Mechanics of Electoral Bribery.* Singapore: Springer.
Mutaqin, Zezen Zaenal. 2018. "Culture, Islamic Feminism, and the Quest for Legal Reform in Indonesia." *Asian Journal of Women's Studies* 24 (4): 423–445.
na Thalang, Chanintira. 2005. "The Legislative Elections in Indonesia, April 2004." *Electoral Studies* 24 (2): 326–332. https://doi.org/http://dx.doi.org/10.1016/j.electstud.2004.10.006.
Nadeau, Richard, Neil Nevitte, Elisabeth Gidengil, and Andre Blais. 2008. "Election Campaigns as Information Campaigns: Who Learns What and Does It Matter?" *Political Communication* 25: 229–249.
Nastiti, Aulia, and Sari Ratri. 2018. "Emotive Politics: Islamic Organizations and Religious Mobilization in Indonesia." *Contemporary Southeast Asia* 40 (2): 196–221.
Ndakaripa, Musiwaro. 2020. "Zimbabwe's 2018 Elections: Funding, Public Resources and Vote Buying." *Review of African Political Economy* 47 (164): 301–312. https://doi.org/10.1080/03056244.2020.1735327.
Nehru, Vikram. 2013. "Survey of Recent Developments." *Bulletin of Indonesian Economic Studies* 49 (2): 139–166. https://doi.org/10.1080/00074918.2013.809840.
Nordholt, Henk Schulte. 2004. "Decentralisation in Indonesia: Less State, More Democracy?" In *Politicising Democracy: The New Local Politics of Democratisation*, edited by John Harriss, Kristian Stokke, and Olle Törnquist, 29–47. New York: Springer.
Norris, Pippa. 2002. "Do Campaign Communications Matter for Civic Engagement? American Elections from Eisenhower to George W. Bush." In *Do Political Campaigns Matter? Campaign Effects in Elections and Referendums*, edited by David M. Farrell and Rudiger Schmitt-Beck, 127–144. London: Routledge.
Norris, Pippa, and Andrea Abel Van Es, eds. 2016. *Checkbook Elections?: Political Finance in Comparative Perspective.* Cambridge: Cambridge University Press.
Nurhidayatuloh, Nurhidayatuloh, F. Febrian, Achmad Romsan, Annalisa Yahanan, Martinus Sardi, and Fatimatuz Zuhro. 2018. "Forsaking Equality: Examine Indonesia's State Responsibility on Polygamy to the Marriage Rights in CEDAW." *Journal Dinamika Hukum* 18 (2): 182–193.
Nye, Joseph S. 1990. "Corruption and Political Development: A Cost-Benefit Analysis." In *Political Corruption: A Handbook*, edited by Arnold J. Heidenheimer, Michael Johnston and Victor T. Le Vine, 963–983. New Brunswick: Transaction Publishers.
Olaniyan, Azeez. 2020. "Election Sophistication and the Changing Contours of Vote Buying in Nigeria's 2019 General Elections." *The Round Table* 109 (4): 386–395. https://doi.org/10.1080/00358533.2020.1788762.
Ott, Brian L., and Greg Dickinson. 2019. *The Twitter Presidency: Donald J. Trump and the Politics of White Rage.* New York: Routledge.
Panebianco, Angelo. 1988. *Political Parties: Organization and Power.* Cambridge: Cambridge University Press.
Pemilu. 2014. *Hasil Pemilu Legislatif 9 April 2014.* Pemilu. http://www.pemilu.com/berita/2014/05/hasil-pemilu-legislatif-9-april-2014/ (site discontinued).
Penders, C.L.M. 1974. *The Life and Times of Sukarno.* London: Sidgwick and Jackson.
Pereira, Carlos, and Marcus Andre Melo. 2014. "Reelecting Corrupt Incumbents in Exchange for Public Goods: Rouba Mas Faz in Brazil." *Latin American Research Review* 51 (1): 1–44.
Peterson, Daniel. 2020. *Islam, Blasphemy, and Human Rights in Indonesia: The Trial of Ahok.* London: Routledge.
Petrocik, John R., William L. Benoit, and Glenn J. Hansen. 2003. "Issue Ownership and Presidential Campaigning, 1952–2000." *Political Science Quarterly* 118 (4): 599–626. https://doi.org/10.1002/j.1538-165X.2003.tb00407.x.

Philp, Mark. 2008. "Peacebuilding and Corruption." *International Peacekeeping* 15 (3): 310–327. http://www.informaworld.com/10.1080/13533310802058786.
Phongpaichit, Pasuk, and Christopher John Baker. 2004. *Thaksin: The Business of Politics in Thailand*. Copenhagen: NIAS.
Popkin, Samuel L. 1991. *The Reasoning Voter*. Chicago: University of Chicago Press.
Pradhanawati, Ari, George Towar Ikbal Tawakkal, and Andrew D. Garner. 2018. "Voting Their Conscience: Poverty, Education, Social Pressure and Vote Buying in Indonesia." *Journal of East Asian Studies* 2018: 1–20.
Prihatini, Ella S. 2019. "Women Who Win in Indonesia: The Impact of Age, Experience, and List Position." *Women's Studies International Forum* 72: 40–46. https://www.sciencedirect.com/science/article/pii/S027753951830428X.
Purnomo, W. A. 2013. "Politik Uang Dinilai Tanggung Jawab Partai." *Tempo.co*. December 13. https://nasional.tempo.co/read/537189/politik-uang-dinilai-tanggung-jawab-partai.
Putnam, Robert D. 1966. "Political Attitudes and the Local Community." *The American Political Science Review* 60 (3): 640–654. https://doi.org/10.2307/1952976.
Querubin, Pablo. 2016. "Family and Politics: Dynastic Persistence in the Philippines." *Quarterly Journal of Political Science* 11 (2): 151–181. https://doi.org/10.1561/100.00014182.
Ratnawaty Chotim, Endah. 2019. "The Practice of Vote Buying in Legislative Elections in Indonesia in 2019: Case Study in Belitung Regency." *International Journal of Humanities and Social Sciences* 8: 123–130.
Redlawsk, David P. 2004. "What Voters Do: Information Search During Election Campaigns." *Political Psychology* 25 (4): 595–610. https://doi.org/10.1111/j.1467-9221.2004.00389.x.
Reeve, David. 1985. *Golkar of Indonesia: An Alternative to the Party System*. Singapore: Oxford University Press.
Reuter, Thomas. 2015. "Political Parties and the Power of Money in Indonesia and Beyond." *TRANS-Trans-Regional and National Studies of Southeast Asia* 3 (2): 267–288. https://doi.org/10.1017/trn.2014.23.
Ricklefs, M. C. 2001. *A History of Modern Indonesia Since c.1200*. 3rd ed. Stanford, CA: Stanford University Press.
Rieber, Steven. 2001. "Vote Selling and Self-Interested Voting." *Public Affairs Quarterly* 15 (1): 35–49. http://www.jstor.org/stable/40441274.
Rini, C. L. 2013. "NasDem Rebut Ketidakpercayaan Masyarakat Terhadap Elite Parpol." *Republike Online*. July 7. https://nasional.republika.co.id/berita/mpkp89/nasdem-rebut-ketidakpercayaan-masyarakat-terhadap-elite-parpol.
Robertson-Snape, Fiona. 1999. "Corruption, Collusion and Nepotism in Indonesia." *Third World Quarterly* 20 (3): 589–602. https://doi.org/10.1080/01436599913703.
Robison, Richard. 1981. "Culture, Politics, and Economy in the Political History of the New Order." *Indonesia* 31 (April 1981): 1–29. http://www.jstor.org/stable/3351013.
Rohrschneider, Robert. 2002. "Mobilizing Versus Chasing: How Do Parties Target Voters in Election Campaigns?" *Electoral Studies* 21 (3): 367–382. https://doi.org/http://dx.doi.org/10.1016/S0261-3794(00)00044-5.
Rolisman. 2012. "Representasi Pemberitaan Kasus Korupsi Muhammad Nazaruddin dalam Surat Kabar Media Indonesia:Kajian Analisis Wacana Kritis." Skripsi - 000115096. Sarjana I, Fakultas Ilmu Budaya, Universitas Padjadjaran. http://repository.unpad.ac.id/frontdoor/index/index/docId/115096.
Rose, Jonathan. 2018. "The Meaning of Corruption: Testing the Coherence and Adequacy of Corruption Definitions." *Public Integrity* 20 (3): 220–233. https://doi.org/10.1080/10999922.2017.1397999.

Rose-Ackerman, Susan. 2008. "Corruption and Government." *International Peacekeeping* 15 (3): 328–343. http://www.informaworld.com/10.1080/13533310802058802.
Rosenberg, Shawn W., Shulamit Kahn, Thuy Tran, and Minh-Thu Le. 1991. "Creating a Political Image: Shaping Appearance and Manipulating the Vote." *Political Behavior* 13 (4): 345–367. https://doi.org/10.2307/586121. http://www.jstor.org/stable/586121.
Ross, Monique. 2014. "Facebook Turns 10: The World's Largest Social Network in Numbers." *ABC News*. February 4. https://www.abc.net.au/news/2014-02-04/facebook-turns-10:-the-social-network-in-numbers/5237128?nw=0.
Sadikin, Rendy. 2014. "Hasil Pemilu Legislatif 2014: Suara PDIP Lebih Rendah dari Perkiraan Survei." *Tribunnews*, May 10. http://www.tribunnews.com/pemilu-2014/2014/05/10/hasil-pemilu-legislatif-2014-suara-pdip-lebih-rendah-dari-perkiraan-survei.
Salna, Karlis, and Viriya Singgih. 2019. "Election Cash Splash Spurs Indonesia's Economy." *Bloomberg*. March 25. https://www.bloomberg.com/news/articles/2019-03-25/election-cash-splash-spurs-southeast-asia-s-biggest-economy.
Sampson, Steven. 2010. "The Anti-Corruption Industry: From Movement to Institution." *Global Crime* 11 (2): 261–278. https://doi.org/10.1080/17440571003669258.
Samuels, David. 2001. "Money, Elections, and Democracy in Brazil." *Latin American Politics and Society* 43 (2): 27–48. https://doi.org/10.1111/j.1548-2456.2001.tb00398.x.
Schatz, Edward. 2013. "Ethnographic Immersion and the Study of Politics: Introduction." In *Political Ethnography: What Immersion Contributes to the Study of Power*, edited by Edward Schatz, 1–22. Chicago: University of Chicago Press.
Schedler, Andreas. 2002. "The Menu of Manipulation." *Journal of Democracy* 13 (2): 36–50.
Schmitt-Beck, Rudiger, and David M. Farrell. 2002. "Do Political Campaigns Matter? Yes, But It Depends." In *Do Political Campaigns Matter? Campaign Effects in Elections and Referendums*, edited by David M. Farrell and Rudiger Schmitt-Beck, 183–193. London: Routledge.
Schütte, Sofie Arjon. 2009. "Government Policies and Civil Society Initiatives against Corruption." In *Democratization in Post-Suharto Indonesia*, edited by M. Bunte and A. Ufen, 81–101. New York: Routledge.
——. 2012. "Against the Odds: Anti-Corruption Reform in Indonesia." *Public Administration and Development* 32 (1): 38–48. https://doi.org/10.1002/pad.623.
——. 2016. "Two Steps Forward, One Step Backwards: Indonesia's Winding (Anti-) Corruption Journey." In *Routledge Handbook of Corruption in Asia*, edited by Ting Gong and Ian Scott, 42–55. New York: Routledge.
Schwarz, Adam. 2004. *A Nation in Waiting: Indonesia's Search for Stability*. Singapore: Talisman.
Sebastian, Leonard C. 2012. "Special Focus Political Parties and Democracy in Indonesia: Introduction." *South East Asia Research* 20 (4): 463–472. https://doi.org/10.5367/sear.2012.0132.
Selinaswati, Selinaswati. 2014. "Rekrutmen Perempuan Sebagai Caleg dan Wajah Maskulin Partai Politik." *Jurnal Perempuan:Untuk Pencerahan Kesetaraan*. April 4. http://www.jurnalperempuan.org/blog/rekrutmen-perempuan-sebagai-caleg-dan-wajah-maskulin-partai-politik.
Setiyono, Budi, and Ross H. McLeod. 2010. "Civil Society Organisations' Contribution to the Anti-Corruption Movement in Indonesia." *Bulletin of Indonesian Economic Studies* 46 (3): 347–370. https://doi.org/10.1080/00074918.2010.522504.
Setuningsih, N. 2013. "Latest Corruption Index Shows Most Graft Committed by Lawmakers: KPK." *Jakarta Globe*. December 16.
Setuningsih, N., and A. Cahyadi. 2014. "Ex-MK Chief Justice Akil Accuses Mahfud M.D. of Involvement in Election Scandal." *Jakarta Globe*. February 22.

Shair-Rosenfield, Sarah. 2012. "The Alternative Incumbency Effect: Electing Women Legislators in Indonesia." *Electoral Studies* 31 (3): 576–587. https://doi.org/https://doi.org/10.1016/j.electstud.2012.05.002.
———. 2019. *Electoral Reform and the Fate of New Democracies: Lessons from the Indonesian Case*. Ann Arbor: University of Michigan Press.
Shattuck, John, and Mathias Risse. 2020. *Reimagining Rights & Responsibility in the United States: Towards a More Equal Liberty*. Cambridge, MA: Carr Center for Human Rights, Harvard Kennedy School.
Sheafer, Tamir. 2008. "Charismatic Communication Skill, Media Legitimacy, and Electoral Success." *Journal of Political Marketing* 7 (1): 1–24.
Sherlock, Stephen. 2002. "Combating Corruption in Indonesia? The Ombudsman and the Assets Auditing Commission." *Bulletin of Indonesian Economic Studies* 38 (3): 367–383. https://doi.org/10.1080/00074910215532.
———. 2013. *Indonesia's Third Democratic Transition: Are the Parties Ready for the 2014 Presidential Election?* Canberra: Australian National University.
Siegel, James T. 1998. "Early Thoughts on the Violence of May 13 and 14, 1998 in Jakarta." *Indonesia* 66 (October 1998): 75–108. http://www.jstor.org/stable/3351448.
Simandjuntak, D. 2012. "Gifts and Promises: Patronage Democracy in a Decentralised Indonesia." *European Journal of East Asian Studies* 11 (1): 99–126.
Slater, Dan. 2004. "Indonesia's Accountability Trap: Party Cartels and Presidential Power after Democratic Transition." *Indonesia* (78): 61–92. https://doi.org/10.2307/3351288.
Smith, Theodore M. 1971. "Corruption, Tradition and Change." *Indonesia* 11 (April): 21–40. http://www.jstor.org/stable/3350742.
Snyder, James M. 1989. "Election Goals and the Allocation of Campaign Resources." *Econometrica: Journal of the Econometric Society* 57 (3): 637–660.
Soares, S. 2014. "Netizens Protest against Light Sentence for Atut." *Tempo.co*. September 5. https://en.tempo.co/read/604812/netizens-protest-against-light-sentence-for-atut.
Stiers, Dieter, Jac Larner, John Kenny, Sofia Breitenstein, Florence Vallee-Dubois, and Michael Lewis-Beck. 2019. "Candidate Authenticity: 'To Thine Own Self Be True.'" *Political Behavior* 43: 1–24. https://doi.org/https://doi.org/10.1007/s11109-019-09589-y.
Stokes, Susan C., Thad Dunning, Marcelo Nazareno, and Velria Brusco. 2013. *Brokers, Voters, and Clientelism: The Puzzle of Distributive Politics*. New York: Cambridge University Press.
Straits Times. 2019. "Indonesia 'Money Politics' Greases Election Machine." April 9. https://www.straitstimes.com/asia/se-asia/indonesia-money-politics-greases-election-machine.
Stratmann, Thomas. 2005. "Some Talk: Money in Politics. A (Partial) Review of the Literature." In *Policy Challenges and Political Responses: Public Choice Perspectives on the Post-9/11 World*, edited by William F. Shughart and Robert D. Tollison, 135–156. Boston: Springer US.
Subkhan. 2013. "Suap Daging Impor, KPK Kembali Periksa Maharani." *Tempo.co*. July 8. https://nasional.tempo.co/read/494386/suap-daging-impor-kpk-kembali-periksa-maharani/full&view=ok.
Subritzky, John. 2016. *Confronting Sukarno*. London: Springer.
Sugiana, Astrid Meilasari, and Dianingtyas M. Putri. 2018. "Indonesian Women's Participation in Politics and Governance: Challenges and Opportunities." 18th International Conference on Future of Women, Petaling Jaya, Malaysia.
Sukarno. 1964. *Indonesia's Political Manifesto 1959–1964*. Djakarta: Prapantja.
Sukma, Rizal. 2009. "Indonesian Politics in 2009: Defective Elections, Resilient Democracy." *Bulletin of Indonesian Economic Studies* 45 (3): 317–336. https://doi.org/10.1080/00074910903301647.

Sulaiman, Yohanes. 2014. "Indonesia Farewells SBY and His Years of Wasted Opportunities." *The Conversation*. October 16. https://theconversation.com/indonesia-farewells-sby-and-his-years-of-wasted-opportunities-32561.

Sule, Babayo, and Mohammed Kwarah Tal. 2018. "Impact of Money on Nigerian Politics: Exploring the General Elections in the Fourth Republic." *Asia Pacific Journal of Education, Arts, Sciences* 5 (2): 89–98.

Swartz, David. 1997. *Culture and Power: The Sociology of Pierre Bourdieu*. Chicago: University of Chicago Press.

Tanuwidjaja, Sunny. 2010. "Political Islam and Islamic Parties in Indonesia: Critically Assessing the Evidence of Islam's Political Decline." *Contemporary Southeast Asia* 32 (1): 29–49.

Tapsell, Ross. 2010. "Newspaper Ownership and Press Freedom in Indonesia." Asian Studies Association of Australia Biennial Conference. Adelaide.

Tarrow, Sidney G. 2011. *Power in Movement: Social Movements and Contentious Politics*, edited by Margaret Levi. Cambridge Studies in Comparative Politics. Cambridge: Cambridge University Press.

Tawakkal, George Towar Ikbal, Wisnu Suhardono, Andrew D. Garner, and Thomas Seitz. 2017. "Consistency and Vote Buying: Income, Education, and Attitudes about Vote Buying in Indonesia." *Journal of East Asian Studies* 17 (3): 313–329. https://doi.org/10.1017/jea.2017.15.

Tomsa, Dirk. 2008. *Party Politics and Democratization in Indonesia: Golkar in the Post-Suharto Era*. New York: Routledge.

——. 2009. "The Eagle Has Crash-Landed." *Inside Indonesia*. July–September. http://www.insideindonesia.org/feature-editions/the-eagle-has-crash-landed.

——. 2014. "Party System Fragmentation in Indonesia: The Subnational Dimension." *Journal of East Asian Studies* 14 (2014): 249–278.

——. 2015. "Local Politics and Corruption in Indonesia's Outer Islands." *Bijdragen tot de taal-, land-en volkenkunde/Journal of the Humanities Social Sciences of Southeast Asia* 171 (2–3): 196–219.

Tomsa, Dirk, and Charlotte Setijadi. 2018. "New Forms of Political Activism in Indonesia." *Asian Survey* 58 (3): 557. https://doi.org/10.1525/as.2018.58.3.557.

Tomz, Michael, and Robert P. Van Houweling. 2008. "Candidate Positioning and Voter Choice." *American Political Science Review* 102 (03): 303–318. https://doi.org/doi:10.1017/S0003055408080301.

Törnquist, Olle. 2006. "Assessing Democracy From Below: A Framework and Indonesian Pilot Study." *Democratization* 13 (02): 227–255.

Tupai, R. 2005. *Chronology of Tommy Suharto's Legal Saga: From Playboy Defendant to Fugitive Murderer to Pampered Prisoner & Soon to Freedom*. Jakarta: Paras Indonesia.

Ucu, Karta Raharja. 2013. "Awal Mula LHI dan Darin Mumtazah Saling Jatuh Cinta." *Republika*. June 24. http://www.republika.co.id/berita/nasional/hukum/13/06/24/mow8zj-awal-mula-lhi-dan-darin-mumtazah-saling-jatuh-cinta.

Ufen, Andreas. 2008. "From Aliran to Dealignment: Political Parties in Post-Suharto Indonesia." *South East Asia Research* 16 (1): 5–41. https://doi.org/10.5367/000000008784108149.

Vaishnav, Milan. 2017. *When Crime Pays: Money and Muscle in Indian Politics*. New Haven, CT: Yale University Press.

van der Brug, Wouter. 2004. "Issue Ownership and Party Choice." *Electoral Studies* 23 (2): 209–233. https://doi.org/10.1016/S0261-3794(02)00061-6.

van der Brug, Wouter, and Anthony Mughan. 2007. "Charisma, Leader Effects and Support for Right-Wing Populist Parties." *Party Politics* 13 (1): 29–51.

van der Kroef, Justus M. 1971. *Indonesia After Sukarno*. Vancouver: University of British Colombia Press.
Van de Walle, Nicolas. 2014. "The Democratization of Clientelism in Sub-Saharan Africa." In *Clientelism, Social Policy, and the Quality of Democracy*, edited by Diego Abente Brun and Larry Diamond, 230–252. Baltimore, MD: Johns Hopkins University.
Van Dijk, Teun A. 2008. *Discourse and Context: A Sociocognitive Approach*. Cambridge: Cambridge University Press.
Vatikiotis, Michael R. J. 1993. *Indonesian Politics Under Suharto*. London: Routledge.
Vicente, Pedro C., and Leonard Wantchekon. 2009. "Clientelism and Vote Buying: Lessons from Field Experiments in African Elections." *Oxford Review of Economic Policy* 25 (2): 292–305. https://doi.org/10.1093/oxrep/grp018.
Vincent, Joan. 1978. "Political Anthropology: Manipulative Strategies." *Annual Review of Anthropology* 7 (1): 175–194.
Walgrave, Stefaan, Jonas Lefevere, and Michiel Nuytemans. 2009. "Issue Ownership Stability and Change: How Political Parties Claim and Maintain Issues through Media Appearances." *Political Communication* 26 (2): 153–172. https://doi.org/10.1080/10584600902850718.
Wanandi, J. 2004. "The Indonesian General Elections 2004." *Asia-Pacific Review* 11 (2): 115–131.
Wantchekon, Leonard. 2003. "Clientelism and Voting Behavior: Evidence from a Field Experiment in Benin." *World Politics* 55 (03): 399–422. https://doi.org/doi:10.1353/wp.2003.0018.
Warren, Mark E. 2004. "What Does Corruption Mean in a Democracy?" *American Journal of Political Science* 48 (2): 328–343. https://doi.org/10.1111/j.0092-5853.2004.00073.x.
Weiss, Jeffrey H. 1988. "Is Vote-Selling Desirable?" *Public Choice* 59: 177–194.
Weiss, Meredith L. 2016. "Payoffs, Parties, or Policies: 'Money Politics' and Electoral Authoritarian Resilience." *Critical Asian Studies* 48 (1): 77–99. https://doi.org/10.1080/14672715.2015.1126139.
Welch, Susan, and John R. Hibbing. 1997. "The Effects of Charges of Corruption on Voting Behavior in Congressional Elections, 1982–1990." *The Journal of Politics* 59 (1): 226–239. https://doi.org/10.2307/2998224.
Wertheim, W. F. 1963. "Sociological Aspects of Corruption in Southeast Asia." *Sociologia Neerlandica* II (1963): 129–154.
Wie, T. K. 2003. "The Indonesian Economic Crisis and the Long Road to Recovery." *Australian Economic History Review* 43 (2): 183–196.
Wilson, Geoff A. 2014. "Community Resilience: Path Dependency, Lock-In Effects and Transitional Ruptures." *Journal of Environmental Planning and Management* 57 (1): 1–26. https://doi.org/10.1080/09640568.2012.741519.
Wilson, Ian. 2014. "Resisting Democracy: Front Pembela Islam and Indonesia's 2014 Elections." In *ISEAS Perspective: Watching the Indonesian Elections 2014*, edited by Ulla Fionna, 32–40. Singapore: ISEAS.
Winters, Jeffrey. 2013. "Oligarchy and Democracy in Indonesia." *Indonesia* 96 (October): 11–33. http://muse.jhu.edu.ezproxy2.library.usyd.edu.au/journals/indonesia/toc/ind.96.html.
Witoelar, Wimar. 2014. "The Jokowi Effect: No Breakthrough Against Oligarchy." *New Mandala*. April 10. https://www.newmandala.org/the-jokowi-effect-no-breakthrough-against-oligarchy/.
Wlezien, Christopher. 2005. "On the Salience of Political Issues: The Problem with 'Most Important Problem.'" *Electoral Studies* 24 (4): 555–579. https://doi.org/http://dx.doi.org/10.1016/j.electstud.2005.01.009.

Xue, Song. 2018. "Ethnic Mobilization in 2015 Local Elections in North Sumatra, Indonesia." *Asian Ethnicity* 19 (4): 509–527. https://doi.org/10.1080/14631369.2018.1433021.

Yogi Prabowo, Hendi. 2014. "To Be Corrupt or Not to Be Corrupt." *Journal of Money Laundering Control* 17 (3): 306–326. https://doi.org/doi:10.1108/JMLC-11-2013-0045.

Zulkarnain, A., and Syamsuddin Harris. 2017. "Fenomena Blusukan Dalam Model Kepemimpinan Politik Joko Widodo." *POLITIK* 13 (1): 1928–1942.

Index

Abdurrahman Wahid, 32, 54–56
Akil Mochtar, 62–63
anticorruption institutions. *See* institutions, anticorruption
anticorruptionism: definitions of, 9–11; historical use of, 50–52, 58, 60; use of, 15–17, 139–140, 147–148, 153–154, 157, 160–162
Asian Financial Crisis. *See* economy
authoritarian legacies. *See* legacies, authoritarian

Bansos, 129, 144
bersih. *See* candidate: clean
B. J. Habibie, 27, 53–54
blusukan. *See* campaign: strategy
brokers, 44, 136, 145–146, 150–151

campaign: context, 36–45; embodiment of candidates in, 12, 20, 140–141, 160; issues, 10, 41–43; norms, 39–41, 147, 153–154, 160; purposes, 136–141; resources, 16, 37, 43–44, 143–146; strategy, 14–17, 36–37, 46; tandem, 102, 104, 109, 129, 138
candidate: anticorruption, 1, 3–4, 9–10, 14, 42, 147, 159–160; celebrity, 34, 140; clean, 1, 15, 67–68, 91–92, 114, 140, 153; context, 36–45; decision-making, 8, 14–17, 147–148, 154–155, 162–163; eligibility of, 26, 173nn18–19, 177n2; image of, 12, 44–45, 140–141; incumbent, 127–130, 144, 152, 161, 165, 173n22; morality of, 4, 14–15, 45, 68, 94, 148, 165–166; motivation of, 12, 17, 93–94, 147–148, 161–163; New Order, 28–29; strategy, 15–17, 40–41, 82–85, 95–97, 123, 143–144, 147–152; party list ranking of, 33, 98, 100–101, 142; party relationship with, 13, 30–31, 33–35, 38, 43–44; values (*see* candidate: morality); voters' opinions of, 3–4, 13–15, 71–73, 117, 146–147
clientelism, 6–7, 40, 152, 178n11.
See also patronage; vote buying
Commission of Four. *See* institutions, anticorruption; New Order

consolidation, democratic.
See democratization
corruption: cases of, 58–64; definitions of, 4–6; history of, 29, 47, 49–53; public opinion of, 63–67
Corruption Eradication Commission.
See institutions, anticorruption: KPK

dana aspirasi, 129, 144, 159, 177n6
dapil. *See* district, electoral
decentralization, 30, 172n10
democratization: 1998, 6, 25–27, 30–31; impact on elections, 30–33
district, electoral, 26, 30–32, 35
DPD, 28, 155, 173n12
DPR, 28, 30–34, 71, 155, 173n12

economy, 27, 50, 175n14
election: history of, 27–33; direct vs. indirect (*see* institutions, political); law on, 7–8, 30–33
elections: 1999, 30–32; 2004, 32–34, 57–58; 2009, 33, 58–60; 2014, 65–67, 139, 142–143, 146, 158; 2019, 168; presidential, 54–55, 57
Electoral Commission. *See* institutions, political: KPU
electoral districts. *See* district, electoral
elites: gatekeepers, 26, 77–80, 140; New Order, 25–26, 52–53

gatekeepers. *See* elites: gatekeepers
Gerindra. *See* parties, political
Golkar. *See* parties, political
golput, 146

Hanura. *See* parties, political

identity, 44–45, 89, 140–141; Batak, 122–126; Bugis, 85; gender, 107 (*see also* institutions, political: gender quota); Javanese, 93, 106; *putera daerah*, 90, 145; religious, 89, 96, 123–125, 142
institutions, anticorruption: KPK, 54, 57–59, 61, 62; New Order, 52–53

199

institutions, political: electoral thresholds, 31–33; gender quota, 26, 93, 171n2; KPU, 34, 177n2; party eligibility, 30–31. *See also* election: law on

Joko Widodo, 76, 104

keterbukaan, 53
KKN. *See* corruption: history of
KPU. *See* institutions, political: KPU

legacies, authoritarian, 25–27
legislative elections. *See* legislative elections

Media, links to political parties, 39, 72; social, 39, 103–104; strategy, 103–104, 128
Megawati Soekarnoputri, 32, 56–57
money: politics, 4–8, 15–16, 41, 65, 142–143; candidate attitude towards, 15–17, 146–148, 153–155
morality. *See* candidate: morality
MPR, 27–28, 54

Nasdem. *See* parties, political
national legislature. *See* DPR
national parliament. *See* DPR
New Order. *See* regimes, political: New Order

Old Order. *See* regimes, political: Old Order
openness, period of. See *keterbukaan*
open-party list, 33–35, 168; intraparty competition and, 35, 142–143. *See also* candidate: party list ranking of

parliament. *See* DPR
Partai Demokrat. *See* parties, political

parties, political: Demokrat, 31, 57–58, 59–60; eligibility, 30–33; Gerindra, 31–32; Golkar, 28–29, 31, 35, 62–63; Hanura, 31–32, 173n15; Nasdem, 31–32; New Order, 28–29, 30–31; PDIP, 30–31, 32, 54, 56; PKS, 60–62; relationship to candidates (*see* candidate: party relationship with; institutions, political)
patronage, 6–7, 26, 29, 47–48, 53, 147. *See also* clientelism; vote buying
PDIP. *See* parties, political
People's Consultative Assembly. *See* MPR
pesta demokrasi, 28–29
presidential eligibility, 31–33, 34. *See also* elections: presidential
putera daerah. *See* identity: *putera daerah*

regimes, political: New Order (1965–1998), 26–29, 51–53; Old Order (1945–1965), 49–51; Reformasi (1998–), 29–34, 54–57
rhetoric, anticorruption. *See* anticorruptionism

Suharto, 26, 27–29, 51–53; family corruption, 52–53, 54–55
Susilo Bambang Yudhoyono, 57–58, 60, 64–65, 158

tandem campaigns. *See* tandem campaigns
Tommy Suharto. *See* Suharto: family corruption
transition, democratic. *See* democratization

vote buying, 6–8, 11, 15–16, 22, 35, 41, 148, 153–155. *See also* money: politics
voters, 11–12, 15–16, 34–35, 41–42, 137–139, 146–147, 165–168; depoliticization of, 28–29
vote selling, 8–9, 167–168

www.ingramcontent.com/pod-product-compliance
Lightning Source LLC
Chambersburg PA
CBHW032214230426
43672CB00011B/2552